959.7043 Birdwell, Dwight W.
BIR
        A hundred miles of
        bad road.

$24.95

DATE			

98

10/97

BAKER & TAYLOR

A HUNDRED MILES OF BAD ROAD

Other Books by Keith William Nolan

A HUNDRED MILES OF BAD ROAD

An Armored Cavalryman in Vietnam, 1967–68

Dwight W. Birdwell
Keith William Nolan

PRESIDIO

To all who served and their families

Copyright © 1997 by Dwight W. Birdwell and Keith William Nolan

Published by Presidio Press
505 B San Marin Drive, Suite 300
Novato, CA 94945-1340

Library of Congress Cataloging-in-Publication Data

Birdwell, Dwight W.
   A hundred miles of bad road : an armored cavalryman in
Vietnam, 1967–68 / Dwight W. Birdwell and Keith William
Nolan.
      p.   cm.
   ISBN 0-89141-628-5 (hardcover)
   1. Vietnamese Conflict, 1961–1975—Personal narratives,
American. 2. Vietnamese Conflict, 1961–1975—Tank warfare.
3. Birdwell, Dwight W. I. Nolan, Keith William, 1964–   . II. Title.
DS559.5.B5   1997
959.704'342'092—dc21   97-11000
                                              CIP

Printed in the United States of America

CONTENTS

ACKNOWLEDGMENTS

My first contact with Dwight W. Birdwell, the subject of this combat odyssey, was a matter of happenstance. In July 1994, while researching a book on the 1968 Tet Offensive, I wrote to Maj. Jerry Headley, U.S. Army (Ret.), President of the 25th Infantry Division Association. I was hoping that Headley could put me in touch with Association members who had served with the division's ground reconnaissance squadron—the 3d Squadron, 4th Cavalry Regiment (Armored)—during Tet when it demolished a regimental assault on Tan Son Nhut Air Base near Saigon. Headley, himself a platoon leader and troop commander in the unit after Tet, did just that, providing the names and addresses of almost two dozen veterans of Tan Son Nhut.

I sent requests for interviews to everyone on Headley's list, including Dwight Birdwell, a tank crewman during Tet with Troop C, 3/4th Cavalry. Married and the father of two grown children, he is now a lawyer in the oil business in Oklahoma City, Oklahoma.

Dwight agreed to help. Bearing in mind that he is not active in the Association, belonging only casually to the 3/4th Cav Chapter, and was extremely reluctant to relive the Battle of Tan Son Nhut— more on that later—I am especially grateful for the information he provided by mail and phone. Besides describing his own experience, Dwight also devoted much time to tracking down several key C/3/4th Cav veterans not on the rolls of the 25th Infantry Division Association.

Their story is told in my eighth campaign history, *The Battle for Saigon: Tet 1968* (Pocket Books, 1996). Previously, having finished one project, I always moved on to a new, unrelated topic. I could not do that in this case. Dwight, possessed of an invaluable, nearly photographic memory confirmed by unit records and other vets, could speak to many historic moments not included in the Saigon book because they were unrelated to Tet, but which nevertheless needed to be recorded for future scholars and students of the Vietnam War.

Thus, this narrative represents Dwight Birdwell's entire tour of duty in Vietnam. I first spoke to Dwight on the morning of August 12, 1994, when he called upon receiving my original correspondence. We have had innumerable phone conversations since. I interviewed him in his law offices on the weekend of January 27–28, 1996, and, back on the phone again, cleared up most remaining fine points by March 1996.

I have the 3/4th Cav and 25th Infantry Division after-action reports that cover the period of Dwight's service. For further background information on the unit and the area in which it operated, I've turned to the classic war novel *Close Quarters* by Larry Heinemann (Farrar, Straus & Giroux, 1977), and William E. Merritt's memoirs, *Where the Rivers Ran Backward* (University of Georgia Press, 1989). Two splendid histories by Eric M. Bergerud, Ph.D., were also invaluable: *The Dynamics of Defeat; The Vietnam War in Hau Nghia Province* (Westview Press, 1991), and *Red Thunder, Tropic Lightning: The World of a Combat Division in Vietnam* (Westview Press, 1993).

I am indebted to Gen. Glenn K. Otis (Ret.), the 3/4th Cav commander during Tet, who reviewed the rough draft of this work. Thanks are also due to Jerry Headley, who offered a perspective from Troop B, and to these Troop C veterans who shared their memories: Col. Theo F. Hardies, NJARNG; Lt. Cols. Anthony R. Adamo (Ret.) and Leo B. Virant II (Ret.); Capt. Richard A. Thomas (Ret.); 1st Sgt. George S. Breeding (Ret.); Sfcs. John R. Danylchuk (Ret.) and James Dean (Ret.); MSgt. Gary D. Brewer, USAF (Ret.); ex-SSgt. J. Steven Uram; ex-Sgts. Russell H. Boehm, Daniel W. Czepiel and Robert D. Wolford; ex-Sp5s Dean A. Foss and Russell A. Gearhart; ex-Sp4s R. Franklin Cuff, H. Jackson Donnelly, Lucio Herrera, Richard Johns, and John F. Rourke.

Keith William Nolan
Maplewood, Missouri

INTRODUCTION

Birdwell was a real kidder and an easygoing guy, but in battle his tank was devastating. He had the instincts under fire that were essential; he did the right things, and he did them unselfishly.

He was a great soldier.

—Sp4 John Rourke, C/3/4th Cavalry

Dwight Birdwell's story is compelling from several perspectives. To begin with, he is an articulate witness to war at the level of the anonymous enlisted man. He was a nineteen-year-old specialist fourth class when he arrived in Vietnam in September 1967. He served as an infantry squad leader, tank gunner, and, after being promoted to spec five shortly before turning twenty, as a tank commander. "Dwight was down where the rubber meets the road, and his perspective is more 'real' than mine, just by virtue of the fact that I was a lieutenant. The guys didn't tell me a lot of things that went on," notes Tony Adamo, formerly a platoon leader in Charlie Troop. Unshielded by rank or position, Dwight saw the war at its most basic. "Dwight was a rugged guy, and he had an awful lot of presence for a spec five. He exuded a combat-experienced aura," says Adamo. The platoon leader was amused that instead of wearing the standard jungle fatigues, Birdwell—a dark-eyed, black-haired, part-Cherokee kid from hardscrabble rural Oklahoma—occasionally suited up in Stateside-issue utilities with a bright red-and-gold 25th Division patch. He had a second set of utilities he sometimes wore in the rear that were decorated with the insignia of an earlier tour in Korea, to include an Indian-head pocket patch from a scout school. "Dwight was into being a little different. I won't say he exactly swaggered, but he did a little bit," Adamo laughs. "Dwight took pride in what he was, and what he was was an exceptional combat soldier. He was one of those solid guys that were the strength of the unit when I got there. He and that handful like him were the ones that were bringing us new guys along, keeping our eyes open, and keeping us going."

Former Charlie Troop GIs recall Dwight as a conscientious, battle-wise, by-the-book soldier, and as a great and loyal friend. "He's a damn good person," says Bob Wolford with simple clarity.

"If Dwight liked you, he'd do anything for you," remembers Jack Donnelly, the loader on Birdwell's tank after Tet. "He seemed like a quiet fella, but when push came to shove he knew what to do. If I was ever to go back into combat, I'd want to be with him."

The memoirs of common soldiers are always vital. Dwight Birdwell's are of special import because the entire history of the U. S. Army in Vietnam is summed up in his tour. During his first five months in-country, the 3/4th Cavalry—like most units of the day—was superbly led by West Pointers and seasoned Regular Army noncommissioned officers (NCOs) whose experience was invaluable at the platoon level. Morale was high, the troops confident and aggressive. Tasked with securing Highway 1, the main supply route (MSR) running northwest from Saigon toward the Cambodian border, the squadron owned the day, and encountered only the infrequent homemade mine or quick, hit-and-run ambush from a nocturnal foe. Friendly casualties were few and far between, and it went without saying that the best army in the world would inevitably crush Victor Charlie—the underequipped, raggedy-ass guerrillas in the black pajamas known more properly as the Viet Cong (VC).

Then came Tet. On January 31, 1968, the first day of the nationwide communist offensive, C/3/4th Cav was dispatched from the division base camp at Cu Chi to Tan Son Nhut, which was then under attack. It was assumed that the air base was being hit by guerrilla raiders. In fact, a VC regiment, its ranks bolstered with North Vietnamese Army (NVA) regulars, had breached the perimeter. Caught unawares, Charlie Troop was shot to pieces on Highway 1 just as it reached Tan Son Nhut. In that moment of crisis, Dwight Birdwell, taking the place of his wounded tank commander, whom he had helped to cover under heavy fire, laid down such a barrage of cannon and machine-gun fire as to keep the enemy from overrunning the burning column. He was peppered with fragments in the face and chest, but continued to fight from his tank until he had expended every round of ammunition it carried, by which time reinforcements were finally arriving to roll up the enemy's flank and secure Tan Son Nhut.

Numerous dead VC and NVA were found sprawled behind the hedgerows into which Dwight had been firing. "Birdwell was supposed to have been written up for the Medal of Honor for Tan Son Nhut," recalls George Breeding, a staff sergeant who joined Troop C on the second day of Tet. "Everybody was talking about what he had done, and the other NCOs said they had enough paperwork and endorsements that they thought it would go through."

The recommendation was downgraded, and Dwight instead received the Silver Star. Meanwhile, Gen. William C. Westmoreland, the theater commander, declared Tet a great victory. It was. Emerging from the shadows, the Viet Cong had been decimated in their attacks on Saigon and the other urban centers of South Vietnam. They had faced the full fury of U.S. firepower, and had lost. Their spirit, however, had not been broken. Fallen guerrillas were replaced by fresh NVA coming down the Ho Chi Minh Trail, and heavy fighting continued across the country as the enemy had to be dug spiderhole by spiderhole from the rural hamlets they'd seized during Tet. Villages cleared once had to be cleared again, then again, and the enemy aggressively initiated contact at every turn, even in broad daylight.

The pressure was relentless. "You couldn't go through a tobacco patch after Tet without getting in a fight," notes Adamo, who joined Charlie Troop in March 1968. "The enemy was everywhere. . . ."

Casualties were heavy, especially among leaders. As the firefights continued in grinding succession, the unit never getting a chance to catch its breath, morale sank in C/3/4th Cavalry. Everything turned ugly. Dwight was a true believer—there to defend the Vietnamese from "communist aggression," he never called them "gooks"—and he watched in horror as stressed-out GIs began brutalizing prisoners and civilians unlucky enough to get in their way on a bad day.

Dwight Birdwell soldiered on, winning a second Silver Star in a miserable battle-wrecked hamlet called An Duc. Some in the unit performed equally well. Others did not. Already demoralized by their losses, they saw less and less purpose in what they were doing after President Johnson suspended the bombing of North Vietnam and entered into the Paris Peace Talks. Replacements brought with them the problems boiling over back home. Drug use flourished, in the rear and the field—Dwight never touched marijuana, being an original "Okie from Muskogee"—and lines began to be drawn between blacks and whites, hippies and hawks. The only cause that remained was survival. "One night we were sitting outside Cu Chi, waiting to join the rest of the squadron as it came by on Highway 1," remembers Adamo. "One of my guys was up on top of a tank, playing with his .45 pistol. When I walked away from him, I thought to myself, I know what he's doing, and it wasn't ten minutes later I heard a bang. He'd shot his thumb off. He was pretty cool about it. He said it was an accident. He had to get dusted off, and that was it, he was gone. Maybe it was an accident, but I was angry because I thought he did it on purpose. I was also jealous. You know, you didn't want to die, and all it took to get out was to take a damn pistol and stick it against your hand and pull the trigger. Go through life without a thumb, what the hell. I couldn't do that, but I was jealous of him."

Dwight, wounded three times by the end of his tour, did not go home on schedule. With nine months still remaining on his three-year enlistment at that point, he instead extended for four more months in Vietnam to take advantage of an early-out program. He was reassigned to Cu Chi. "We spent a fair amount of time together, and reached a simpatico that wasn't exactly spec five to captain," says Tony Adamo, who was also back in the rear then as the newly promoted troop executive officer. "There were nights when we drank our way into some real heavy discussions. Dwight was a deep guy. He wanted to know things. When I found out that he had gone to college and law school after the war, I wasn't surprised."

This ex-GI's star has risen high. In addition to running a small law practice where his wife keeps the books, Dwight—who has gone gray and round, an intense but warmhearted man with a certain shy and wry humor—serves as Chief Justice of the Cherokee Nation. He was originally appointed to the Cherokee Nation Judicial Appeals Tribunal in 1987 by Principal Chief Wilma P. Mankiller.

To describe Dwight Birdwell as the poor boy who pulled himself up by his own bootstraps is accurate but incomplete. His was a soul-searing war, and a quarter of a century later he remains draped with a melancholy shroud. "Dwight is pained," Adamo says sadly. "He's a man that went out and did well in the world, but he was carrying Vietnam with him every step of the way. Lot of baggage. . . ."

The first time Dwight called after getting my letter about Tet, he was angry. He has a temper, and I had unwittingly asked him to open a box he had been trying to close. He did agree to an interview, though, because "the thought of helping a young man achieve a goal that was important to him appealed to me—even if it meant letting a few demons loose." Describing that fiery hour at Tan Son Nhut was bad, but bearable. The idea of walking through his entire tour for this narrative, even if he was to be compensated as a coauthor, was not. It took much unfair pressure from me to convince Dwight to do so for the sake of history. "It just tears my damn heart out to talk about it," he explained, even as he agreed to help once again. It has been a painful process, not at all cathartic as I had hoped. Like many good men, he blames himself for things that were beyond his control, and is haunted by memories of dead comrades. He carries the dog tag of one who was especially close to him on his key ring. Recounting that friend's agonizing death—the man was burned over his entire body when a rocket set off the white phosphorus shells in their tank—he is angry again, eyes wet in a hard face. There is nothing to say to him, and there is little justification for what I am doing. My only rationale is to hope that the raw truth in Dwight's undimmed and tragically unhealed memories will counterbalance those books, many of mine included, which give war "a polish and a glow that it did not have at the time," to quote James Jones. "The process of history always makes me think of the way the Navahos polish their turquoise. They put the raw chunks in a barrel half filled with birdshot, and then turn the barrel and keep turning it until the rough edges are all taken off and the nuggets come out smooth and shining. Time, I think, does the same thing with history, and especially with wars."

That problem does not exist here.

To understand who Dwight Birdwell was in Vietnam, and who he is today, it is necessary to understand the people and the mean rural poverty from which he came. "My wife tells me that the reason I survived Vietnam was because of where we grew up. Vietnam was just an extension of a hard and violent life. . . ."

Dwight is an Okie, but his mother, Lois, originally hailed from the cotton and tobacco country of central Arkansas. Her father, Howard Smallwood, a farmer of meager means, had pulled up stakes around 1921 when she was four or five. He left under a cloud. "He had killed a man. The deceased had significant family in the community, so my grandfather moved west," notes Dwight, retelling a tale his mother told him only once, when they were picking berries together on their farm the summer after he came back from the war, and which she refused to talk about again. The trouble had apparently begun when Lois's infant brother injured himself with a cap pistol and died of blood poisoning. In his anguish, Smallwood blamed his wife—the cap pistol had been a present from her brother. "There was a fellow who sensed this rift, and he started stopping at the house and talking to her while she was on the porch. It got under my grandfather's skin." Smallwood was driving his wagon down a dirt road one day, little Lois sitting beside him, when he came face to face with his rival, who was on horseback. There was a confrontation. The other man reached for his rifle. "My grandfather grabbed his Winchester quicker, and dropped him. As he was going down, he yelled, 'You son of a bitch,' so my grandfather pumped a few more into him for good measure," says Dwight. Smallwood was arrested for murder, and justice was meted out backwoods style. "He had to sell his farm to pay his lawyer, and the judge, who wanted a 'bounty' for ruling the shooting self-defense. It was an outright bribe. The judge's philosophy was that 'if I have to take the heat from the dead man's family for letting you go, by God, I'm going to make some money for my troubles.'"

Howard Smallwood divorced his wife and, taking custody of Lois, who favored him over her mother, became a roughneck in the oil fields of Oklahoma and Texas. Following the booms, he ended up in Amarillo, Texas, in the mid-1930s, working for Phillips 66.

Father and daughter were still there in 1945 when Lois met a new oil-field worker named Tom Ward. She was a striking, blue-eyed woman with long black hair. A mixed-blood Cherokee, he was, or so he said, an ex-Marine just back from the Pacific. They were soon married, and Dwight Wayne Ward was born on January 19, 1948. The marriage crumbled soon thereafter. "My father was a womanizer and a brawler and a hard-drinking man," says Dwight. "To put extra money in his pocket, he would sell the furniture. My mother would come home from work, and the house would be empty. He would get abusive. He would beat her, and drag her around by her hair."

Lois hated her ex-husband. Nevertheless, she felt it important for Dwight to know his relations, so once a year they would take the bus to Tom Ward's home area of Bell, Oklahoma, a Cherokee community in the forested foothills of Adair County near the Arkansas border. During their stay when Dwight was three, Lois met an older gentleman named Ed Birdwell. At the time, his sick and elderly mother was living with him on his farm, as was the mother's female attendant. The woman had marital designs on Birdwell, and did not appreciate his sudden interest in younger, still-striking Lois Ward.

While visiting at Ed Birdwell's place one day, Dwight began pulling up the flowers the attendant had planted around the house. The woman snapped, "I'm going to beat him within an inch of his life!"

Lois snapped back, "I'll box your jaws if you do."

Infuriated, the woman ran inside, snatched up a large wood-stove poker, and coming back out, hit Lois with it before she could rise from her chair. "My mother picks up this big rock," Dwight recalls. "She's going to come down on this woman, but sense prevails, and we all leave. We were down there with my relatives, so there's like fifteen of us trekking up the hill, going back to my aunt's place."

The spark had not been extinguished, however. "About a month later, that old man shows up in Amarillo, and the next thing I know we're in his Ford pickup truck, headed for Oklahoma. . . ."

Lois was thirty-four when she married again. Eddie B. Birdwell was a once-widowed, twice-divorced, gray-haired but iron-bodied fifty-five-year-old, with a long, stern face that spoke to his English ancestry. Hailing from Arkansas, he had been a farmer, mechanic, blacksmith, and one-room schoolhouse teacher, as well as a mule-driving Army teamster at Jefferson Barracks, Missouri, during the Great War. When Lois joined him, he was making his living as a water-well driller, and lived in a small, ramshackle house—this is where Dwight grew up—on the 219 acres he owned in the Bell area. "I was a defiant little soul even then, and we didn't get along well at first, but after a year or so I developed a strong love for this man, and he liked me too," says Dwight, still bemused by eccentric, hard-headed old Ed Birdwell. He was a white man who chose to live in an Indian area so isolated that it would not have phone service for another two decades. He was an outspoken Republican in a part of the state controlled by the Democrats. "He was just a different sort of guy. He was always going against the wind. He was a very independent man—never asked anybody for anything."

There was a creek running through their property, and Dwight spent many a great summer day playing along it with his friends. Ed Birdwell loved the woods, and Dwight learned to appreciate nature from him. "He taught me how to use a gun, but he wasn't a hunter in the sense that he got a buzz from killing. He believed you should only kill game when you were truly hungry and had no other source of food," explains Dwight, who credits being a good soldier when the time came with his stepfather "working me real hard on our farm, and taking me out in the woods, showing me how to track game, and sit silently and wait, and make your shots count, and so on and so forth. I remember sometimes when we would go to town we wouldn't have the money to buy a box of .22 shells. A box of shells was maybe a quarter! They actually sold them individually. My stepdad would buy ten of them, and, boy, he'd get mad at me when I wouldn't hit a target. 'You're wasting that stuff! . . .'"

• • •

Ed Birdwell had chickens, pigs, and cows. He and Dwight would be up every morning at four to feed the animals and milk the cows, and by six Ed would be off in his truck to his latest drilling site. Back by dinner, he would work his fields into the night. "He was a hard worker, but a lousy businessman. He would drill wells for credit and never get paid," says Dwight. Ed finally sold his drilling rig around 1960, and returned to farming full time. Dwight had been in the fields himself since he was five. "My legs were too short to manipulate the clutch and the brake pedals on most tractors, so Ed got me a John Deere that had a hand clutch," he remembers. They raised corn, strawberries, sweet potatoes, and black-eyed peas. Dwight and his mother joined the poorest of the Cherokees—who were their closest friends—picking strawberries in the spring and beans in the summer and fall. Lois finally got a minimum-wage job on the canning line at Stilwell Foods, in Stilwell, the largest town in the area. "We did without. We'd take ten dozen eggs into town, and maybe they'd give you a sack of flour at the grocery store, or we'd sell them ten or fifteen chickens for two dollars. We had a cream separator. It's a device that you crank and crank and crank, and it separates the cream from cow's milk. We'd sell the cream to a little creamery. We did all kinds of little hustling things to make money any way that we could."

It was a get-nowhere existence. "My stepdad had a real bleak view of life, and my mother's was even bleaker," Dwight sighs. "Their attitude was you work and work and work, don't expect anything nice, and thank God for whatever you can put in your mouth."

Dwight wanted out. He wanted to do something with his life. His heroes included Audie Murphy, and he dreamed of going to West Point. "I loved my mother dearly, but she simply accepted her place in society, and thought that I should too. For me to want anything better went against her Bible," he says of this rock-ribbed Baptist. "When I looked at anything that glittered, she and Ed told me I was stupid, that we were poor, and that's the way it was. It created an incredible amount of frustration and hostility in my little heart. . . ."

As a boy, Dwight walked a mile or so to Bell Grade School. The students were mostly Cherokees, most of the teachers white women.

Two were practically saints to Dwight, but he describes the rest as indifferent or incompetent if not mentally ill. "It was hell. It was hell for eight fucking years," he spits, remembering the teachers who smacked him and jerked him around by his hair, and the high school dropouts with the ducktails, homemade tattoos, and cigarette packs rolled up in their T-shirt sleeves "who were always hanging around and screwing with us little kids. Bullyism was just a fact of life. You had to take care of yourself. You had to fight, and if you didn't, you'd get beat up and beat up bad. Every day you were getting the shit beat out of you, or beating the shit out of somebody else. The other kids had brothers and sisters to help them out. I had nobody. It was just me by myself, and I grew up pretty rough."

In isolated communities, some grudges never die. The man who owned a certain little grocery store in Stilwell, for example, was related to the woman Dwight's mother had pushed out of the way when she married Ed Birdwell. "I hated it going into that store because when my dad wasn't looking, that man would pinch me or kick me to get back at my mother," remembers Dwight. "To get *him* back, I'd go through with my knife and cut his sacks of feed open. Once he told me to get something out of a refrigerator that he knew would shock me because the wiring was faulty, and it shocked me. He laughed real big about it, but I was a little older by then and when he turned his back, I booted him in the ass real hard. I was too big for him to do anything about it."

Dwight had another small-town cross to bear. Tom Ward, his natural father, still lived in the Bell area, and though they had no meaningful contact, Dwight was shamed by him nonetheless. Ward had a reputation for fighting, drinking, stealing cows, and generally raising hell. During one of his periodic stays in the county jail, he started a fire in his cell, and another time it was duly reported in the local paper that he had stuffed his mattress into the toilet of his top-floor accommodations and flooded the entire courthouse building.

"The sins of my father were mine to carry," says Dwight. "Other kids would see him laying out beside the road drunk or beaten up, or both, and I was constantly taunted about that. . . ."

Alcoholism was a major problem in the community, and cheated out of a stable life at home and even a semblance of an education at the grade school, many of Dwight's peers dropped out. Dwight did not, and after graduating at the top of the class from Bell he took the bus to Stilwell High School. It was a real school, and these by comparison were happy days. Dwight was Class of 1966, and though a good student popular with teachers and classmates—he was elected to student council, and was once even Student of the Month—he tended to hang out with the toughs, such as they existed at that time and place, cigarettes dangling, shirttails pulled out in defiance of school rules. They loved beer, fast cars, and Elvis. They weren't hard core juvenile delinquents, but they had little respect for traffic laws, and Dwight still smiles when recalling certain adventurous fender-benders, car hoods that tended to fly up when you hit ninety, and one semi-inebriated turn that resulted in multiple barrel rolls right in front of all the girls and hot-rodders parked in the local Dairy Cup.

Many of Dwight's friends were white. He was actually less than half Cherokee himself, but he looked like a full blood and that made all the difference in certain quarters. "I desperately wanted to go to college, but when I asked my high school counselor about college, she told me that there were lots of good jobs out there like driving trucks, unloading trucks, things like that," he remembers. That was subtle. More blunt were "some of the rednecks who would tell me that I wasn't anything but a 'fucking Indian' whenever I excelled in school activities, and that it didn't matter what I did because in time I would be drunk, dead, or in prison like the rest."

Dwight burned with hopeless rage. "It was hard to have any confidence in myself. I started drinking, and drinking, and drinking. I went from the top ten percent of my class to somewhere in the middle. I was in a funk. I never drank to party. I drank to get to the bottom of that bottle, because when I did it really eased the pain."

During his junior and senior years, Dwight worked from eight at night until three in the morning, six days a week, in the big chicken houses across the border in Arkansas. It was an exhausting schedule. He was off Saturday nights, however, and he and some of the badass Bean brothers—there were a bunch of them, Cherokee boys as crazy as he was—would hit the taverns with fake IDs. The nights usually ended in gouging, kicking, bloody-knuckled, split-lip brawls. "My stepdad and I weren't getting along at all at that time. He was telling me I was no good, and my mother always sided with him," Dwight says. His mother wanted him to stop his foolish talk about college. She was furious about his drinking and fighting. "She had no confidence in me. When she would get angry, she would compare me to my natural father. I looked like him, she said I was acting just like him, and I was really beginning to feel that it was my destiny in life to be a failure because of my personal circumstances. It was a constant fear of mine that I would end up an alcoholic like my natural father."

When Dwight Birdwell was sixteen, he and a white buddy followed up an afternoon of drinking by driving to a night football game the Stilwell team was playing in neighboring Westville. The chief of police of the small town spotted the cheery pair in the bleachers, waved them down, and told them to walk out quietly with him. He said he was going to put them in his car and take them to jail for being drunk in public. "Well, hell, as soon as I get out the gate, I take off," Dwight recounts. The chief, a gruff, tough good old boy, drew his revolver, and with some hyperbole told Dwight's buddy to bring him back or he would drop him. The buddy caught up with Dwight, "but I'm really pissed, the cop is really pissed, and when we come back this cop pulls out his big old black stick and starts beating me with it. We got into it really big. I had him down on the ground, but he managed to get handcuffs on me. He throws me in the back of his car, but he cuffed me with my hands in front, so when he jumps in the driver's seat, I drop my arms over him, and drag him into the backseat, and we're going after it again. By the time the dust settled, I was a pretty messed-up guy. That stick had really done a job on my face. . . ."

Dwight was brought before the justice of the peace the day after his arrest. Friends were on hand to testify that present circumstances notwithstanding, he was not really a juvenile delinquent—even the arresting police chief, being hard but fair, testified that "somewhere in that drunk body I think there's a good boy"—and the magistrate released Dwight with only a twelve dollar and fifty cent fine, and the promise, not kept, that he would never set foot in Westville again. Dwight's friends raised the money. That was all well and good, but Dwight knew there would be other incidents if he stayed where he was. He needed an escape. "My mother and step-dad had told me that I was to get out of the house as soon as I graduated. When I got out of school, there I was, with no funds, and no way to go to college—so I signed up. I thought, go do the Army, and get that GI Bill."

Dwight excelled at soldiering, and loved the Army.

He volunteered for Vietnam.

Author's note: Commentary from co-author Keith William Nolan and C/3/4th Cav veterans appears in the text in italics.

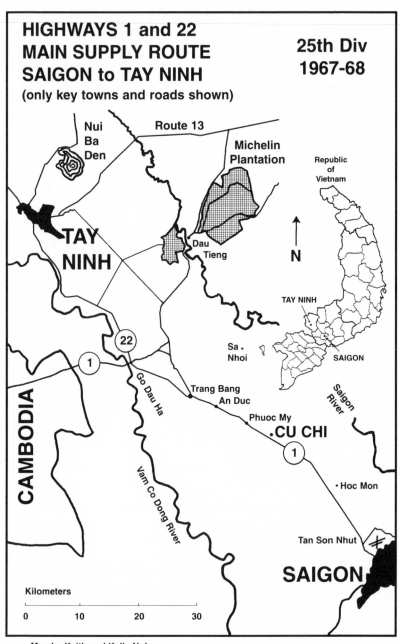

HIGHWAYS 1 and 22
MAIN SUPPLY ROUTE
SAIGON to TAY NINH
(only key towns and roads shown)

25th Div
1967-68

Nui
Ba
Den

Route 13

Michelin
Plantation

Republic
of
Vietnam

TAY
NINH

Dau
Tieng

N

TAY NINH

Sa .
Nhoi

SAIGON

22

1

Go Dau Ha

Trang Bang
An Duc

Saigon
River

Phuoc My

.CU CHI

CAMBODIA

1

Vam Co Dong River

· Hoc Mon

Tan Son Nhut

SAIGON

Kilometers

0   10   20   30

Map by Keith and Kelly Nolan

Part One
CHASING SHADOWS
(SEPTEMBER 1967–JANUARY 1968)

Chapter One

A t our altitude, there was no war. Everything below was lush and green and beautiful. Coming in by commercial airliner, like tourists, we had been attended to during the long flight by miniskirted stewardesses. Some of us had been somber during this cushioned passage, some of us excited—we filled every seat in the plane, row upon row of short-haired GIs in short-sleeved khakis—but the only visible reminder of where we were going was in the face of one of the stews, a lovely, shapely thing, who was as pleasant and efficient as her sisters, but a little solemn, too, as she went about her duties. She had a pair of jump wings pinned to her chest, and I imagined that she was in love with and worried about a young airborne trooper who had earlier taken his own flight to Vietnam.

We landed at Tan Son Nhut. Donning our garrison caps and hefting our duffel bags, we were directed onto olive-painted Army buses with screen-covered windows and were soon rolling through Saigon en route to the 90th Replacement Battalion in Long Binh.

We really were tourists at that point. I was amazed to see beautiful European women strolling down the crowded sidewalks—I assumed they worked at the various embassies in the capital—and thought that they and the other sights and sounds sweeping past were all great and marvelous and exotic. This is my big adventure, I thought.

I was there because in my mind America was right. I also wanted my piece of the war. I wanted to do my ancestors proud. I wanted to nail that coonskin to the wall for LBJ. Raring to go, my only concern when we unloaded the buses and got in line at the replacement center was being assigned to the right outfit. I hoped that I wouldn't end up in the 25th Division. Not that I knew anything about the unit. I just didn't like its patch. Nicknamed The Tropic Lightning after its quick wrap-up of the Guadalcanal campaign, the division's yellow-outlined insignia was a yellow lightning bolt on a red taro leaf. The subdued version worn in Vietnam was black on olive-drab. Either way, it was the ugliest damn patch in the combat zone and was mocked as the electric strawberry. I had thoughts of staying in the army and didn't want to be sentenced to wearing that unheroic blob on my right shoulder as my combat patch for the rest of my military career.

Predictably, when I got up to one of the clerks behind one of the desks, he said, "You're going to the 25th Division."

Was there any way to change those orders? "Nope," he shrugged. My Military Occupational Specialty (MOS) was 11E for Armor Crewman. "They need 11Es, and that's where you're going."

I tried to plead my case, but he looked past me to the next GI in line. Heartless, soulless bastard! Why couldn't he have assigned me to the 1st Cav or the Big Red One?! I thought of offering the clerk a bribe, but didn't, and walked away fuming to myself that I was going to wait until he got off duty and then stomp his ass. The impulse passed.

Sometime the next day, a group of us, newly outfitted in jungle gear, were shuttled to nearby Bien Hoa Air Base for a hop by C123 transport plane to the 25th Division base camp at Cu Chi. While we were waiting at Bien Hoa, a bunch of go-go type USO performers came through the terminal. These were American girls. They were really built upstairs, and some nearby ARVN—that is, our allies, soldiers from the Army of the Republic of Vietnam—just went wacko. I thought GIs were bad, but these guys absolutely flipped. They'd never seen anything like it before, or at least acted like they hadn't.

Going to Cu Chi was, finally, like going to war. The C123 was a roaring, rattling cattle car, prop driven, and we replacements sat on webbed seats inside the bare fuselage, facing each other in two long rows. The back ramp remained partially open the whole way. It was a short flight—Cu Chi is twenty-five kilometers northwest of Saigon, straight up Highway 1—but long enough. That we had crossed an invisible line was obvious as soon as we disembarked. There were a squad's worth of green body bags lined up to one side of the runway, awaiting transportation back the way we had just come, and that's when it really hit me that this is it, I'm finally here.

It had taken me fifteen months. I had joined the U.S. Army while a senior in high school and reported for active duty on May 24, 1966, two weeks after graduating. I went through Basic Training at Fort Polk, Louisiana, and Advanced Individual Training (AIT) in armor at Fort Knox, Kentucky. In October 1966, I was posted to Camp Beard, Korea, with the tank battalion organic to the 2d Division—and, God, how I would have loved to have worn *that* big and bold patch in combat! In any event, my Korean service was invaluable. I was in a great platoon with great NCOs. Our gas-engined M48A2 tanks were almost identical to the diesel M48A3s used in Vietnam—both had 90mm main guns, but the former was equipped with a .30-caliber coaxial machine gun (MG), the latter a 7.62mm—and we learned just about everything there was to know about how to fight and maintain those big mothers. In addition, we conducted dismounted exercises north of the Imjin River on the Demilitarized Zone, operating with live ammunition, this being a time of numerous border incidents. My platoon was never fired upon, but on many a freezing night the North Koreans broadcast unnerving propaganda to us from across the DMZ, citing the names and hometowns of individual GIs—how they got this information, I'll never know—and bemoaning how much they were missed by their families and friends. We were wary of unmarked minefields left over from the war, and once while digging a tank position we unearthed a skeleton wearing a rusty helmet and moldy fatigues, the remains of some poor soldier missing at least fourteen years, buried, it seemed, by the near miss of an artillery shell while crouching in a mortar pit. The mortar tube was still there too.

I really grew as a soldier in Korea. I shot expert with the pistol and rifle at the range. I had never been in better physical condition. When we humped the mountains as infantrymen—and Korea has some big-ass mountains—I could literally run to the top ahead of everyone else in the unit, even in full gear with an M14 rifle.

I was promoted rapidly enough, making E2 out of Basic, E3 soon after joining my unit, and E4 as a top graduate of the Imjin Scout School. I also did well on various aptitude tests—"With scores like this, you've chosen a combat arm? What the hell is *wrong* with you?!" the recruiting sergeant had exclaimed when I first joined the Army—and was selected to attend the U.S. Military Academy prep school. I ultimately turned down this opportunity, partly out of self-doubt, partly because even though I was 70 percent of the way to deciding on a military career, I was hesitant to commit to five years of school and the four years of service required of West Pointers.

Instead, I volunteered for Vietnam. My request for a transfer, known as a 10-49, was approved in July 1967. We were back at Camp Beard at the time, working on our tanks in the motor pool, when a sergeant came down the hill toward us from the barracks area.

"Birdwell! Birdwell!" he was shouting. "Get your stuff packed. Your 10-49 came through. You're going to Vi-et-nam!"

Everyone just froze and looked at me. The sergeant walked me up to the orderly room, and, sure enough, there were the orders. I left two or three days later, and the platoon, tight group that it was, had a surprise party for me at 2d Division Headquarters to see me off after presenting me with a little plaque. In my prime, I should have gone straight to Vietnam. However, granted a forty-five-day leave, I went home to Oklahoma first. Big mistake. For one thing, I fell in love. She was a Cherokee girl, and this whirlwind affair—which went unconsummated, given the fact that though we talked of marriage we decided to wait until I came back from Vietnam—dulled my edge a bit. I was still gung-ho, but a little less inclined to heroics. My leave quickly ran out, and my stepfather accompanied me in the beat-up station wagon that functioned as a taxi between Stilwell and Tahlequah, where I needed to catch the Continental Trailways bus to the Oklahoma City airport. Just as I was about to board the bus, I grabbed my stepfather's hand, shook it, and, addressing him by his first name, for I never called him Dad, thanked him for all that he had done for me. This hardheaded old man who never showed any emotion, and with whom I had fought so badly before I joined the army, started crying, and hugged me for the first time in our lives. The driver of the station wagon, a veteran of World

War II, and just as hard as hell himself, started crying, too, as did the fifteen or twenty people on the bus. I will never forget that moment.

Off I went, but by the time I disembarked from that C123 transport plane at Cu Chi—I had flown from Oklahoma City to Travis Air Base in California, catching my flight to Vietnam around the first of September 1967—I had come to regret my leave even more. It was bad enough that I had become mentally distracted. I had also hurt myself, dropping a heavy piece of metal on the big toe of my right foot while helping my stepfather do some welding in his little workshop on the farm. I was barefoot at the time, and it really bruised and mashed the toe, tearing off part of the nail. It had not healed before I arrived in-country, and after two days in the heat and humidity of Vietnam it was in even worse shape, swelling to twice its normal size.

I was limping badly, and one of the sergeants at the 25th Division replacement center barked, "What the hell's wrong with *you?*"

I pulled my boot off, he took a look, and the next thing I knew I was in a jeep headed for the 12th Evacuation Hospital in Cu Chi. The doctors put me under and made an incision to drain the infection. I spent the next several days recuperating in the replacement center, going back to the hospital for checkups. It was an experience that burned off another layer of my gung-ho sheen, given the shot-to-hell guys I saw as I hobbled through the wards with a crutch. I was also disheartened by the seasoned-looking GIs who'd sidle up to us replacements—we really stood out in our bright new jungle fatigues—and after establishing their credentials as seen-it-all, done-it-all combat veterans, would tell us in vivid detail how new guys were always getting zapped, greased, wasted, or otherwise blown away. "Buddy, you're dead. You're going to get killed," one told me with casual finality, as if trying to help me accept reality. Too late not to have been taken in and terrorized by this sadistic ritual, I came to understand only later that these troops were base camp heroes who knew not of what they spoke. "What's your MOS? *Armor!* Oh, man, let me tell you, there was an armor track out there on the perimeter the other night that got hit by an RPG—that's a rocket-propelled grenade—and it burned 'em all alive. *Burned 'em to a crisp!"*

• • •

Though I expected the worst, the war actually began very slowly for me. The truck ferrying replacements to their units let me off outside the orderly room, a sandbagged tent with a wooden floor, of the armored cavalry troop to which I had been assigned. I swung inside with a crutch under one arm and presented my orders to the first sergeant. He made no effort to welcome me to the unit. The best he could muster was a grimace at my bandaged foot as if marking me down for a malingerer. The two clerk-typists in the tent were equally cold in their attitude. Fuck you, they seemed to sneer as they glanced over—we're all heroes here, and you ain't shit.

The top sergeant assigned me to SSgt. William J. Kampe, the Communications NCO in Headquarters Platoon. "Help Kampe until you get healed up," he said before dismissing me with a shrug.

Welcome to Troop C, 3d Squadron, 4th Cavalry. . . .

Sergeant Kampe wasn't overjoyed to see me, either, when I showed up at his hootch, but he enthusiastically sought me out later that afternoon. "Goddamn, I've gone through your record book, and you are one bright guy!" he said. "I need a radio repairman. Let me train you, and you can be part of my section—and you'll have something to make a living with when you get out of the army."

It was thus that I sat out the first month of my so-called adventure, fiddling with broken radios in the Commo Shack. It would have been worse than it sounds if short, wiry Kampe—a flinty but soft-hearted career man, prematurely gray at age thirty—hadn't taken me under his wing. He was, incidentally, a German from San Antonio, Texas, and could carry on some hellacious conversations in Spanish with the Hispanic GIs—or so it appeared when they were drinking!

Charlie Troop turned out to be not such a bad outfit. The first sergeant might have been three-quarters asshole, but the other NCOs reminded me of the pros I had served with in Korea. One day I listened in as several E6s and E7s who had been with the unit from its first days in-country—arriving as C/1/10th Cav, 4th Division, in October 1966, the troop had been redesignated C/3/4th Cav, 25th Division, after an interdivisional swap of units in August 1967—reminisced about the first sergeant in charge when they had originally shipped out from Fort Lewis, Washington. They said he had been a prick in the States and a prick in Vietnam—except when he went out to the field. There, he was a smiling old top, passing out cold beers to his boys. The bastard was covering his ass, they laughed, afraid that if he didn't he would get blown away for the way he rode people in the rear. I chalked it up as the kind of talk to be expected in a field-wise unit that didn't have time for lifer chickenshit.

In October 1967, at the end of the rainy season, Troop C, support elements included, established a temporary laager site somewhere in the Tay Ninh–Dau Tieng area north of Cu Chi. I was back on my feet by then and was determined to escape my rear-echelon fate. I got my chance when a guy I'll call Art Parsons, a baby-faced track driver in the 3d Platoon—a "track" was an M113 Armored Personnel Carrier (APC)—reported that his headset wouldn't hook up to the radio in his hatch. Employing a trick Kampe had taught me, I spit into the rubber jack before plugging the headset in. Parsons was taken aback, but that little bit of moisture was all that was needed to complete the connection.

Before returning to where the commo section was set up in the perimeter, I complained to Parsons that "I don't like this shit I'm doing. I want to get in one of these line platoons."

"Man, you need to get to know Sergeant Dean," Parsons said. "I bet he'd really like to have you, since you're a radio expert."

With that, Parsons walked me over and introduced me to Sfc. James Dean, the 3d Platoon Sergeant of C/3/4th Cavalry. "Howdy, how you doin'?" this rangy old soldier asked by way of greeting, surprising me with his friendly country-boy informality. Dean listened sympathetically to my plight, then said, "Hell, come on over."

When I explained that Kampe considered me a full-fledged member of his section, healed foot or not, Dean said, "We'll take care of it." He did. That day or the next, Kampe came up to me mad as hell. "Goddammit, you didn't have any training as a radio repairman. I could have gotten somebody who was already trained, but I took *you*, and kept *you* out of the field," he shouted, furious that he had wasted his time. "You're *fucking* me. You're fucking me, and I don't appreciate it one bit. I thought you were a better man than that."

"I'm sorry," I said, "but I've *got* to do this."

"Well, get your ass out, then," he said, meaning it.

I packed my gear and joined my new platoon.

The name of the game was convoy security. Headquartered in Cu Chi, the squadron rarely went to the field as a force unto itself. Nor did its three ground cavalry troops. Instead, we usually operated as platoons. There were three line platoons to a troop, and on a typical day most would be outposted along Highway 1—the main supply route, which ran twenty-five kilometers from Saigon to Cu Chi, then another twenty-five to Go Dau Ha—and Highway 22, which continued for thirty klicks up to Tay Ninh. These were highways in name only. Mostly unpaved and in poor condition because of heavy use by heavy military vehicles, they were elevated several feet above the endless rice paddies so as not to disappear underwater during the rainy season. We sat at widely separated positions to secure the MSR, an acceptable risk given that the VC operated only in small bands in our area. The duty was quiet, the only diversion the women gliding past on mopeds and bicycles, filmy, split-legged *ao dai* skirts billowing, the kids switching magnificent water buffaloes along, the trucks rumbling toward the capital with loads of lumber, and the overcrowded old buses that counted pigs and chickens and ducks as passengers. The Vietnamese we saw seemed to be a happy and friendly people.

On a rotating basis, one platoon would escort the morning supply convoy from Saigon to Tay Ninh. Each was led by a single military police V-100 armored security vehicle with four oversized tires and twin .30-caliber machine guns in a little turret. Our vehicles—each cav platoon had three M48s and seven M113s on paper, but usually only two tanks and four or five tracks were operational on any given day—would fall in at intervals as the convoy passed Cu Chi. Protected by this armor and a few MP gun jeeps, and with scout helicopters from our air cavalry troop buzzing along the flanks, these massive convoys of 150 to 200 trucks stretching out for twenty or thirty kilometers were never ambushed in our AO.

The day was indeed ours. Convoy duty was, nevertheless, dull and dusty and unrewarding; as Capt. Leo B. Virant II, the commander of C/3/4th Cavalry, later wrote: "Ten VC held down our thousand-man squadron."

At least, though, I was finally in the war. When I walked over from Kampe and reported to 1st Lt. Bobbie J. Young, the 3d Platoon Leader—and he was a good one, a tall, muscular, deep-voiced ex-NCO who had gone to Officer Candidate School (OCS)—he assigned me to a track, and that very night I was out on an ambush patrol, wondering how many mosquitoes could possibly feast on me at the same time. I had probably been enjoying a beer at that time the evening before.

I was squad leader on the infantry track. Spec Four Mike Christie was the actual track commander, and as "TC" he manned the .50-cal MG. In addition, we had a driver and two M60 machine gunners. My seven-man squad rode on the back deck with the gunners during our kidney-jolting patrols through the tree lines and across the dry rice paddies of our area. We always sat up top for fear of mines.[*]

Teamed up as we were, Mike Christie and I became very close. Broad shouldered and ruggedly handsome, Mike had been a leather-jacketed hood back home in New York—his forearms were heavily tattooed, and his hair combed back greaser style—but he was also dead-serious, all business, and a natural leader. Mike took me out on that first ambush to show me how it was done. When he talked, people listened, and he didn't take any shit from anybody. He unwound only in the rear, and it was obvious when he had clandestinely gotten smoked up with some of his like-minded buddies because his eyes would look like red road maps. Welcome to Vietnam. . . .

"Have you been smokin' that shit again?" I would tease him.

"Birdy, you just don't know what you're missing," Mike would snort in his street-smart jive, making fun of the naive Okie.

---

[*]Each vehicle had a bumper number. Ours was C-38. The letter identified our troop, the first number our platoon, and the second our specific vehicle according to a system used in all cavalry platoons: 0 was the platoon leader's track; 1, 2, 3, and 4 were scout tracks; 5 was the platoon sergeant's tank; 6 and 7 were additional tanks; 8 was the infantry track; and 9 a mortar track with a built-in 4.2-inch mortar tube on a rotating base plate that could be fired through the top hatch.

Other vices were satisfied in the field. Whenever we stopped for more than five minutes, mamasans would materialize with soda and beer—these women with the white blouses, black pants, conical hats, and red teeth from chewing betel nut also sold sandwiches and sliced pineapple—and prostitutes wearing sunglasses and miniskirts would come putt-putting in on mopeds. The sodas and beers were hot, the women cold. They were better than nothing, however, and once when we were up around Tay Ninh and a girl set up shop on a poncho liner in a foxhole between two APCs—it was five dollars a pop—even a certain lieutenant took a turn, his one and only as far as I know. He was a family man, and an otherwise solid, by-the-book leader. He reemerged buttoning his trousers, and, suddenly embarrassed and probably a little angry at himself, he snapped at the platoon, "Don't tell anybody about this. You didn't see anything."

The lieutenant lit a cigarette and quickly walked away. I didn't get in line myself. I wasn't exactly an innocent after my tour in Korea, and I pass no judgments on the prostitutes—this was a poor country; you had to make a living—but I couldn't get too excited about having sex with a woman after ten other GIs had, and I didn't want VD.

Though the days ticked by uneventfully, many nights did not. The night was not ours. To prevent the Viet Cong from mining Highway 1 under cover of darkness, we conducted Night Thrust operations. This was better known as Running the Road. Spread out and moving fast in single file so as not to give some VC with an RPG an easy shot, each platoon would cruise up and down its ten- or fifteen-kilometer section of highway all night long, led by a tank with a blazing searchlight mounted atop its 90mm main gun. We would occasionally stop, herringbone on the road—that is, one vehicle would pivot to the right, the next to the left, and so on down the line—and while the crews catnapped, one GI would remain on watch behind the .50-caliber MG of each vehicle and scan the field on his side with a night vision device known as a Starlight Scope.

The civilians were under a dusk-till-dawn curfew, so anything spotted at night was considered hostile. When we approached the little villages along the road, we would dismount, leaving only a driver and .50 gunner in place, and sweep forward on both flanks in advance of the column to disrupt possible ambushes. We actually went through people's houses with flashlights. Sometimes they appeared terrified when they awoke, but usually they were stoic, and on occasion when a trooper gestured to unlock the tall cabinets found in many of the houses, cabinets big enough for someone to hide in, an irritated homeowner might gesture in return that he didn't know where the key was. You had to point your weapon at the lock before he would climb out of bed and unlock the cabinet. There was never anyone in there.

My first enemy contact came at the end of a Night Thrust operation on Highway 1. It was about four or five in the morning, and we were returning to base camp, when an RPG was suddenly fired at Sergeant Dean's tank, the last in line—we usually had a tank front, tank middle, and tank drag when running the road—from a blacked-out village just outside Cu Chi. It was a common enemy tactic to snipe at the rear vehicle because if they hit it, great, and if they missed, that was fine, too, because by the time the rest of the column realized what was happening and turned around to fire back, the ambushers would be long gone, able to try again somewhere else some other night.

In this case, the enemy scored a hit. Instead of slamming directly into the hull of Dean's tank, however, the RPG detonated against a section of runway matting called Pierced Steel Planking (PSP), that our tanks were rigged with; it was a rectangular piece hanging from hooks down the length of the treads on either side. Rocket-propelled grenades were shaped charges that did their damage by burning a hole through armor and setting off the ammo and fuel inside. They were damn effective, and the runway matting was there to give our tanks some stand-off protection.

This unconventional extra armor having done its job, Dean, his tank suffering only superficial damage, was able to swing his 90 about and begin returning fire. The track directly ahead of Dean pulled around and behind him, and the TC raked both sides of the road with his .50-cal in case the ambushers had darted across the highway while trying to make good an escape. The rest of us herringboned, and though there had been only that one rocket, we also opened up, laying down a blanket of protective fire in case we had entered an ambush zone. When the lieutenant managed to get everyone to cease fire, my infantry squad clambered off our track and moved into the village for a hootch-to-hootch sweep. We came up empty handed, and our unflappable platoon sergeant joked, "Hell, that was just some kid that stole his daddy's RPG and went out for a little fun!"

The first time I actually saw the enemy was also during one of our Night Thrusts. Dean was in the lead as we sped toward a ville where movement had been reported, and when we neared it, he flipped on his searchlight, sending a laser beam of white light down the highway. Two Viet Cong were captured in the blinding glare, crouched over the mine they were planting in the road maybe a quarter of a mile downrange—and in the next instant, they disappeared in a flash and a bang, one of the startled guerrillas having stepped on their own mine as they tried to escape. The explosion put a big crater in the road. The two guerrillas were both killed. Pulling up and dismounting, we found them sprawled off in an adjacent field, wearing only shorts, missing a limb or two, and otherwise chewed to pieces. I stared down at my enemy. They didn't have horns; they didn't have tails. They were young. I imagined them to be energetic and dedicated to their cause just like me, and I felt sorry for them more than anything else. Each had a mother and other family somewhere who were going to grieve terribly for them. They were poor misguided souls as I saw it, fighting for the wrong banner, and I thought there was some tragedy in the fact that a lot more of them were going to end up like these two before the rest had the sense to call it quits. We climbed back aboard our vehicles, mission accomplished.

I might have empathized with the enemy as fellow soldiers, but I was appalled at what they were capable of in the name of the National Liberation Front. On numerous occasions when we moved out in the morning, we would roll past civilians—schoolteachers, village officials, and the like—who had been murdered during the night by political cadre, their bodies left beside the highway as a warning to others. Sometimes the victims were women. They were usually murdered individually, sometimes in pairs. The scene was always the same. The victim's hands would be tied behind his or her back, and from the gunshot in the back of the head there would be a great circle of dark brown blood dried in the dust. Grieving family members would be slumped beside the body, crying and wailing.

I can't say that my fellow GIs were outraged by these atrocities. I think most were indifferent. They were good soldiers, but apolitical, and though not abusive to the civilians, they didn't have much use for the Vietnamese. Superhawk that I was, I was infuriated—especially the time I saw a dead child on display alongside his dead parents. How dare they do this, I thought. We've got to prevail, we've got to win, we can't let this go on! I was angry that these systematic murders by the communists didn't seem to get much play in the papers and, relating it to back home, considered how terrible it would be if two or three sets of town officials were assassinated over a two or three month period, how disruptive it would be to the community, and how intimidating for anyone else to step up and try to provide effective leadership. I thought how brave and committed these murdered men and women must have been, and how their deaths validated to me exactly why we were in Vietnam.

Chapter Two

S ome nights, instead of running the road, the platoon would simply herringbone in place on the elevated highway. With the tanks and tracks thus positioned for immediate backup, my infantry squad would conduct ambush patrols designed to catch guerrillas slipping in to mine the MSR. Lieutenant Young would point to some spot on the map, usually a klick or so out, through which higher command had divined the Viet Cong might move, assign us a general route, and the seven or eight of us would slide off the road at nightfall with bush hats, ammo bandoliers, and plenty of grenades, so caked and streaked with orange-brown road dust that we didn't bother with camouflage paint. Moving single file through the hushed darkness, the ambush would include an M60 team and a troop with an M79 grenade launcher—in addition to the M16 rifles the rest of us carried, I always humped the radio and the Starlight Scope—and after finding some concealing vegetation at our assigned site, we would arrange ourselves in a little circle, all approaches covered, terrain permitting, by the claymore mines that another designated trooper carried out in a pack and set up. Stinking of insect repellent, oily, pungent stuff that only seemed to work for an hour no matter how much you smeared on, we would lie low, swarmed by mosquitoes who could draw blood through the canvas of our jungle boots, waiting miserably for dawn when we could pack up and return to the platoon.

Most ambush patrols passed in such quiet solitude that the guys developed a real fuck-it-let's-get-some-sleep attitude. Half should have been awake at any given time—locked, cocked, and ready to blow away a hapless enemy at a moment's notice—but my tired, pissed-off troops would not have tolerated such adherence to the book. Instead we rotated watch, one man up, an hour at a time. Since I was used to working an ungodly number of hours back home, I'd stay awake during the entire ambush—it was just too risky to put the security of the entire squad in the ability or willingness of one guy to stay awake after a hard day—and often when the trooper on guard fell asleep, as he usually did, I wouldn't rouse his replacement. It would be just me, sitting there in the dark with the radio, and my squad, wrapped tightly in ponchos against the mosquitoes, sound asleep. They were gone. They were just corpses waiting to be declared dead.

I never wore a poncho. They were too clumsy; they'd slow you down if you needed to react quickly. Instead, I sat uncovered night after night, being eaten alive. The others took ambush patrol a little more seriously themselves in the area of An Duc, a bigger-than-average village on Highway 1 up toward Go Dau Ha. It was a bad place. When we rolled through during the day, the hostility was palpable—people would stare with hatred, or turn their heads, refusing to even look at us—and at night we were always catching some sniper or rocket fire in there. Mining incidents were also frequent, so to interdict these nocturnal saboteurs, my squad slipped into an ambush position one night just outside An Duc. We set up where two terraced rice paddies joined together in an open area with good fields of vision about two hundred feet away from the edge of the village. It was as still and quiet as a cemetery in there. The smell of incense drifted to us. I was under the impression that the villagers burned it at night to ward away the mosquitoes, which must have plagued them as badly as us.

I know my asshole was tight that night. I think everyone else's was, too, but I'll be damned if I didn't catch one of my guys, a goof-off named Good, asleep when I crawled over to check him. He was supposed to have been watching the rear. I gave him a shove to wake him up, but when I checked on him again during that same hour he was supposed to be on watch he was again sleeping.

"Good, if I come back here again and find you asleep," I whispered hard in his ear, "I'm going to blow your fucking brains out."

When I came up on him a third time ten or fifteen minutes later, he looked dead to the world, curled up with his head on the ground. I unholstered my .45-caliber pistol in a cold fury and thumbed back the hammer. I was so crazy angry I might have squeezed off a round next to his ear, giving us all away in the process—but Good must have heard me, because he suddenly whipped around, whispering hoarsely, "I'm awake, I'm awake, God-dammit! Put it up! Put it up!"

There was no contact that night. We never actually ambushed anyone in An Duc, but just being out there was a draining and nerve-jangling experience. We felt eyes on us in the dark. We were always tense, waiting for a shadow to suddenly loom up with a grenade. During one of those long nights, Ray Hines—this incompetent tank crewman was still a spec four after six years in the army, and for that reason I am not using his real name here—was attached to my squad. He almost got us all killed. The night having passed without incident, Young gave us the word to come on in at about four in the morning. Gladly, I thought, but we were just a few hundred meters from the safety and security of the platoon when Hines suddenly whispered that he had left his pistol behind. I didn't know why he had pulled the damn thing out, and how he could have been so stupid as to just leave it laying on the ground was beyond me, but I reported the loss to the lieutenant—and he instructed us to retrieve the weapon. Having to turn around and go back was excruciating. As we tiptoed back in, a squad of us in the enemy's backyard, we were convinced that they were probably already scavenging our ambush site for anything we might have forgotten. Every one of us wanted to kill Hines. We found the pistol and tiptoed right back out.

I'm not sure if we ever ambushed anybody. There were two or three nights in locations other than An Duc when I spotted passing Viet Cong—or at least through the rubber eyepiece of my Starlight Scope, which cast the world in a green glow, I *thought* I saw them—and we'd squeeze off the claymores at these ghostly images, but we never found any bodies, we never found any blood trails, we never found any weapons, and we never found any equipment.

Contact being rare, it was hard to stay sharp at all times, and there was a certain laxness in our operations. When we herringboned for an hour or two while running the road, some guys would grab some sleep. Others would sit up top, quietly talking and smoking. The enemy, if they were really out there at all, could already see the silhouettes of our tanks and tracks on the elevated highway, so a cigarette glowing in the dark wasn't the end of the world—though I thought it unwise to pinpoint your skull so perfectly for some ambitious sniper. Not all the guys were smoking Marlboros. It was out there on the highway, not in the rear, that I first caught a whiff of marijuana. People weren't open about it, and the number of those who indulged was small, but I was shocked nonetheless. I associated marijuana with antiwar protesters at Berkeley and thought smoking it in the combat zone was utterly un-American. It transpired, however, that even the 2d Platoon leader, a lackluster officer who rotated out less than two months before Tet, was a pothead, or at least tolerated its use right under his nose. We passed his parked command track in the field once and saw that thick marijuana smoke rolling up from the open cargo hatch. That lieutenant's no-sweat attitude was contagious, and one night when his platoon swept a roadside village, some of his guys looted their way through a row of little stores. They helped themselves to sunglasses and beer and whatever else caught their eye, and the next morning our embarrassed troop commander had to deal with a crowd of angry villagers demanding compensation.

I once had a trooper fire up a joint during a night ambush. He was the driver of the infantry track and was without a doubt the most undisciplined, out-of-control soldier in the platoon. He didn't want anybody fuckin' with him, as he used to say, and fuckin' with him meant telling him what to do. He simply could not take orders. That could be a problem because he was a big, strong stud of a guy from rural Virginia, and he was willing to get physical with people, rank be damned. He was also a bully with the civilians. I'll call this wild man Norman Smith—he was killed on the first day of the Tet Offensive, and I shouldn't slander the dead—and say in his behalf that when he didn't feel that he was being abused by the powers that be, he was a genial enough fellow. He had a funny, joshing side and could be downright buddy-buddy at times. It was around Christmas when some of the guys received care packages from patriotic citizens who had picked names and addresses at random from some type of list of servicemen overseas. Norman got a big metal can full of potato chips from a gentleman in Florida, and unlike the others who hoarded their manna from heaven, he shared with everybody on the track.

But Norman was Norman, and the night Dean's tank took that RPG, he went a little crazy when Christie, who was up behind the .50 in the TC hatch, tried to get him to pivot the track in a specific direction so he could return fire. Orders in combat usually come out clip and fast, but Norman took it personally, and he rebelled at Christie's instructions, screaming back over the intercom and jerking the APC around like a bucking bronco. Christie finally had to slam Norman in the back of his head with the butt end of his M16.

Spec Four Norman Smith was sometimes attached to my infantry squad, and he told me up front, "Don't pull any lifer shit with me. I'll do what you want, but if I ever think you're *ordering* me, I'm not going to do it—and there's going to be hell to pay."

When we set up ambushes, Norman immediately crashed for the duration. You didn't want to wake him for his turn on watch because he would have made such a commotion as to give away the whole show. He was in his own orbit, and I left him there—except for the night he fired up that joint. We were operating as a troop at that time in the Michelin Rubber Plantation near Dau Tieng. Only a few nights before, we had spotted hundreds of little green lights in the far distance, moving through the rubber trees like fireflies, and someone had told me that those were North Vietnamese and Viet Cong with some type of filter on their flashlights as they slipped through the darkness toward Saigon. We called artillery fire down on the lights.

None of this worried Norman. We had no sooner gotten into position than he produced a joint and snapped his Zippo. I crouched down beside him. "There's not going to be any of that," I whispered. "If you don't do anything else for me, don't do that."

"Birdy, don't fuck with me," he glowered.

"You're not going to do it," I said firmly. "Norman, you can kill yourself, but you're damn sure not going to kill me."

Norman got loud, not giving a shit where we were and how few of us there were. He was a heavy pothead, and I was ruining his night. It got tense for a moment, but I held my ground, and Norman finally offered a compromise: "Hell, I'll smoke it under my poncho."

"That'll cover the light," I countered, "but you can *smell* that shit a mile away. Charlie will know exactly where we are."

"Okay, okay," he snapped in disgust, giving up.

My troubles with Norman were minor in comparison with those of SSgt. John R. Danylchuk, who displaced the underranked Christie as the infantry track commander upon joining us in December 1967. Small and wiry, Danylchuk was a Scotsman by birth—when we cranked up, he would shout "Tally-ho!" in his improbable accent—and had served as a sixteen-year-old cadet-soldier in the Black Watch before immigrating and joining the U.S. Army. When he transferred into Charlie Troop, he had already survived a hair-raising tour with the Long-Range Reconnaissance Patrol attached to our air cavalry troop. He was an excellent NCO. He was also a little nuts. He was still a kid at heart, I think, and the war was his playground. He loved to take out our night ambushes, bush hat crushed down low on his head, his short-barreled CAR15 submachine gun held ready at the waist, a .45 on one hip, and a big Bowie knife on the other. He also had a razor sharp Gerber knife strapped ready to go on the shoulder harness of his web gear, and sometimes went so far as to wear knee-high Indian moccasins, the better to tread quietly through the brush. He thought he was Errol Flynn, rakish mustache and all.

Scotty Danylchuk sported all the airborne and ranger badges and had been decorated once with the LRRPs. He was decorated twice more with us, once for chopping down two guerrillas with his CAR15 during a Night Thrust firefight on Highway 1—things started heating up a bit as Tet approached—once again for leading a dismounted daytime patrol that bagged four more VC while they were cooking rice in a little hootch, their captured M16s and M79 leaning off to the side. Danylchuk's little group advanced right at them through the elephant grass in a skirmish line and cut loose at fifty meters.

I respected Danylchuk. On the other hand, Norman Smith hated anybody who tried to make him do his job, and being a lot bigger than our ninety-eight-pound track commander, Norman didn't mind showing his displeasure. We were moving cross-country one night when Danylchuk instructed Norman to cut the APC left then right in quick succession, and Norman, feeling abused again—actually, I think Scotty was just keeping an eye on the terrain—gave it the gas and roared us around in circles, slinging several of my troops off the back deck. Equipment went everywhere. Everyone was pissed, but no one wanted to tangle with Norman, and the guys kept their mouths shut as they dusted themselves off and climbed back aboard.

The rebuke had no impact, but Danylchuk did chew Norman out once for a bit of spastic craziness on his part that allowed a squad of Viet Cong to live to fight another day. Our ambush patrol was spread out along a paddy dike that night, watching a village. Unaware of our presence, the guerrillas were crossing the paddy in front of us. Danylchuk was watching them through the Starlight Scope as they walked toward us. We had them dead to rights—and then, before they were within range, Norman sprang up with a shout and lobbed a hand grenade. It exploded harmlessly in the paddy and the shadows spun around in their tracks, disappearing back into the darkness. Danylchuk suddenly clambered over the dike, shouting at us to catch them. We tried. We ran through the night in headlong pursuit, but the best we came up with were a pair of Ho Chi Minh sandals one of the guerrillas had kicked off in flight. Danylchuk held them up, laughing that we had chased the bastards right out of their shoes, but it had been a reckless stunt. We could have run off the edge of the world out there, and no one in the whole squadron would have tried it but Danylchuk.

It was scary to be led by someone so brave.

Chapter Three

Sometime in December 1967, Alpha Troop made contact along a stretch of highway where the rubber trees and heavy brush had been cleared back a quarter mile on either side to discourage convoy ambushes. Charlie Troop came through the next day, looking for trouble, but as far as I know the only result of this combined sweep was a single guerrilla killed in the initial fray. The dead man lay sprawled in the bulldozed debris to one side of the road, naked except for a pair of shorts. He had several bullet holes in him. He was big, the biggest Vietnamese I ever saw, and had a fierce, determined look about him. He appeared to be in his thirties, and it was obvious that this wasn't some raggedy-ass farmer-by-day-guerrilla-by-night. This was a hard-core mother, and the sight of him chilled my blood.

Lieutenant Young had rotated to the squadron staff by then, having completed his six months of command time. Officers spent only half their tours in the field. It was our brand-new platoon leader, 2d Lt. Donald J. Russin, who told me to move down the side of the road for several kilometers with my squad and see what else we could find. What we found was a bunker complex. It was so expertly camouflaged that I didn't notice the first log-reinforced bunker until I had actually walked up on top of it. We counted seventy or eighty more of them. They were freshly made, but no one was home, thank God.

I reported the complex and its location by radio. "I didn't mean for you to go that far," Russin answered. "Get your ass out of there. . . ."

The enemy was everywhere and nowhere. We found their bunkers and made souvenirs of the propaganda leaflets and little paper Viet Cong flags they sometimes scattered along the road, but they themselves were always just out of reach. Danylchuk or I would eagerly climb headfirst into the tunnels we sometimes uncovered, a .45 in one hand and flashlight in the other. They were always empty. On Thanksgiving Day, the troop was up around Dau Tieng, and I was flying back to it aboard a Huey resupply helicopter, having been dispatched to pick up an engine part or something in Cu Chi. We were passing over the Michelin when the door gunner suddenly caught sight of movement down in the rubber where the plantation bordered the Saigon River. His eyes were afire as he leaned over his M60, pumping away, and I was excited, too, pulling against my seat belt to get a look, even as I held on tight while the pilot swooped down toward our quarry. I was hoping we had caught hundreds of them. The helicopter circled low, reconning by fire, but the enemy had disappeared again, and we eventually pulled back up and continued toward Dau Tieng.

Late in the year, we began doing less convoy security and more of the aggressive search-and-destroy operations we had been trained for. We were finally taking the war to Charlie. The situation, however, remained frustrating. "We had overwhelming firepower," writes Captain Virant, "but couldn't find the enemy to shoot at. . . ."

They could always hear us coming. Running the road at night, we would suddenly encounter hastily made roadblocks of brush and little chopped-down trees. Assuming them to be booby trapped— we once had to medevac a sergeant with a bellyful of shrapnel when he messed with a roadblock—we tore them down with a grappling hook attached to a long rope or blew them away with plastic explosives.

Following a sweep operation one day, we were coming back on the same trail we had earlier used to enter the area. The lead track commander, SSgt. Gary D. Brewer, who was second only to Dean among the NCOs in the platoon, told his driver to pull to the side as soon as the heavy vegetation allowed, uneasy about using the same route twice. Sure enough, there was a mine just ahead. Only an hour had elapsed since we had first come in on that trail.

The enemy challenged us in strength only once before Tet. First Lieutenant Ted Hardies and the 1st Platoon were running the road south of Cu Chi one rainy night when two VC squads ambushed them from inside a village near the Hoc Mon Bridge. The results were predictable. The platoon immediately herringboned and leveled such return fire that the ambushers quickly fled, leaving behind one dead VC who was found sprawled atop his RPG launcher. Blood trails led off into the high sugarcane fields behind the village.

In open battle, we were simply unbeatable. When we did take casualties, and we lost five men killed during my first five months, it was always in incidents in which we had no chance to defend ourselves. On October 25, 1967, the entire troop was moving up Highway 1 at dusk toward the Go Dau Ha fire support base when a scout track in Hardies's lead platoon ran over a mine. The enemy used simple, homemade mines—a burlap sack stuffed with C4 plastique and buried with a pressure-type detonator of tin and bamboo connected to a battery with cheap wire—but they were devastating. The scout track was actually the fifth or sixth vehicle in the column, but the driver veered slightly out of the tread marks of the tank and APCs ahead of him, and thus hit the mine the others had unknowingly just missed. There was a terrific explosion, which blew off the tread and some of the road wheels on that side of the vehicle, and sent the track flipping upside down and backward with a hole in its belly. The driver was killed in his hatch, pinned underneath the thirteen-ton personnel carrier. He never knew what hit him.

We lost the others in hit-and-run ambushes. On November 28, the rear tank of Hardies's platoon was RPG'd while running the road near An Duc. The rocket penetrated the turret, and a quick fireball flashed inside it from the propellant charge of several main-gun rounds. The tank commander and his loader, who always sat up top when not actually in action for fear of being burned alive in just such a situation, jumped or were otherwise thrown clear by the blast. The driver clambered out of his hatch, but either tripped or was shot as the ambushers covered their retreat with automatic-weapons fire, and falling right in front of his still-moving tank, he was run over and killed on the road, his head crushed by one of the treads.

The other ambush that resulted in casualties was also more freak accident than firefight. On December 17, Virant was accompanying the 2d Platoon during a routine running-the-road operation when an RPG team, again ensconced in a village, took a potshot at the infantry track as it went past. The guerrillas aimed too high and missed the vehicle, which would have been the end of it—except that the rocket hit three GIs riding on the back deck and blew them to pieces. Almost everyone else on board was badly wounded. The enemy slipped away, unseen in the dark. Afterward, the captain joined those troopers who had to police up the mangled bodies and body parts in ponchos, and happened upon something dark lying in front of a hootch, which, he was shocked to realize when he picked it up, was a bloody hunk of scalp. It was a terrible moment for everyone, and the guys, growing to hate the people as much as the guerrillas who swam among them, decided among themselves in their frustrated anger that the next time they went through that village, they were going to open fire at the first sign of trouble and keep firing until everything was flat.

The first three months of my tour overlapped with the last three of the incumbent squadron commander. His is a blank face in my memory, as might be expected given our different stations. His conventional performance nevertheless stands in marked contrast with the dynamic leadership of Lt. Col. Glenn K. Otis, USMA 1953, who assumed command of the 3d Squadron, 4th Cavalry, 25th Division, in December 1967. Otis was a small, athletic man with penetrating blue-gray eyes and the blunt manner of the upstate New Yorker he was. He was also a brilliant combat commander—none of us who observed him during Tet were surprised when he eventually made four-star general. Otis was everywhere. We could be at the most isolated location in the squadron area, but he would show up out of the blue aboard his high-backed M577 command track to talk informally with us about whatever operation was in progress, how they were feeding us, and what we needed. He traveled without security vehicles, even at night when checking on our lonely little outposts along the highway. It was awe inspiring. I was uptight running the road even in platoon strength, and when we asked him after the war why he took such chances, he brushed the implied compliment aside, saying that he hadn't done anything we hadn't. That's the kind of man our commander was.

The first time that I saw Otis was a night soon after Danylchuk took over C-38. We were positioned by ourselves off the MSR near An Duc when another APC pulled up—and here was this colonel asking us how everything was going. This was definitely something new!

Otis had a Starlight Scope, and he casually remarked, "Sergeant, I think I see a couple of guys mining the road down there."

Being the hyperkinetic type anyway, Danylchuk went crazy with excitement as he ordered the driver to "get those gooks!" Otis joined the chase in his APC, and though the VC heard us coming and high-tailed it into the night, eluding our best efforts to find them, they did leave behind some of their explosives and gear. "I'm proud of you men," Otis said before continuing on his way. "You did a great job preventing this mining incident. I'm glad you spotted them."

Hell, I thought, *you* spotted them! It wasn't us!

Captain Leo Virant, our troop commander, was also a super professional, but was not as beloved as Otis. It was a matter of style. The son of a career officer, Virant graduated from West Point in 1963. He was tall and slender, male-model handsome with his expensive sunglasses and his sandy hair parted to the side. Articulate and polished, a man whose dry wit was much enjoyed by his fellow officers—though they were astonished by the silk kimono he sometimes wore around the officer's hootch in Cu Chi—he was also something of a loner with an aloof and arrogant side. When finding fault with us troopers, which he often did given his properly high standards, he had a quick and vicious mouth. He could tear your flesh off, and it would take you five minutes to figure out it was gone. He always maintained an immaculate appearance, and when I first joined the unit and saw him prancing around, being sarcastic, looking cool and smug behind his shades, I thought, what an asshole. . . .

My attitude toward Virant mellowed in time—his military skills demanded respect—but he always intimidated us. Take the afternoon we were sweeping an area west of An Duc, my infantry squad dismounted and on line ahead of the tracks. We stumbled across several AK-47 assault rifle ammunition magazines that had been wrapped in plastic and hastily buried. I suspect we had startled a group of guerrillas who ditched the magazines before scattering.

A trooper named Barry Lewis proudly radioed in that "We've captured some banana-style AK-47 magazines."

"Really?" Virant replied, noting that *all* AK-47 magazines were banana style. "Perhaps I'm wrong," the captain continued as Lewis deflated like a balloon. "Perhaps you've discovered something unique and new that no one else has seen before. . . ."

I thought well of our green platoon leader, Lieutenant Russin. A lot of the guys didn't like him, but I wanted to give him a chance. He was impetuous and gung-ho, a little too quick to plunge ahead, throwing caution to the wind—proud of his OCS bars, he didn't listen to his NCOs—but I thought he had the makings of a good combat leader given some experience.

In the meantime, it was stocky, muscular, soft-spoken Sergeant Dean, who had a weathered, old-for-his-age face, to whom we looked for leadership. He was an old Regular Army NCO, complete with a massive tattoo of a naked woman covering his left forearm. Dean had originally enlisted in 1948 right out of high school—"I got tired of smelling that old horse's tail," he joked, noting his days behind a plow on his father's dirt farm in Thaxton, Virginia—and arrived in Korea in August 1950, a platoon sergeant in the tank battalion assigned to the 1st Cavalry Division. He fought on the Pusan Perimeter, survived the debacle in North Korea, and won the Silver Star in the spring of '51 for piling up bodies in front of his tank as fast as the enemy could come out of the night during a human-wave Chinese attack on a hill defended only by his platoon and the Greek battalion to which it was attached. Dean was shot off his tank by a sniper some time thereafter while standing behind the turret, returning .50-caliber fire. The bullet barely missed his heart. Dean returned to his unit as the acting platoon leader, having made master sergeant on his twenty-first birthday, and was recommended for a battlefield commission by his outgoing battalion commander. The new colonel quashed the recommendation when Dean refused the battalion commander's order to place his platoon out in front of the line without the attached infantry unit Dean had argued that they needed to protect themselves in such an exposed position. He came home in November 1951.

Sometimes when we were drinking beers back in Cu Chi, Dean would talk about Korea. He had seen the dark side of war. The enemy often mixed with the refugees that came through their lines during the bitter winter of 1950–51, and, intimidated by their presence, the civilians would not point them out. Dean saw GIs and South Korean troops brutally beat refugees with rifle butts during so-called field interrogations, and once when an enemy soldier in civilian garb suddenly threw a grenade from out of a large group of refugees moving past, the fed-up tankers opened fire into the crowd.

Were many civilians killed? "Who cares—you're protecting yourself," answered Dean, who always contended that the civilians in Vietnam were well treated in comparison to those in Korea.

Dean was probably right. I remember another old NCO story I had heard along the way which had sickened me: "When we were checking the roads for North Korean infiltrators, if we ran across any good-lookin' woman, her ass was grass. We'd get her behind the tank and work her over. . . ."

Treating us like sons, Sergeant Dean made us want to perform at our best without saying a word. If you didn't, he would frown, his big hound-dog eyes sad with disappointment—and if that didn't work, his voice would drop into a bearlike growl, and he'd tear your ears off! When we ran the road, Dean's tank was always leading the way or in the drag position, the two most dangerous spots in the column. His was never the middle tank. He never ran over a mine in the dark, which was simply a matter of luck, and became an expert at spotting them during the day—the burlap sacks in which the charges were buried, as well as the black powder the enemy sometimes used, soaked up the morning dew, leaving wet circles on the unpaved highway. He always rode point when we moved out in the morning for this reason. Upon spotting a mine, Dean would have the column halt at a prudent distance while he called Brewer forward, then the two sergeants would approach the wet spot on foot, dig up the mine with bayonets, snip the wire running to the detonator with wire cutters—hoping all the while that the mine wasn't command detonated or otherwise booby trapped—gingerly carry it to the roadside ditch where blowing it up wouldn't further crater the highway, place a plastic explosive charge beside it, light the fuse, and finally saunter back, joking with each other along the way. It was a hell of a show.

* * *

Near the end of the year, Sergeant Dean informed Mike Christie and me that he was going to promote us both to E5 pending our completion of the Tropic Lightning Combat Leadership Course he was scheduling us to attend in Cu Chi. Mike had been trained as an infantryman—MOS 11B—and would be promoted to sergeant. My situation was more complicated. I was an 11E tanker, but had been serving as an infantryman. If I wanted sergeant stripes, I would have to change my MOS to 11B and remain on the infantry APC.

As an armor crewman, I rated the less prestigious rank of specialist fifth class and was ineligible for the coveted CIB—the Combat Infantryman Badge—no matter how many dismounted patrols and ambushes I went on. "If you stick with your armor MOS, I'd very much like for you to join my tank," Dean offered. "You've got some great leadership skills. If you go with me, I'll work with you, then give you your own tank to command. You'll make E6 in no time."

My own tank! I jumped at the offer and watched as Dean walked over to explain the switch to Sergeant Danylchuk. I couldn't hear what they were saying, but Scotty glanced over at me sharply when he got the news. He was quite animated as he pled his case, but he lost, and immediately stomped up to me and said that I had let him down.

I felt guilty as hell. I had been Danylchuk's right-hand man on the infantry track. The other guys in the squad really didn't give a shit about soldiering, and Norman Smith was in open rebellion by that point, appalled that Danylchuk actually expected him to clean his weapon and stay awake on guard. I wasn't threatening to beat Danylchuk up, or calling him "Chunky," like Smith did. I wasn't making fun of him because of the way he talked. I wasn't mocking his weird weapons. I followed his orders and helped him any way that I could. He trusted me, and I respected his rank—and now I was leaving. Danylchuk felt totally abandoned.

The Bob Hope Show arrived around Christmas, and from my seat atop an army ambulance I had a grand time watching Raquel Welch show some leg. Back at Cu Chi again on the last day of the month, Troop C ushered in New Year's Day 1968 with star-cluster flares. Beers were popping, too, and the mood being what it was,

Good and Bob Wolford—a shy, quiet, solid soldier who I counted as one of my best friends—decided to hit the NCO tent with smoke grenades. Bob might have been low key, but he definitely had a sense of humor. The plan was to lob the grenades over the top of the sandbagged tent so that the slight night breeze blowing toward them would carry the smoke back on through it. Bob and Good pulled the pins and let them fly—but one of the canisters, marked in the dark by its burning fuse, hit some communications wire running through the area and bounced back onto the roof of the tent. The roof caught fire. Good took off in one direction, Bob in another, cutting several tents down the row into one where a bunch of guys were playing cards. Thinking fast, Bob grabbed a seat and a handful of cards, and when an angry sergeant burst in moments later, Bob tried to look innocent despite his pounding heart while the others replied that no, nobody had come through there. The tent burned to the ground. The culprits were never caught.

I made the move to Sergeant Dean's crew around New Year's Day. Dean was the commander of tank C-35, and already having a loader and driver, he assigned me as gunner. The role of the gunner is to properly sight the main gun and assure target accuracy. It is a key position in traditional tank warfare, but in Vietnam our targets were usually so close that the commander fired the main gun by sight, needing only a loader to keep the shells coming. The gunner was a spare man who sat atop the turret with an M16 or M79 grenade launcher, ready to assist any way he could.

The loader was that screw-up Hines, and I'll call the driver Jim Lancey. I got off on the wrong foot with this hot-tempered, chip-on-his-shoulder GI, and we never got past it. The issue was the new engine—known as a pack—installed at Cu Chi shortly after I came aboard. The engine was air cooled, and Dean told Lancey to make sure to hook it up to the hoses that ran to the filter system. We were back on the road that day or the next, but during a routine maintenance break, I pulled open the grills on the back deck and realized that the hoses were not hooked up. The filters had not been cleaned, either, and the engine compartment was as coated in road dust as the outside of the tank. I hooked up the hoses, but the damage had already been done—not fifteen minutes farther down the road, we blew an oil cooler and started putting out some bad smoke.

The engine was ruined, and after we were towed back to Cu Chi it had to be pulled and replaced. The warrant officer from our maintenance section who oversaw the job knew that the pulled pack was new, and it was obvious, as he checked the dust-clogged engine, what had happened. Seething at the waste, he asked me sharply, "That engine wasn't hooked up properly, was it?"

I had no choice but to say, "No, sir, it wasn't."

"I'm going to court-martial whoever's responsible for this."

Ultimately, that was the tank commander, so I told Dean what the warrant officer had said. "Okay, you're going to have to cover for me," Dean replied. "You're going to have to change your story."

Feeling dishonorable, I lied to the warrant officer when he came back to take statements. He was furious, but the issue died without anyone losing a stripe—I think Dean had a lot of pull in the network of senior NCOs running through the division. In any event, new pack in place, we blasted up to Dau Tieng to rejoin the rest of Charlie Troop. When we shut down in the base camp, I told Lancey to give me a hand. Tank maintenance was never ending, and it required a lot of physical work, but he wasn't in the mood. He intended to go get a cold beer, and when I told him that he wasn't going to shrug off his duties again—I was still mad about the blown pack—he told me in two words to fuck off. I swung on him, and we went down slugging and kicking. It was a dead serious fight, and at first I was winning, but Lancey got on top of me as we grappled and was beating the daylights out of me when the guys broke us apart. We were speaking again a few hours later—not friends, but we could get along.

I was still new to the tank crew when the platoon, operating near the same area where we had found the buried ammo magazines the month before, bulled through some thick hedgerows right into a group of Viet Cong. At least, I think they were Viet Cong. They were all military-age males, and they acted like guerrillas—as stunned to see us as we were to see them, they scattered in all directions—but they didn't appear to have any weapons. The situation was too confusing to open fire, especially given the strict rules of engagement under which we operated. We were allowed to fire only when fired upon or given permission by higher command. The hell with it, I thought as I focused on an individual evading quickly through the brush about a hundred feet away—I'm going to drop him! From atop the tank turret, I swung my M16 up and snapped back the slide to chamber a round—and the damn thing jammed. The figure disappeared an instant later, leaving me boiling with frustration.

We swept the area. Crossing an open field, we discovered a little enemy camp back in a tree line. There was a thatch-roofed hootch outside of which someone had been cooking rice and several camouflaged bunkers, including one that had apparently served as a first-aid station; it was littered with bloody bandages. Jumping off his track, Danylchuk charged into the hut before anyone else—to hell with booby traps—and found numerous rifles, hand grenades, and rocket-propelled grenades cached inside. Lancey joined him and suddenly held up a magnificent Viet Cong flag that Danylchuk had somehow missed. They got into an argument over it. Lancey won. We had no way of knowing that within a few weeks, we'd have more enemy equipment, weapons, and flags than we ever wanted.

Tet was coming.

Part Two
INTERLUDE
(JANUARY 1968)

Chapter Four

Mike Christie and I reported to the Tropic Lightning Combat Leadership Course on January 22, 1968. The commandant was a first lieutenant, the instructors all E6s and E7s with combat experience. There were about fifty of us in the class, mostly infantrymen drawn from units throughout the division. The school occupied a small compound in the division base camp, and though it was loose and casual in comparison to the hard-core Imjin Scout School, the training was excellent. In addition to various drill and marching exercises, and lectures about leadership and tactics in classrooms and outdoor bleachers, we would also be trucked out to the field in full combat gear to do map and compass work, lead patrols, and learn how to call in artillery fire. We didn't actually bring in the rounds ourselves, but huddled around whatever instructor was on the radio and listened in as he went through the live-fire drill with the artillery back at Cu Chi.

We were an especially attentive class. The USS *Pueblo* was seized by the North Koreans while we were at the Leadership Course, and we wondered if we would be going to war in Korea next.

The instructors were good guys, but they were definitely different. One had a pet python, and during one ten-minute break when we were out in the bleachers, he produced a chicken—so, lucky us, we got to observe how a python kills and swallows a chicken.

Another instructor was a somewhat chubby Southern lifer who had been reassigned to the school after being wounded in a line unit. Young for his rank, he was extremely proud of his E6 stripes. He was friendly in a hearty, cock-of-the-walk way, and though an expert in the ways of war what he really liked to talk about was sex. He repeatedly held forth on the subject of going down to satisfy your girlfriend. If you didn't, he lectured, they would leave you. He described in detail how he did it for his girlfriend, said that if we didn't do it for ours, he would be glad to fill in, and one night he set up his little projector in our barracks and showed us his porno movies. Some of the stars were dogs, which was too damn much for me.

The war was heating up at this time. After dark on January 20, a platoon from Troop A was ambushed on the dirt road that connected the division base camp with Cu Chi village. To the shock of those who were hit, the VC had boldly set up less than a kilometer from the base camp, virtually right outside the gate. They initiated the ambush with a volley of RPGs, and within seconds, five APCs were burning on the road like torches. Nine GIs were killed and twelve wounded, and the guerrillas, their losses unknown but probably minimal, faded away as a reaction force sped toward the fray.

Some days thereafter, Lieutenant Russin's track driver took their vehicle through an opening in a hedgerow running along a berm and right over a mine. It was dark at the time, and Troop C was returning from a sweep operation north of Cu Chi. There was a huge fireball, and the troop commander, in the following APC, thought he had lost the entire crew. Explosions always looked worse than they were at night, however, and the track wasn't even disabled. Russin survived with damaged eardrums, a ringing headache, and superficial fragment wounds, then walked back under his own power to report to the captain that no one had been seriously injured. Russin and several similarly banged-up crewmen were put on light duty in Cu Chi.

On January 28, Captain Virant was accompanying the 3d Platoon of C/3/4th Cavalry as it swept south through the paddies, hedgerows, forests, and scattered hootches of a farming community called Sa Nhoi about fifteen kilometers northwest of Cu Chi. The rest of the troop was in blocking positions. The dismounted lead troops of the attack platoon pushed into a thickly vegetated area. "As we moved along, we would scrape the ground with our knives, clearing away the leaves and looking for signs of the enemy," recounts Pfc. John F. Rourke, who found just such a clue when he checked out a clump of bamboo. Several stalks had been cut off at the base. "I should have called for help, but I didn't. Instead, I got down on my hands and knees and started scraping away the leaves. I had made about three sweeps with my knife when I uncovered the corner of a trap door."

Rourke stood up slowly as he tried to remember his training, but before he could make his next move the top of the spiderhole popped open and a VC inside hurled a hand grenade straight at his head. *"I ducked, and the gook jumped back down in the hole while I went screaming through the bamboo to my right,"* says Rourke. *"I hugged old mother earth. I was sure I was done for, and when the grenade went off, I waited to feel the warmth of the blood on my side."*

Realizing he was unscathed, an amazed Rourke scrambled to his knees just in time to see a VC darting from the spiderhole. *"He was only five feet away from me. I opened up—and got him!"*

There were three guerrillas in that position, armed only with grenades. All were wounded, captured, and dusted off. *"Later, we understood they died,"* notes Virant. *"I was against dusting off VC in any event. The VC would fire at medevac ships, and I didn't see any point in endangering our people to save a wounded bad guy."*

The sweep continued. The area turned out to be crawling with spiderholes, and a second contact resulted in one wounded prisoner and a dead Viet Cong with a Chinese submachine gun. Next, the dismounted troops discovered a stubborn guerrilla who refused to crawl out of his hiding place. *"We crushed the tunnel, and his feet were sticking out, along with his head,"* says Virant, *"and we thought, we got this guy, he's pinned down in there— but then we began looking at the distance, and joked that either this was one tall sonofabitch, or it was actually two VC. The one with his head sticking out of the dirt was dead, but we pulled the other one out by his feet, and amazingly, he was still alive. He had not yet suffocated."*

At that point, Virant moved his command track into a clearing adjacent to the contact area, where he was joined by Lieutenant Colonel Otis, who arrived aboard his own APC. Meanwhile, Sergeant Dean, having moved about fifty meters into a nearby bamboo thicket, knelt beside the leaf-covered trapdoor concealing another spiderhole, and with his .38 Smith & Wesson revolver at the ready, flipped the board off. Luckily, the Viet Cong inside didn't have an AK-47, or that would have been the end of Dean, but he did have a U.S.-issue hand grenade, and having already pulled the pin, when his overhead cover lifted up he instantly threw it out, hoping to take an American with him.

Everything happened fast. Dean emptied his .38 into the spiderhole—he and the diehard were looking right at each other—then spun around to leap for cover just as the grenade exploded. Dean went down hard, as did Sergeant Danylchuk and Pfc. Albert L. Roby, both of whom had been covering Dean. Roby's leg was shredded. Danylchuk caught most of the blast, and with his stomach torn open, he was holding his intestines in with one hand while he fired his CAR15 with the other at a second guerrilla who had sprung from the hole and was rushing through the trees, trying to get away.

Danylchuk missed. Moments later, however, the fleeing guerrilla collided with Sergeant Brewer, who was charging up to help. Brewer threw him to the ground, pinned him with his knee in his chest, and, afraid that this VC might also have a grenade, instinctively swung the dull bayonet he had been probing for spiderholes with down into his throat. It wasn't a deep wound, but Brewer realized an instant later that he needn't have stabbed the enemy soldier at all. The man was unarmed and in a daze, having apparently been peppered with fragments from the grenade his comrade had thrown.

Turning the bedraggled prisoner over to some other troops who had come forward, Brewer scrambled up to the spiderhole and chucked a grenade inside, praying that he wasn't on top of an ammo cache. He pulled two bodies out when the smoke cleared—the diehard and a woman whom the GIs presumed had been serving as a guerrilla nurse. She might actually have been a cook, scout, ammo bearer, or all of the above, or she may have been an RPG gunner for that matter.

Dean was bleeding heavily down the front of his fatigues from fragment wounds in his chest, arms, and legs as he walked back to the clearing, and finally he asked one of the boys to help him sit down. That was it. He couldn't get back up; he was loaded aboard the medevac on a stretcher. He passed out shortly after the Huey lifted off.

The guerrilla who had been stabbed was not dragged out of the bamboo in time to be dusted off. There was no urgency in calling in a second medevac, and the prisoner, losing blood from a wound the medics had no interest in treating, lay in the clearing under the hot sun. "He was really in bad shape, but he managed to crawl some thirty feet into the shade of the colonel's track," recalls Virant, who was shocked to realize how indifferent he and his men were to the suffering of this enemy soldier. There were ten or so troopers standing there, watching the VC drag himself along, "And this is not a criticism, this is an observation—but I looked at them, and they were all just *looking at that guy with cold, blank expressions. No offer of help, no sympathy. These were fine young decent guys who would be fine young decent citizens when they went home, but that was what the war did to them. The attitude was that the only good gook is a dead gook. This was a bad guy; this was the sonofabitch that killed my buddy. He might have been the one who blew those three guys to pieces the month before, and so he lay there, and the medevac never came, and he finally just died."*

The sweep wasn't over yet. Captain Virant rushed to the scene when another guerrilla discovered in yet another spiderhole popped a grenade out before trying to get away, wounding a trooper in the face. Making sure the GI was okay, Virant then took off in hot pursuit. "This VC had run across a little cultivated field with eighteen-inch-high green crops of some type," he remembers. "I sent a sergeant around the field to cover one exit, and I told somebody else to go the other way, and then I crawled out into the field itself."

The troop commander, armed with an M16, was about thirty feet in and ten feet over when he spotted his quarry. "The VC turned and saw me coming up behind him, but he was wounded. I don't know how that happened, if he got hit by his own grenade or by return fire from some of the dismounted troops. In retrospect he was probably too far gone to have done anything to me—but as soon as I saw him, I stood up and emptied my magazine into him. I was probably in a state of shock or temporary insanity, emptying the whole magazine like that. It was almost like the bad guys were invincible, that you had to put eighteen rounds in them to make sure they were dead."

I heard about the Sa Nhoi contact from Mike Christie. Being career motivated and super gung-ho, I didn't go off limits, but Mike was always sneaking out of the barracks at the Leadership Course at night to get red eyed with his buddies over in the Troop C rear area. They told him what had happened, and the next morning we got permission to visit our wounded in the 12th Evacuation Hospital.

I was shattered that we were losing Sergeant Dean.

I was also sorry about Roby, a strong, silent type, and dedicated soldier from Tennessee who wore a Western-style pistol that his family had sent to him.

Danylchuk was in the worst shape of all and lay heavily bandaged in his hospital bed, a tube in his nose, a catheter in his penis, and

IVs in both arms. He lashed out at me in his pain: "You let me down big time, Birdy. If you had been there, this wouldn't have happened. . . ."

I didn't know what to say. Scotty was in a world of hurt. Being thin of frame, the grenade fragments had literally blown away what flesh and muscle he did have in the area of his wounds. His chest and stomach were shredded. He had a gaping hole all the way through his right thigh, and his left kneecap was cracked. I mumbled to him that I was sorry and would only be able to console myself, in retrospect, with the thought that Danylchuk had actually been lucky to have been wounded when he was. Given his charge-first-and-ask-questions-later style, he never would have survived Tet.

On the late afternoon of January 29, a gunship from D/3/4th Cavalry, the air cavalry troop, rolled in on several VC in the Ho Bo Woods north of Cu Chi. Inserted to search the bodies, the Aerorifle Platoon (ARP) landed right in a hornet's nest. Five ARPs were killed, and the survivors, including their gut-shot lieutenant, were pinned down in a bomb crater until an hour after midnight when a two-company infantry task force that combat-assaulted into the area at dusk was able to fight its way through. Three infantrymen had been killed. The enemy body count was sixty-six. The storm clouds were gathering.

Our class graduated from the Leadership Course on January 30, and Christie and I caught a jeep ride back to our unit that evening. There was some hard partying going on inside the Charlie Troop tents at that time, complete with tape players, beer, and bottles of Jim Beam and Seagram's whiskey. There really wasn't much to do in the rear except drink. The guys were probably a little looser than usual because we were under the impression that the Tet holiday truce was in effect. We didn't know it had actually been canceled because of major enemy attacks in the central part of South Vietnam.

I wasn't up to a party, and after sitting on my cot, catching up with some buddies, I crashed early. I was anxious to get back on my tank and was very much looking forward to moving out the next morning. Everyone was in a good mood about the move, in fact, because the word was that we were heading up to Tay Ninh, and then over to Dau Tieng. Though I hated the base camp at Tay Ninh—it was hot and dusty, sitting in the middle of a flat piece of nowhere with nothing around—Dau Tieng was another matter. We loved the place. It was an oasis from the war. The base camp occupied the western edge of the beautiful Michelin Plantation, the old French mansions serving as headquarters buildings. Morale among the troops stationed there was high. There was even a concession stand on the base, housed in what had once been servants' quarters, where you could buy hot dogs and Kool-Aid. The whole area was tranquil, the picturesque hamlets and the orderly rows of rubber trees attractive to the eye and soothing to the spirit. The people were friendly and industrious. Wagons and logging trucks shared the road with us, and mamasans sold delicious vegetable sandwiches made with tomatoes, cucumbers, and soy sauce on French bread. I always felt close to home at Dau Tieng.

Part Three

TET

(JANUARY 31, 1968)

Chapter Five

The day did not go according to plan. When SSgt. Ron E. Breeden, the acting platoon sergeant, pulled back the flap to our tent and told us to saddle up, we were not surprised that it was still pitch black outside—it was about half past four in the morning, not an unusual time to move out—but the word circulated as we rolled out of Cu Chi that we weren't going to Dau Tieng.

We were headed instead for Tan Son Nhut.

There had been some type of enemy attack on the giant air base and command center, and Captain Virant wisely decided on a cross-country approach to avoid possible ambushes and mines along the MSR. Lieutenant Colonel Otis kept an eye on us from a Huey whose crew dropped parachute flares to light the way. Virant's command track accompanied the 2d Platoon, which was on point. The 3d Platoon followed in loose column formation. The 1st Platoon was not part of the reaction force, having been outposted the day before to the Hoc Mon Bridge, which was roughly equidistant between Cu Chi and Tan Son Nhut on Highway 1.

The ground became marshy as we neared the bridge, and after one tank bogged down—another tank attached towing cables and pulled it free—Virant decided to wheel onto the highway, which was paved at that point and elevated several feet above the flat and open terrain.

We moved down the blacktop as fast as we could in the dark, but did not actually expect to make heavy contact at the end of the line. Except for the fact that our objective was in the Saigon area, which was about as far back in the rear as you could get, the mission seemed so routine, in fact, that hard-charging Lieutenant Russin, who would have risked exacerbating his injuries had he thought we were heading into a real battle, elected instead to remain in base camp.

Sergeant Brewer was acting platoon leader in his place. I rode atop the turret of Breeden's tank, which he had inherited from Dean—it was in the middle of the column, leading our platoon—along with Hines and Sp4 Dean A. Foss, the platoon mechanic. Lancey was driving. It was still dark when we passed through the 1st Platoon's positions, but the sky grew lighter as we entered the built-up outskirts of the capital—dawn was an overcast luminescent gray—and the squadron commander's helicopter peeled off at that point, not only because we no longer needed flares, but also because our two-platoon force had come under the operational control of the ARVN command in Saigon shortly after crossing the Hoc Mon Bridge.

Sergeant Breeden stood shirtless, tanned, and hard muscled in the commander's cupola of C-35. Based on what he could catch over his radio headset, he reported to us that "the word is there's a squad of VC breaking into the wire at Tan Son Nhut."

Hines exclaimed, "We're going to kick ass!"

Charlie Troop can handle a squad of VC any day, I mused, not unhappy with the prospect of racking up some enemy bodies. This is going to be like shooting fish in a barrel. . . .

It was not going to be like that at all. We did not know that the world had turned upside down at three o'clock that morning, the communists taking advantage of the festive Tet holiday that ushers in the Lunar New Year to launch a massive win-the-war wave of assaults against almost every major city in South Vietnam.

We did not know that the Mekong Delta was on fire. We did not know that sappers had penetrated the U.S. Embassy compound in downtown Saigon, or that an NVA division had run up a red flag with a gold star over the old imperial capital of Hue.

We did not know why we passed no civilian traffic as we headed south, or why all the houses along the way appeared deserted. We didn't even know what was happening at Tan Son Nhut. An advisor from an ARVN training center south of the Hoc Mon Bridge had been detailed to guide us to the specific gate on the air base perimeter where we were needed—he was waiting for us in a jeep along

Highway 1—but could provide no information on the enemy action itself. Virant directed the advisor to join the rear of our column.

The lead platoon had no operational tanks. Because we were heading into the unknown, Captain Virant placed one of our platoon's three M48s at the head of the column as we pressed on. Leading from the front, he had his track fall in directly behind that point tank. Virant then made radio contact with the senior U.S. Army advisor at Tan Son Nhut. Had that lieutenant colonel been fully informed of the situation—and given the fog of war, he was not—he could have told Virant that we were about to face not a squad of guerrillas, but the 271st Regiment, 9th VC Division. After setting up a command post in the Vinatexco textile mill directly across north-south Highway 1 from the west side of Tan Son Nhut, and after slipping into the hamlet that ran south from the factory down the same side of the road, the assault force had used satchel charges to blow paths through the perimeter wire and minefield. The nearest air force security police bunker firing on the attackers was taken out with RPGs, and after putting more rockets through the perimeter fence and the gate on that side of the base, the lead enemy battalion flooded in and charged toward the runway. Stopped at its edge by a thin line of security police who hastily formed up on the opposite side, the enemy inside the fence hunkered down behind cover and engaged the airmen in a nose-to-nose exchange of fire, while those battalions still in the hamlet across the highway prepared to renew the push as the sun came up. The guerrillas were reinforced with a foe we had never faced before—regulars of the North Vietnamese Army.

Chapter Six

The Battle of Tan Son Nhut began for us in a state of utter confusion. The lead tank had just drawn abreast of the knocked-out perimeter bunker, and the rear of the column had just cleared the textile mill, when a wall of fire erupted from the long and narrow hamlet on our right flank. Troops from the point platoon recount that the column was still moving when the firing started. That is not my recollection. I have an image of our well-spaced column stopping on the road—there being only a clearing to our right, Sergeant Breeden had Lancey herringbone slightly so as to face that part of the roadside ville parallel to the personnel carriers ahead of us—and of a brief calm before the storm as we tried to assess the situation we had just rushed into. It was not at all clear what was going on, given the roar of our 690-horsepower engine and the dust hanging in the air from the passage of the point platoon. Unnerved, Hines dropped to cover inside the turret after blurting, "I don't like the way this looks!"

Breeden pulled off his headset to hear better even as he squinted into the hazy gray twilight. "They're saying there's VC up there," he remarked, turning to me. "Hell, I don't see a damn thing. Do you?"

"Goddamn, man, look—*they're everywhere!*"

Though it was an overcast morning, the top of a tank on the elevated highway provided a commanding view. There was movement to our left inside the air base—our column was hemmed in by the perimeter wire running down that side of the road, and the hamlet running down the other—and to the right-front I could see more silhouettes darting into positions among the hootches and hedgerows opposite the point platoon. The figures were clearly armed, but none were firing, apparently stunned at our arrival.

50

I shouted at Sergeant Breeden to open fire. He hesitated, worried about hitting civilians in this heavily populated area on the edge of Saigon. Being court-martialed for firing without permission or otherwise violating the rules of engagement was a constant worry, especially for career men like Breeden, but he finally pumped thirty to fifty .50-caliber rounds downrange, then put the main gun into action. I was thunderstruck by what happened next. The sky lit up with tracers—hundreds of them, *thousands*—and it made no sense because they were green, and we used red tracers. Orange balls of fire also streaked out of the hamlet, and explosion after explosion rocked the point platoon. The scene looked just like one of our Mad Minute demonstrations at the armor school in which sixty seconds of concentrated main gun and machine-gun fire were directed at targets on a firing range, and it took me a stunned moment to grasp that something was terribly wrong. We were supposed to be the ones that gave it to *them,* but this furious scythe of tracers was coming at *us.*

Breeden was hit almost immediately. He let out a scream and collapsed into the turret. Dropping down through the loader's hatch, I pulled his hands away from his face. He was in agony, a bloody hole where his left eye had been. He had another ragged hole, apparently an entrance or exit wound, below the base of the left side of his skull. I climbed topside again, hauled the platoon sergeant up through the loader's hatch, and, with rounds snapping past all around, hurriedly helped him down to cover on the left side of the elevated highway.

I took Breeden's place in the commander's cupola. Breeden, right before I got him out of the tank, had actually told Spec Four Hines to take over—Hines had six years in this man's army to my twenty months—but given what a foul-up he was, I had interjected, "Wait a minute, wait a minute—*I'm* the E5 here!"

After a pause, Hines mumbled, "No, I'll do it—"

"No, you won't!" I barked harshly.

I put on a combat vehicle crewman helmet, connected it to the tank communications system—the CVC had a radio-intercom switch box and a boom mike that snapped down in front of your mouth on the left side, and a short cord that plugged into the long telephonelike cord running up from the radio built into the turret—and commenced firing with the main gun and the heavy machine gun, hands wrapped around the wooden grips, thumbs on the butterfly trigger in between.

As focused as I was, I didn't realize that the point platoon had been utterly destroyed in the opening shock-wave of fire. Captain Virant had just shouldered his M16 when a metal fragment hit the back of his head, fracturing his skull. He was lying unconscious inside the command APC. His artillery lieutenant had lost several fingers and had a massive gunshot wound in his thigh, but had slammed shut and locked the hatches and was hunkered inside with his .45-caliber pistol out and ready. Their driver was dead. Their track commander was dead.

The 2d Platoon sergeant was dead too. The lead tank had taken several rockets, which wiped out the entire crew, including Norman Smith, I later learned, and most of the APCs following like ducks in a row had also been RPG'd and now sat dead on the road belching smoke and flame, the ammunition inside cooking off.

Frantically returning fire, all I knew in the heat of the moment was that the .50-cal MG on my tank had no armor shield. You made yourself an outstanding target when you put it into action, and as I pumped away—sitting on the opened cupola hatch cover, head and chest in full view—there was a constant and terrifying buzz from rounds whining past or ricocheting off the turret. Several RPGs seemed to fly right at me, but at the last moment one overshot the tank and the others sailed past to the left to explode in the air base.

I bellowed at Dean Foss, our hitchhiking mechanic, to unass the tank and take cover. Tough nut that he was, Dean had been standing beside the turret, blasting away with his M16. Meanwhile, Hines—that balding, overage-in-grade loudmouth who wanted to get back to the beer-and-frauleins life of a tanker in Germany—was in a panic. I had fired only ten or so 90mm rounds when he began screaming that we had to pull back before we all got killed. He wasn't loading the main gun. I shouted at him to calm down, forced to rely on the .50 as our only firepower. Hines finally got back to work, and it was then as I put the main gun back into action that I suddenly realized that no one was returning fire from any of the vehicles ahead of me. Several were burning. I couldn't believe it, but enemy soldiers had clambered aboard one disabled and abandoned track. They were monkeying with the machine guns, but I put mine on them before they could turn them against us. The tracers snapped downrange as straight as arrows and several of the little figures went flying off the back deck. The rest scurried back to cover on the right side of the highway.

Every vehicle ahead of us had been put out of action. I could see troops from the point platoon keeping low against the left side of the highway as they pulled back toward my tank—we called the narrow strip between the base of the elevated roadway and the air-base-perimeter-wire a ditch—and I kept up a furious rate of fire to cover these survivors. Ten feet tall and twelve feet wide, our fifty-two ton tank shielded the smaller APCs lined up behind us from most of the frontal fire. Thus unscathed from the bulk of the enemy force, our platoon achieved total fire superiority over the lesser number of guerrillas in the hootches running down the right flank between the rear of my tank and the textile factory. Responding instantly to what we thought was an ambush up ahead, our track gunners opened fire before the foe alongside us did—opened fire, in fact, before they had seen a single enemy. The wall of lead literally blew the hootches to splinters, and blindly eliminated camouflaged enemy soldiers before they could do us any harm, to include a machine-gun crew whose bodies were discovered after the battle in a good spot of cover only thirty feet from the platoon command track.

The firing had begun at a word from Sergeant Brewer, our field-wise platoon leader. I thought the world of Brewer. An old soldier to us at the age of twenty-six—he was originally from an Indiana coal town—he had a big handlebar mustache and was shaped like a beer keg. He was laconic, slow-moving, and easygoing. He had pulled a previous tour with a supply unit in Saigon, and through his old contacts could produce beer, steaks, and bottles of the hard stuff. The troops affectionately referred to this laid-back lifer as Brew-baby.

Sergeant Brewer was a bulldog in battle. Taking command of Troop C, he made radio contact with Lieutenant Colonel Otis, who ordered him to pull back. Brewer refused. "We got too many wounded," he said, referring to the casualties from the point platoon who had crawled back to us and the ones still pinned down up front. "I can't leave 'em, and I can't pull 'em back—so I'm going to stay put."

Thus, we hunkered down and fought it out. Informed of the disaster that had befallen our detached reaction force, Lieutenant Colonel Otis had immediately rushed to the scene aboard a Huey and, though he had no authority to do so, took control of the battle from the incompetent ARVN command in Saigon. We would have been destroyed had he not. In coordination with calm, steady, unflappable Brewer, the squadron commander—call sign Saber 6— brought in gunships and resupply-medevac helicopters from Troop D. The enemy had a dozen well-entrenched .51-caliber antiaircraft guns, and they played havoc with the Hueys. Otis was shot down four times—and subsequently awarded the Distinguished Service Cross[*]—but he was quickly picked up each time by another chopper and never lost control of the battle. The gunships kept roaring down our right flank no matter how much battle damage they accumulated during their runs. At Brewer's direction, the tank at the rear of our column ran back and forth over the air base perimeter wire to clear a lane to the perimeter fence, which the tank also plowed through, and Hueys kept landing there to unload ammunition for us no matter how many were shot down in the process. Humping a heavy ammo box on each shoulder, Brewer personally led the teams that hauled the munitions back to the vehicles on the road, and at one point he had a grip on Breeden's arm, ignoring the fire whip-cracking all around as he led the sergeant back through the mashed-down wire to a medevac. Head down to keep from tripping and unable to hear anything for all the noise, Brewer looked up only at the last moment—and realized that he had almost walked right into the rear rotor of the Huey.

---

[*] The 3/4th Cavalry won a Presidential Unit Citation for Tet.

Recommended for the Medal of Honor, Sergeant Brewer eventually received the Distinguished Service Cross. Brewer was everywhere during the battle, keeping the unit organized, and at one point I happened to glance backward and saw that he was standing in the ditch behind my tank. Grinning up at me before he turned around to work his way back down the line, he shouted, "Keep firing, Chief!"

I was doing nothing but. In fact, Staff Sergeant Thomas, the black career NCO commanding the tank at the rear of the column—he was another pro—chimed in appreciatively over the radio for all to hear, "Birdwell's really feedin' that cannon. It's smokin'!"

Enemy fire snapping past or ricocheting off the armor with terrifying whines, C-35 was the locus of Troop C's desperate battle for survival. I was firing like a madman—reinforcements were on the way, we had to hold till they arrived—blasting at hootches and hedgerows and individual enemy soldiers darting from position to position. Most of the ones I spotted were in the bushes and behind a hedgerow that ran along an earthen berm on the far side of a large rice paddy. I kept sweeping that area with the .50, piling up expended brass and grabbing fresh hundred-round ammo boxes from the stack in the bustle rack that wrapped around the outside rear of the turret.

I also concentrated my main-gun fire on that hedgerow. The long and thin gun tube looked wicked as it traversed toward a target. The 90mm was, in fact, a devastating weapon, so loud, the concussion so ferocious, that it just numbed you. I was half deaf as I kept up the fire. I was firing by sight from my seat on the opened cupola hatch cover, using the lanyard we had wrapped around the internal firing handle. You just gave that cord a little jerk and the cannon would roar like thunder, and without having to drop into the turret to use the firing handle and periscope you could really stay focused on your target.

Hines was down inside the smoke-filled turret, reloading the main gun—upon ramming in a fresh shell and closing the breechblock, he would shout, "Up!"—and throwing the empty casing out through the loader's hatch above him. We fired HE, WP, and even HEAT—that is High Explosive, White Phosphorus, and High

Explosive Antitank—plus Canister and Beehive, which were my rounds of choice. Canister was like grapeshot, and Beehive was just wild—each round was packed with eight thousand two-and-a-quarter-inch steel darts that shredded everything before them like a shrieking whirlwind.

Enemy fire on us was constant—a nearby advertising billboard was shot all to hell during the course of the battle—and Hines got panicky again at one point. "Back up, back up, back up!" he screamed to the driver. "Let's get the hell outta here before we all get killed!"

I tried to countermand the order, but got no response from Lancey. I could hear over the intercom, but no one was listening to me, and I couldn't figure it out—I was so pumped up that I didn't realize the microphone had been shot off the side of my tanker helmet. Lancey started backing up as instructed. I glanced behind me. There were numerous wounded huddled in the ditch along the highway, and though I couldn't hear them over the engine, it was obvious from their saucer-sized eyes that they were shrieking at me to stop the tank before it crushed them. In desperation, I unplugged the helmet, jumped down onto the road amid the continuing enemy fire, and banged on the hatch the driver had closed to protect himself from the earsplitting blast of the main gun. Lancey swiveled the platelike hatch open, and when I shouted at him to pull forward into our former position, he did so without hesitation.

Hurriedly climbing back into the commander's cupola, I was reconnecting my tanker helmet when I spotted a small group of enemy soldiers to my left front, falling back toward the perimeter fence from inside the air base. I couldn't traverse the turret to put the main gun on them because the gun tube would have been directly over the troops in the ditch alongside my tank, and the power of the muzzle blast that came out of the two side vents at the end of the barrel was such that it would have injured some of them.

The coaxial was jammed. I couldn't fire the .50 at them either. I had burned the barrel out, and my tracers were veering off in every direction except directly at my targets—so I grabbed my M16. This wasn't the one that had previously jammed up on me—we had recently been issued an improved model with a chrome chamber—

and I squeezed off the magazine in one smooth burst. Two or three of the figures went down in my sights and did not get back up. The rest slipped through the wire down where the lead vehicles were sitting and escaped across the highway into the enemy hamlet.

By that stage in the battle, most of the survivors of the point platoon had made it back down the side of the road to my tank, thanks to Sp4 Russell H. Boehm and Pfc. R. Frank Cuff—great soldiers, they were also the best of friends—who'd laid down a tremendous base of covering fire from their separate tracks, and then, when their vehicles were hit, from the ditch, using hand grenades and loose M16s and the M60 machine gun each had dismounted from his APC.

Boehm set up his machine gun right beside my tank, and later told me that the next time I fired the 90, a redheaded GI squatting beside him grabbed his face, screaming that he'd been hit. It turned out that he'd only caught some road gravel that sprayed backward from under the tank treads. The main gun really was a hell raiser.

I hadn't known Boehm and Cuff very well before that day, but afterward they became two of the most trusted buddies I had in Nam. There were others keeping up the good fight from the mauled 2d Platoon, to include a sergeant who, having been shot in one arm, blazed away one handed with his M16, joking that he was John Wayne. In addition, the platoon's new medic, a soft-spoken, round-faced Indian boy with a thick shock of black hair, hustled up and down the ditch to treat the casualties without any regard for his own safety. Except that he was acting out of concern for his buddies, not bravado, the medic reminded me of a mechanical rabbit at a county fair, running from one side of the target area to another, daring the shooters to blast him.

Many others had ceased to function, however. The green lieutenant in command of the 2d Platoon was in a daze, and other stunned troopers were hunkered down like turtles in the ditch behind my tank. I noticed Good from my old infantry squad sitting there, too, cradling a bloody arm and beaming broadly about his million-dollar wound.

Why in the fuck aren't you sonsofbitches doing something? I thought furiously. Why aren't you returning fire?!

Though we were still under heavy fire, we later learned that the situation inside the base was actually stabilizing at that point. Rushing down Highway 1 from the Hoc Mon Bridge, the 1st Platoon of Troop C—led by SSgt. Roy W. Kennard, the tough platoon sergeant, because Lieutenant Hardies was on R&R with his wife in Hawaii— had turned onto a service road just north of the textile mill and entered the base through a small gate in the perimeter fence. Guided into position by an airman who climbed aboard a tank, the platoon joined the security police in methodically reducing the positions of those diehards still fighting inside the west end of Tan Son Nhut Air Base.

During a lull in the enemy fire from both sides of the highway, an open-topped jeep sped down the unpaved road that followed the inside of the perimeter fence. The jeep stopped about a hundred meters behind my tank, and a man of field-grade age sporting a baseball-style utility cap leapt out and began shouting and gesturing wildly to us. I assumed he was an officer because I could see no stripes on his sleeve, but I couldn't even tell if he and his young driver were from the army or air force. I couldn't make out a word over the tank engine, so I unplugged my helmet again and climbed down behind my tank to ask if anyone in the ditch knew what he was saying.

I was told he was calling us cowards and demanding that we charge the enemy. That might have seemed like a good idea from his side of the fence, but we had too many casualties, and even those GIs who were unscathed were too numb to respond, too numb to give a damn that their courage was being challenged. They were in no condition to do much of anything but hold on, so ignoring what I thought was an unrealistic order I swung back aboard my tank and resumed firing. To hell with him, I thought—if he gets through all that wire between us, you just let him take command of the tank.

Frustrated, the officer jumped back in his jeep and continued down the road on the other side of the fence. He had gone past my tank when an enemy soldier still inside the perimeter suddenly blasted the jeep with a burst of automatic-weapons fire. The officer slumped over. The driver made a hard left and sped away, while the enemy soldier who had presumably done the shooting jumped up from the tall grass he had been hiding in—he was in black pajamas,

and carrying an AK-47—and took off down the perimeter road away
from us. It wasn't funny, but later we kind of laughed about it anyway, remarking that this big shot telling us how to fight might have
been wiser had he kept his mouth shut and exhibited a little more
caution. I have no idea if he was killed or only wounded.

The madness continued. I was booming away with the main gun
to the cheers of some of the guys in the ditch when one of the
rounds failed to fire despite repeated jerks and tugs on the firing
cord. Hines wouldn't touch it. I too remembered the lecture in armor school about how a round might spontaneously discharge
when loaded into the overheated chamber of a main gun that had
been fired without break. Afraid to remove the dud and put the 90
back in action myself—I knew that goddamn shell would explode in
my hands as soon as I got it out—I pulled on a pair of asbestos
gloves, replaced the burned-out machine gun barrel, and opened
up with that instead. I burned the replacement barrel out within
minutes, even as several troopers yelled at me to fire the main gun
again, having no way of knowing there was a defective round sitting
in the chamber.

It was a bad situation, and Hines, already shaky, came totally
unglued. "We're being overrun," he shrieked on the squadron net.
"They're everywhere. . . . We're out of ammo. . . . Please help us!"

He was howling like a stuck pig as he contacted the driver again
on the intercom: "Get out, get out, GET THE HELL OUT!"

Lancey started backing up just like before. Still unaware that my
microphone had been shot away, I was completely baffled that I
couldn't get through to the driver, so, infuriated, thinking Lancey
should know better than to listen to the hysterical loader, I tore my
CVC helmet off and jumped down onto the forward slope of the
tank. I pounded on the driver's hatch and was so angry that when
Lancey opened up, I kicked the man right in the head, furiously
motioning to him over the roar of the engine to move the tank back
into position.

Lancey spun toward me with blood in his eyes. He didn't deserve
an army boot to the head—he had been following the instructions
of the only crew member he could communicate with, and had he
been wearing his sidearm I think he might have unholstered it and

shot me in the heat of the moment—but he pulled forward as instructed, even as I dropped down into the turret to deal with Hines.

I smacked him across the face. "We don't have any choice," I shouted as I laid my .45 upside his head to let him know I was serious. "We're *not* leavin'! We're stayin' here—and we'll have a better chance of getting out if you'll do your fucking job!"

Hines calmed down. At that point, I faced the fact that I had to do something about the defective round in the chamber of the main gun. The longer I ignored it, the more heat it absorbed—and the better the chance it might cook off as I removed it. I told Hines to vacate the turret for his own safety, then opened the breechblock, working the lever several times to extract the stuck shell. I picked it up, ignoring the pain—it was hot, hot, hot—as I frantically clambered up through the commander's cupola, then keeping low, prepared to throw it into the wire behind my tank. I wasn't about to throw it in the paddy to my front because of all the fire coming from that direction.

I still had the round clutched against me when it exploded. At least, I thought it exploded. There was a hell of a roar, and I was confident I was dead, but then I realized that Mike Christie and a trooper named John Cotton had advanced to the side of my tank with a shoulder-fired 90mm recoilless rifle and had just let fly with their first round. Regaining my senses, I waved away the men in the ditch behind my tank and heaved the dud round into the wire.

Back in the cupola, I noticed my asbestos gloves I had worn earlier and cursed myself as a dummy for not having used them when handling that hot shell. Putting the main gun back in action, I got another dud. This time, I was in better control of my emotions. I quickly got Hines out of the turret again, donned the thick gloves, and threw the round in the same area where I had gotten rid of the first one. I resumed firing, while down to my right Christie and Cotton kept exposing themselves around the corner of the tank to fire that damned recoilless rifle. It was unnerving. The weapon was as loud as thunder, its ferocious backblast swirling up dust and smoke behind us in the wire, and every time they punched off another round, I nearly leapt out of my skin, thinking the tank had taken a direct hit.

Chapter Seven

Finally noticing that my tanker helmet was damaged, I tossed it aside and stood bareheaded in the turret as I fired the balance of our main gun ammunition. The tank carried sixty-four 90mm rounds, and except for the two duds we sent every damn one of them into the enemy positions. I also went through all our .50-cal ammo—I had Lancey and Hines evacuate our empty tank at that point—and was finally reduced to popping away with my M16 from the top of the turret, though it didn't take long to use up all my magazines.

"That main gun's a 90-millimeter, right?" Christie asked.

I answered in the affirmative. "This is a 90 too," he shouted, pointing to his recoilless rifle. "Take some of my ammo!"

I didn't think it would work, but Mike insisted that I give it a try, so climbing down to the back deck, I took the rounds that he handed up to me. They were the right size but, unlike tank munitions, had perforated jackets, and I didn't use them, afraid that they might blow up in the breech. The main gun remained silent.

In the middle of this chaos, I realized that there was a diminutive white woman sporting a blond braid taking photographs of the battle from up ahead in the ditch. She was accompanied by a white male—we later heard that they were French newspaper reporters—and the sight of them was as startling to me as if a kangaroo had bounded into view. The pair eventually disappeared back toward the air base.

The situation was desperate. Enemy fire was building to a crescendo, and there weren't many of our guys left who could fight. Lancey was one of those still functioning. He worked his way forward against the side of the highway, darted onto the road itself to recover weapons and ammunition from several of the abandoned personnel carriers, then distributed his catch among the troops in the ditch.

Having picked up several critical hits while orbiting the enemy ville, Lieutenant Colonel Otis's command ship was forced to make an emergency landing at that time. The Huey bounced in hard behind my tank, mashing down the perimeter wire with its skids. Fearing a possible fuel fire, Otis and crew immediately jumped out—I had no idea the helicopter had actually been shot down until I saw the scramble to get away from it—but in short order another Huey swooped in for the colonel and his artillery liaison officer, who had hauled his radio off the downed command ship and kept the support fires coming during their brief interlude on the ground.

The abandoned Huey sat in the wire, its nose almost touching the elevated highway. Hey, I thought, there's two '60s on that thing!

Rushing through the concertina and slicing my legs to ribbons in the process, I was dismounting one of the M60s when a door gunner who had taken cover nearby shouted, "Leave that alone!"

The door gunner was clean shaven. His flight suit was immaculate. "The hell with you," I barked over my shoulder, pulling the M60 free.

I turned one machine gun and a minigun can full of ammunition over to my buddy Bob Wolford, who was on the APC directly behind C-35. I climbed back aboard the tank with the other aviation-style M60—it had twin D-handles and a butterfly trigger—and opening up another ammo can that I had salvaged, I cut loose into the ville with a renewed fury. It didn't last long. The front part of the barrel suddenly disappeared in a dazzling flash, and I realized that I had taken a faceful and chestful of little fragments. Perhaps a rifle grenade had slammed into the machine gun—if it had been an RPG, I would have been blown away—but whatever the case, I now had nothing left but the sidearm holstered against my hip and no choice but to evacuate the tank myself and jump down with the others in the roadside ditch.

Moving forward with Lancey, Foss, and an Ottawa Indian from my old infantry squad, I reached a big tree standing by itself near the disabled lead tank. Captain Virant's track was next in line, and I made repeated attempts to reach it while Foss popped up to cover me with his M16, but was driven back by enemy fire before I could open the back hatch. Unable to rescue the troop commander—we didn't even know if he was alive or dead—we nevertheless held our ground, determined to keep the enemy from coming over the top and overrunning the wounded men strung out in the ditch behind my abandoned tank.

We were the most forward element still firing. "Goddamn, there's three or four hundred gooks over there," my Ottawa buddy finally exclaimed, down to his last one or two M16 magazines. "We ain't gonna hold 'em off! We gotta get back to the rest of the platoon!"

"No!" I shouted. "We've got to *hold* this damn position!"

"We're gonna get killed!"

"Well, so what?" I shrugged.

"Fuck that!" my buddy snapped, and with that, he spun around and scuttled back down the ditch on all fours.

I was so mad I almost shot him. Meanwhile, good old Dean Foss—a pugnacious, hardworking little fireplug of a man from Bar Harbor, Maine, who walked, talked, and looked like Popeye—kept firing his M16 in quick, jack-in-the-box bursts despite the rocket fragment that had grazed the side of his neck like a branding iron.

Having collected ten or fifteen hand grenades from abandoned vehicles, Lancey and I began throwing them across the highway. In response, an enemy machine gunner trained his weapon in our direction. The fire ripped into the tree trunk right above our heads like a chainsaw, and with leaves and branches falling about us, we were completely pinned down, unable to move forward, unable to move back, unable to even raise up anymore to return fire.

This was the end of the line. It was all over. The enemy was going to clamber over the highway at any moment, stitching the ditch with their AK-47s. This isn't real, I thought, looking back through the perimeter fence at the interior of the air base. This was the rear. This was where I came in-country, and where I was supposed to leave from at the end of my tour. I could even see commercial airliners parked on the runway. Here I am, about to die, I thought incredulously—and just behind me are the Freedom Birds! Gripping my .45, I braced myself to fire six rounds when the final assault came, and then to put the pistol to my head and pull the trigger on the seventh and last round in the magazine. I hoped I could do it. I didn't want to be captured.

Dean Foss was Regular Army and had been stationed in Germany before requesting duty in Vietnam. "My mama begged me not to volunteer for any more overseas service," he said grimly. "By God, if I get out of this one, I'm going to listen to her the next time."

He was being dead serious, but I had to laugh.

We did not die, however, because moments later, as if on cue, Troop B came to the rescue, having raced straight down the thirty-nine kilometers of Highway 1 between its security positions at Trang Bang Bridge and Tan Son Nhut Air Base.

Gunships preceded the relief force. Hueys strafed the wire behind us, coming in so close that the three of us in the ditch thought we might be taken out by friendly fire, while others rolled in on the hootches facing us across the highway, pumping rockets. The machine gun that had us pinned down abruptly ceased firing.

More helicopters sailed low over the open fields between the enemy village and the textile mill, laying down a smoke screen to conceal the arrival of Troop B. Directing the unit by helicopter, Saber 6 had it turn off Highway 1 immediately after passing the mill, then execute a left flank so that all its tanks and tracks were on line and facing the top and left-rear of the enemy village at an oblique angle.

Bravo Troop commenced firing. The enemy was chewed to pieces, and I exulted that it was their turn to be the fish in the barrel. Enemy soldiers died in their spiderholes as a dismounted assault element from Troop B pushed into the hamlet. Guerrillas who tried to run across the paddies to the south and west were blown away by the tank and track gunners waiting for them, or blown to bits by the artillery barrages being fired on the escape routes. It was a turkey shoot. We had to keep low in the ditch for all the stray fire tearing through the hootches and hedgerows and passing just overhead to shake the concertina wire behind us. We discovered after the battle that our point platoon vehicles were embedded with metal flechettes from the Beehive rounds fired by Troop B.

Chapter Eight

Lieutenant Russin was furious. He was mad at himself for having remained in base camp because of his injuries when we originally moved out that morning, and, anxious for battle, he was bitterly disappointed that as fast as he had organized a reaction force when informed of the heavy contact we had run into—he utilized troops on light duty and had several headquarters tracks stacked with as much ammunition as they could carry—all that was left when he arrived was to coordinate the medevacs and mopping up. Russin was young; he was proud; he wanted to make his career in the military; and he had missed the big action in which he could have been a hero. He almost seemed to resent those of us who had fought the battle as he got the unit reorganized and was in no mood to listen to my objections when he ordered me onto a medevac. I looked terrible and my shirt was a bloody rag, but I tried to point out that head wounds bleed excessively and that my injuries were actually superficial.

They were, but I was really arguing because I wanted to stay with my buddies. Everyone was smiling, amazed to still be alive. I had no hard feelings for my old Ottawa comrade, and he grinned at me with admiration, shaking his head: "You're crazy, man, you're fuckin' crazy!"

Survivors of the point platoon hugged me and slapped me on the back. "You saved us," they said. "You just kept throwing 'em and throwing 'em and throwing 'em, and you never backed down!"

Captain Virant had been recovered unconscious but alive from his command track and was medevacked out on a Huey. Russin ordered me onto another dust-off, but after climbing aboard the left side of the crowded ship, I simply hopped out the right side. I

65

figured that no one would notice, and that when Russin finally saw me he wouldn't even remember that I was supposed to be gone, given everything else that was going on. I was wrong on both counts. Russin spotted me within moments, and completely out of patience, he shouted red faced that it was up to the medics, not me, to determine how badly I'd been injured, and that he was going to court-martial my ass if I didn't follow orders and remove myself aboard the next medevac helicopter.

Sergeant Brewer was standing there with an amused smile. "You need to go on back and get those wounds taken care of," he said.

The medevacs had been completed by then, so Russin had several troops escort me to a Chinook supply helicopter that had landed near the west end of the runway inside the air base with instructions to keep their eye on me until the chopper got back off the ground.

Bodies were being loaded aboard the Chinook. Troop B had lost three men KIA—Killed in Action—plus seventeen WIA—Wounded in Action. Troop C had twelve KIA and forty-eight WIA.

Civilian casualties had also been gruesome. Some inhabitants of the hamlet facing Tan Son Nhut had been murdered by communist political cadre, many more—women and children included—had been blown away by the massive firepower we had brought to bear.

Against this, the enemy body count, a subject of much conjecture and exaggeration during our little contacts before Tet, was a solid five hundred. Communist weapons and gear were scattered everywhere, and as I walked toward the Chinook, I could see GIs dragging mangled bodies out of the mangled hedgerow into which I had been firing. I was later told that many of the dead VC and North Vietnamese had smoking bullet wounds, which made sense because after expending all my conventional .50-cal munitions, I had been forced near the end of the battle to use a last box of white phosphorus rounds. Reserved for burning down hootches and such, I was under the impression that using such ammunition on human targets was against the Geneva Convention.

On the way to the Chinook, I passed a sergeant who stood atop one of the 1st Platoon APCs inside the wire, sniping with his M16 at stragglers retreating across the fields on the other side of Highway 1. The range was about three hundred meters, so I don't know if he hit anybody, but he was placing his shots very deliberately—and he was laughing as he fired.

Everybody wanted some payback. "We did some things that weren't right," a friend confided to me after the war. "They seemed right then, but not now. . . ."

I'm glad I was not there for the mop-up. I was told that one of our lieutenants—not Russin—pulled a North Vietnamese out of a spiderhole and then furiously slammed the butt of his M16 into the back of his head with such force that the stock broke off the weapon.

It got worse. Troop B sent twenty-four prisoners back to Cu Chi. Charlie Troop policed up six of their own. According to numerous witnesses, the bareheaded guerrillas, their hands tied behind their backs, were forced to their knees in a little clearing in the village, and then several enraged troopers began shooting them in their heads. A lieutenant from Troop B ran over to stop them—"Bravo Troop got there late, and they didn't see what we saw," my friend explained—and one of our guys leveled his M16 at the officer, telling him to mind his own business or he would be next, even as the last of the prisoners was executed in his turn. The incident was never reported, but fearing a possible investigation, several troops cut the ropes binding the dead men's hands so that there would be no obvious evidence of murder.

The trip out was terrible. I was the only living passenger among twenty-three bodies crammed together on the floor of the Chinook. I know there were twenty-three bodies because I counted them, and I counted them because when I was a child I had learned to count by numbering off the calves I helped my stepfather castrate on our farm. The scene in the Chinook evoked those bloody memories. It was like a slaughterhouse in there. The bodies were uncovered. Some were missing limbs. Some were stiffening up. There were more there than our unit had lost, so I had to assume that this helicopter was serving as a meat wagon for other units fighting around Saigon.

I looked at the faces. I recognized the track commander of Captain Virant's APC, my great buddy Richard Rhodes, among the dead. Most of us were just kids, but Richard was a smart, mature, and outgoing man who had been a college football star and was engaged to a schoolteacher. He had had the bad luck of being drafted by the U.S. Army a step ahead of being drafted to play for the Houston Oilers.

That was enough. I looked away from the bodies and would not have looked back, but I realized to my horror that one of the casualties was twitching and mumbling incoherently on the floor of the Chinook. The man who was not really dead was a chubby, popular, curly haired lifer sergeant from the 2d Platoon nicknamed Fatty Arbuckle. He had been shot through his CVC helmet while manning the .50 on his APC.

I rushed up to the crew chief, an older noncom, and pointed at Fatty. "This guy's alive!" I shouted desperately.

"What makes you think so?"

"Shit, man, he's *moving!*"

The crew chief shrugged. "All bodies do that," he said, refusing to come look for himself. The cocksucker was indifferent as hell.

Furious and sick, I sat back down. I looked helplessly at my buddy Fatty, this good sergeant who I'd kidded with and palled with. I looked right at his brain where part of his skull had been shot away, and I thought, My God, how can he be alive, he can't be alive. . . .

When the Chinook touched down at the 12th Evac in Cu Chi, I alerted the medics who met the chopper that there was a survivor among the dead. They immediately wheeled Fatty inside on a gurney, and, hooked to tubes and machines, that poor man lingered in a coma for two weeks before finally succumbing to his injuries.

I ended up sitting on a gurney in one of the wards while a doctor and nurse in green fatigues who looked like they'd had a long day themselves stood before me and used tweezers to pluck out the dozens of little fragments embedded mostly in my head, but also in my face and neck and chest and arms. The doctor quickly moved on to other casualties—my case was trivial compared to the shot-up troopers on gurneys to either side of me—and the nurse finished the job. All the women from home were beautiful, this one more so than most with her brown hair and dark eyes and slim face, and if I was in any pain she melted it away with her kind words and gentle manner as she removed the last of the fragments, wiped the wounds down with iodine, wrapped my forearms with gauze, and taped more in place over the pockmarks in my face and chest.

I walked back to our tent that evening.

Part Four

HOC MON

(FEBRUARY 1968)

Chapter Nine

For my part in the Battle of Tan Son Nhut, I was awarded the Silver Star. There was no ceremony. I was simply called to the troop orderly room one day nearly six months after Tet, and a clerk handed me the medal in its case, along with a blue folder, embossed with the division insignia, which contained copies of the citation.

Feeling cheated, I just threw the stuff in my footlocker. Though the Silver Star is the third-highest valor award and I should have valued it as such—many men who did more than me never received any recognition—the buzz at troop headquarters after the battle had been that I was going to get the Congressional Medal of Honor.

I had made the mistake of getting my hopes up. However, I've since been told by a friend of mine who worked in the orderly room that Lancey and Hines, whose eyewitness testimony would have counted heavily toward a CMH had it been favorable, were still upset with the way I had handled them and described my actions in less than glowing terms. In addition, I don't believe that I was actually submitted for the CMH. Instead, I was put in for the Distinguished Service Cross. At that point, it was up to the division awards section to disapprove or downgrade the recommendation, or, and this is what I thought would happen, to endorse and submit it to United States Army Vietnam, which had the authority to award DSCs, or to forward it as a Medal of Honor recommendation all the way up the chain of command to the Department of the Army.

Fair enough, but by the time the paperwork was in order my old buddy Lancey had been reassigned as the troop awards clerk—incidentally, he also got a Silver Star for Tan Son Nhut—and it is my understanding that he personally wrote the recommendation that was sent to division. It was so bland an account that I should consider myself lucky to have even received a downgraded Silver Star.

I am foolish to dwell on the subject of awards and decorations. My complaints are nothing more than sour grapes. Combat soldiers are not even supposed to care about medals, but I must admit that I did. Being awarded the CMH or Distinguished Service Cross— and, frankly, I felt that I deserved no less, the way medals were handed out over there—would have been a tremendous boost to the military career I was planning. More importantly, having come from the lower rungs of society, a poor boy in whom no one had invested many expectations, I wanted to return home with just that kind of vivid affirmation that I had done good in the army.

My major concern the morning after the battle was not medals, but simply rejoining my unit. Having gone AWOL from the hospital to spend the previous night in our tent at Cu Chi, I was headed for the Troop D helo pad that morning to hitch a ride back out to the field aboard a resupply chopper when our new top sergeant, First Sergeant Delacerda, intercepted me near the squadron mess hall. I tried to tell him that my injuries weren't as bad as they looked, but he cut me off. "I've got medical orders that say you can't go back yet," the sergeant said. "I'm looking right at you, troop. You're torn up."

"Hell, there's nothing wrong with me," I snapped back in a voice that implied he could shove his orders up his ass.

Not smart. Delacerda was a tough little bantam rooster from the Philippines. He demanded total and instant obedience, and, hyperactive and fast talking when upset, he energetically told me to "Get back to your hootch before I court-martial you!"

Delacerda won round one. He won the next few rounds, too, because no matter how many times I snuck over to Delta Troop the next couple days, he either caught me or the resupply ships were too overloaded to take on a passenger. Delacerda finally confined me to quarters with dire warnings about Long Binh Jail.

Being young and hotheaded, I went right back over to Troop D the next afternoon. I was trying to look inconspicuous, just another GI headed back to his unit, but the bandages didn't help. My old platoon leader, Lieutenant Young, who was presently on the squadron staff, happened to be at the pad, and he noticed me as I climbed aboard a Huey. Signaling me to get off, he squinted suspiciously when I told him that the top had given me permission to return to my unit.

To my chagrin, Young got on the horn with First Sergeant Delacerda: "I have an individual here who tells me that you cleared him to go back to the field. I'm just checking. His name is Bravo-India-Romeo-Delta-Whiskey-Echo-Lima-Lima. . . ."

Delacerda was not amused. He was, in fact, ablaze when I reported to the orderly room as ordered and leapt to his feet screaming about my insubordination. I was pretty mad myself, and standing a full head taller than the first sergeant as he berated me and threatened to kick my balls so hard they'd come out my mouth—that's the way he talked—I had the urge to charge over his desk and knock some sense into his thick lifer skull. I had to respect his stripes, though. I also had no interest in going to the stockade, so I took what he had to dish out, saluted sarcastically, marched out, then looked over my shoulder and immediately headed back to the helo pad. Young was gone by then, and without further interference, I found a helicopter headed to my unit. My theory was that once I got back out to the field all the orders about staying in the rear wouldn't make a difference. They didn't.

Charlie Troop was laagered inside the wire at the west end of Tan Son Nhut when I rejoined about the fifth day of Tet. Everything was quiet. There had been no action, in fact, since the squadron had cleared the last of the decimated enemy out of a little village called Ap Dong that faced the north side of the air base on February 2. The mopping up had been accomplished without any friendly KIAs, but unfortunately the handful of wounded included the indomitable Sergeant Brewer, who with Russin back on the scene had been serving as the platoon sergeant on C-35. Brewer had been behind the .50 when he caught a ricochet early in the sweep that flashed off a nearby tin roof and punched into his stomach just below his flak jacket. Feeling little pain, he stayed with the unit until he realized that the warm sensation running down his leg was blood and lots of it. He helped load the other wounded onto a chopper before climbing aboard himself, then shouted to the guys that he would be back as soon as he could, not knowing that his intestines had been badly ripped and that he would be medevacked all the way to Japan, never to return.

Despite such key losses, morale was high when I got back. The feeling was that the worst was over. The enemy had been thoroughly trounced. There would be little opposition, we thought, when we went back to running the roads. Meanwhile, it was party time. Part of the unit had been dispatched into Saigon to help secure the U.S. Embassy and had come back with cases of bottled Coke and even more cases of some type of Vietnamese-made orange and lemon soda pop.

We drank our complimentary sodas to live rock music: Bob Wolford had liberated some electric guitars and speakers from the bombed-out textile mill, and he and a few other musical types in Charlie Troop jammed for us while we were at Tan Son Nhut.

We even ate well. I think it was the morning after I had rejoined the unit when several air force enlisted men came up to us as we sat around cussin' and bitchin' behind our M48s and M113s. "You guys really saved our ass when we got hit," they said. "We'd be proud if you'd come over and eat breakfast in our mess hall."

"Breakfast?!" I sputtered. "It's *nine* o'clock in the morning!"

In an army facility, you either ate breakfast by six or seven or you didn't eat breakfast at all. "No, no, no," our air force buddies explained. "Our mess hall is open twenty-four hours a day."

The whole platoon trooped over. The mess hall was neat, clean, and air conditioned, and my mouth fell open when one of the cooks working the serving line said, "How do you want your eggs?"

I just stared at him. When our mess section choppered out with field stoves to prepare a hot breakfast in the field, the only option was powdered eggs. We usually made do with C-rations. They were left over from World War II—I remember seeing stacks of cardboard cases stamped with 1945 dates—and included canned crap like chopped eggs and ham, and the infamous ham and lima beans.

"How do you want your eggs?" the air force cook repeated. "You want 'em hard boiled, soft boiled, scrambled, or over easy?"

The next cook in the line asked how I wanted my potatoes. I had fried potatoes with my eggs, but can't remember if I put a glass of milk, coffee, orange juice, or hot chocolate on my tray. They were all available, and at that moment I realized that I'd made a terrible mistake: I should have joined the United States Air Force!

The enemy dead were bulldozed into a mass grave in the field off the west end of the runway. Following a ceremony conducted by a Buddhist monk, the spot was marked with a memorial sign in English and Vietnamese. Charlie Troop filled a disabled personnel carrier from top to bottom with captured weapons—pistols, SKS carbines, AK-47s, and RPGs—and dragged the dead-lined APC behind another APC until we returned to Cu Chi. The communist pistols and carbines were great trade items among the rear-echelon types, as it was legal to take them home as souvenirs. It was not legal to take AK-47s out of the country, but we figured that the air force personnel who were buying them for seventy-five bucks apiece must have found a way to smuggle them out aboard transport planes. They actually had not, and about the time the price for a mint-condition AK-47 had reached three hundred dollars, the word got around that you couldn't take them home and the bottom fell out of the market. We still had a stack of them that wouldn't fit into the disabled track and ended up destroying them all before we left Tan Son Nhut Air Base.

Chapter Ten

Pulled off my tank to fill a hole in the crew of another, I was serving as gunner on C-36, which was commanded by a Staff Sergeant Truxel, when Charlie Troop moved out of Tan Son Nhut at daybreak on February 6. The unit went one way. We went another. Specifically, our tank had been detailed to Lieutenant Young of the squadron staff, who had come down to the air base to check on some matter or the other and needed an escort back to Cu Chi. It would have been an easy dash up the highway had Young not been towing a big rubber fuel blivet. The blivet might have been barrel shaped, but I don't guess it had been designed to be dragged behind a personnel carrier at the end of a nylon cord. It didn't roll. It jerked and bumped and thumped along. It careened from side to side, going off the road at times and bouncing off roadside hootches in the hamlets through which we passed. It finally started to peel apart, and Young pulled off into a field, unhooked the ungainly blivet, and turned it into a ball of fire with an incendiary grenade before we jumped back on Highway 1.

Continuing on our merry way, we were nearing the large and prosperous village of Hoc Mon, the heart of which was situated a kilometer east of the main supply route at the hub of several lesser roads, when squadron headquarters directed us into a blocking position west of Highway 1. Distinctly aware at that point that we were just one tank and one track off in the middle of nowhere, we pulled into a little grove of trees surrounding a Buddhist temple that was itself surrounded by a vast expanse of open rice paddies. The paddies provided us fantastic fields of fire, and there we sat, concealed and virtually unreachable, waiting as instructed for the rest of the unit to link up with us after sweeping through Hoc Mon.

The deserted temple was elaborate and beautiful, and several of us were looking it over when a crewman listening to the radio on Truxel's tank suddenly shouted, "Hey, they're in heavy contact!"

We gathered around the radio: C/3/4th Cav and a company from the 27th Infantry Regiment, known more famously as the Wolfhounds, had run into what was later determined to be a VC/NVA battalion that had seized Hoc Mon on the first day of Tet.

Charlie Troop was shot to pieces. We could not hear the battle itself, but listening in on the radio—and it was strange to be sitting in a tranquil little oasis on that bright and sunny morning, eavesdropping on our unit's destruction—we could hear automatic-weapons fire behind the frantic transmissions. We were stunned—we had thought the war was all but over—and sick at heart. We wondered if we should try to hook up with our guys, but given that our two vehicles would have been vulnerable to an easy ambush if we had struck out toward the action, squadron headquarters prudently instructed us to hold our position and simply watch for enemy movement. If we detected any, we were not to engage directly, but to call in air strikes.

The day and the night passed for us without incident. We still had to escort Lieutenant Young to Cu Chi, and when we hit the road the next morning, we passed scenes of destruction at dismayingly frequent intervals all along Highway 1. It was a mess. There were bodies strewn along the roadside—enemy bodies, the bodies of dead civilians, bodies that defied identification—and burned-out trucks and personnel carriers sitting abandoned on the highway itself or off on the shoulder where they had come to rest after being shot up. We drove right past a ferocious firefight to our right, and it was like seeing a war movie in a drive-in theater. Tanks were pushing through a flattened village. Infantrymen were firing from foxholes in the rubble. There was nothing left of the village; they were blowing the pieces to pieces, but the enemy was dug in deep and their fire was so intense that we had to keep low as we sped past because of all the stray green tracers snapping across the highway from right to left.

Turning onto the unpaved road that led to the division base camp from the highway, we passed through the town of Cu Chi. It was a shambles—the communists had also overrun this town on the first day of Tet and had been pushed out only after bitter fighting—and we were thankful when we finally made it into base camp.

Having dropped Young off, Sergeant Truxel's tank moved out alone on February 8 for a hairy cross-country run to rejoin C/3/4th Cavalry. We found the unit laagered in a field south of Hoc Mon. The guys were shell shocked after two major battles in one week. "We gotta get out of here," some of them mumbled. "We're all going to get killed. I gotta get off the line. I gotta get a job in base camp. . . ."

Hoc Mon had been as bad as Tan Son Nhut. As I understood it from talking to the guys, the Wolfhounds had been hit first on February 6. Pinned down with three KIAs, they requested armor support. Charlie Troop formed on line, and Lieutenant Russin gave an eager battle cry over the radio—"Third Platoon, let's show 'em how it's done!"—as the M48s and M113s gunned through the bamboo growing thickly along a dike separating them from the Wolfhounds. "As we came down on the other side," recounted my buddy John Rourke, who was on the mortar track, "Charlie let us have it hard—RPGs, machine guns, and small arms. They had us where they wanted us. Ahead of us, I saw an infantryman behind a gravestone waving for us to go back. Too late now. I spotted a machine gun just ahead of us about thirty yards giving us a steady spray. I stood up and fired a burst at the smoke pumping from the barrel and got back down. I popped up again to fire another burst, but no smoke was pumping now."

The enemy was entrenched in camouflaged spiderholes in the next hedgerow. Rourke saw the track commander to his left get nailed in the head even as he was firing his .50-cal MG. "Then I glanced to my right just in time to see Lieutenant Russin's head snap back too," he said. The APC to the left took an RPG an instant later. "Everyone jumped off and started running to the rear. The driver on the lieutenant's track turned chicken and threw it in reverse, then turned around and took off with Russin slumped over backward. . . ."

I mourned the loss of Lieutenant Russin. Sporting a big aviator's mustache, he was cocky and overly aggressive, but I thought he had what it took to make a good combat leader once his greenness wore off. As it was, he died green. The guys hated him. "That son of a bitch Russin put us all in that spot," cursed Rourke. "He should have called in the gunships first, and then had us move in. I guess the dirty bastard got his medal, but he took a lot of good men with him. . . ."[*]

Charlie Troop took ten KIA at Hoc Mon. The unit pulled back in disorder, leaving behind numerous bodies and blown-up APCs. Staff Sergeant James D. "Papa" DeForest, our thirty-seven-year-old, grizzly bear-sized troop motor sergeant, bravely took his track back into the kill zone to check for stragglers. Among those he rescued was our platoon mechanic Dean Foss, then serving as a track gunner. Numerous gung-ho support troops had, in fact, volunteered to go to the field because of the heavy casualties suffered at Tan Son Nhut. Two supply men were killed on Foss's APC, along with the track commander, and Foss was all alone with one other surviving crewman when DeForest pulled up. They climbed aboard and got the hell out of there.

Sergeant Kampe, my old boss in the commo section, had also been on line at Hoc Mon, and he told me a terrible story about one of his communication troopers named Joe Grigsby who wanted a piece of the action and ended up taking my place on C-35. When one of the other replacement crewmen had his lower jaw blown away, the rest of the guys deserted the tank, leaving behind Grigsby, who steadfastly manned the .50-cal MG. Perhaps he thought the unit would move back up and rejoin him. It didn't, and Kampe said that they watched Grigsby through binoculars as he expended all of his machine-gun ammunition, paused fatalistically to light a cigarette, then continued to fire on the enemy with an M16 from atop the turret until killed.

The enemy overran the tank. Fearing it had been booby trapped, Charlie Troop called an air strike on C-35 before recovering its dead and its abandoned vehicles without contact on February 7. The

---

[*]This anger was understandable, but misdirected: Russin wasn't running the Hoc Mon operation; he was responding to orders himself.

trauma of the battle and the unnerving anticipation of the next attack—although the guerrillas had slipped away from the scene of
the ambush, Hoc Mon itself was still in enemy hands—had a bad effect on C/3/4th Cavalry. It was either on the day Truxel's tank rejoined the outfit, or the next, that I first saw a civilian abused by GIs.
We were laagered near a militia outpost in a hamlet on the outskirts
of Hoc Mon. When a Vietnamese man on a bicycle came down the
dirt road running past our position, two troopers—one black, one
white, both of them big guys with bulging biceps who did what they
wanted when they wanted—stopped him to check his ID card. They
started questioning him, which was standard procedure, but the animosity and tension were such that the next thing we knew they
were slapping the man around, then shoving him back and forth
between themselves as they punched him in the face. They beat
him bloody.

The Vietnamese man knew better than to try to defend himself
and barely raised his head as they worked him over. "Hey, knock
that shit off," some of us shouted, outraged. "Let him go!"

Finally, an ARVN captain stormed down from the militia compound, and raising hell with the two GIs, he sent the Vietnamese
man on his way. Most of the guys were too numbed out by all that
had come before to think much about the incident, but some—the
smart ones, the compassionate ones—were upset, and the first subtle line had been drawn between the soldiers of Charlie Troop.

Such abuse eventually became common. The war had changed.
Attitudes were hardening. Everyone around us was the enemy now.
John Rourke was not a participant in the abuses, but he could tell a
tale about the return to base camp at the end of the Hoc Mon operation that reflected the new mood: "We were going real slow
through this one village on the way back, and every time the column
stopped to wait for civilian traffic to get out of the way, the driver of
the track ahead of mine would start throwing C-rations to the kids
asking for handouts along the road. He was laughing and waving
and just having a good old time. This track was from the Headquarters Troop. The crew hadn't got their asses shot at like we had.

"I started fuming inside. The next time the column stopped and
that driver started throwing more rations, I told my TC I'd had

enough and climbed off the track. I walked up to the Headquarters track and yelled at the top of my voice for that kid to get out of the track. He looked at me like I was crazy. I screamed again. He got out. I looked up at his TC—he was an E6—and I pointed at him and yelled, 'You stay right there!' Then I turned to the driver and put my nose in his face and proceeded to tell him that these kids' fathers were our enemy, and he was feeding them and giving them cans to make booby traps with. The driver turned white and stood at attention. I told him to get back in that driver's seat and stay there and drive. I looked at his track commander again and said, 'You got anything to say?' He shook his head. I went back and climbed into my track. The column soon moved on. I don't know why I did that. Total frustration, I suppose. I felt good. The two of them never moved a muscle they shouldn't have the rest of the way back. I imagine they could feel my eyes burning the back of their heads. . . ."

On February 9, Charlie Troop was working through a deserted hootch area on the outer fringe of Hoc Mon when an RPG flashed without warning from a tree line several hundred meters away. It came right at Sergeant Truxel's tank, atop which I was sitting with a captured AK-47 across my lap. Along with a spare gunner, Sgt. Warren G. Harding, Jr., I instantly jumped down to the ground—we didn't have any function in operating the tank, we were just meat up there—and was frantically scrambling off to the right for cover while my buddy scrambled off to the left when the RPG went nose first into the ground and exploded harmlessly about fifty feet short of the tank.

There was a smattering of small-arms fire, but Sergeant Truxel immediately opened up with the .50, and after he traversed the 90 and put a couple HEs into the tree line, that was the end of that.

Feeling like fools and realizing that some of the guys were looking at us as if we were cowards, Harding and I climbed back aboard the tank. We had no more contact during our reconnaissance in force. The main push that day was made by Bravo Troop and three companies of Wolfhounds on the southern side of Hoc Mon. Enemy resistance was stubborn, and the infantry-cavalry force pulled back so the area could be softened up with massive firepower.

As we laagered in at dusk, we could see gunships rolling in on Hoc Mon. In response, big green tracers from several enemy anti-aircraft guns laced the darkening sky. Those .51s had an incredible reach, and the gunships began firing from higher and higher altitudes. Refusing to play it safe, a prop-driven A1 Skyraider from the Vietnamese air force made repeated low-level passes right through all the tracers to put automatic-cannon fire on the target. I don't know if that brave pilot took the gun crews out, or if they had the sense to lie low until he banked away for home, but the enemy fire eventually dried up.

Artillery fire boomed into Hoc Mon all night long.

Chapter Eleven

The troop executive officer, Capt. Daniel D. Patterson—a pseudonym—was the acting Troop C commander when we went back into Hoc Mon on February 10, 1968. Patterson was not a combat officer. Neither was he a career man. He was instead a nice, nervous, well-regarded administrator and logistician with an ROTC commission—he was distinctly middle class and should have been in a business suit instead of army green—who had never commanded a line platoon like most execs and he had probably never wanted to. What Patterson wanted to do was go home. He was two months short when Tet broke, and, hastily dispatched to replace Virant, he was, it was obvious to all of us, extremely distressed by this sudden turn of events. He was shaky, uptight, and in way over his head. He inspired no confidence in us, and I doubt that he had much confidence in his own abilities after that disastrous first attack into Hoc Mon.

This time we were going in from the northeast, and we hooked up with an element of the Wolfhounds in a hamlet about three klicks out of Hoc Mon. The enemy positions were not fixed. They shifted rapidly, and instead of driving for the heart of the crossroads town, our objective now was a forested area the guerrillas had slipped into that was almost a kilometer in length and perhaps a third of a klick wide. It showed up as a small green oval on our topographical maps.

Between the long side of the woods and the hamlet was a clearing. The Wolfhounds had already tried to launch an assault across it but had been forced back, and when we came in from their rear, they were hunkered down among the trees at the edge of the village.

Sergeant Truxel stopped our tank near one of the hootches. "Hey, Three-Quarter Cav!" a nearby Wolfhound GI shouted up at me.

The grunt was sitting beside several bloody and bandaged fellow Wolfhounds, one of whom appeared to be dead. The man who had called to me was begrimed and sweat soaked, a green towel around his neck. He looked beat to hell, but hard and angry too.

"You want this monkey?" he asked harshly, indicating a little pet monkey he had on a leash. "He'll eat, shit, and drink with you." The grunt's eyes flashed with fury. "Eat, shit, and drink," he spat. "That's about all you Three-Quarter Cav assholes are good for!"

I said nothing. I knew why he was mad: During the chaotic fighting of the last few days, a tank had backed up over a Wolfhound, crushing him to death under its treads, and several other grunts had been killed and wounded by uncoordinated fire from B and C/3/4th Cavalry.

As we got organized for the next assault, the Wolfhounds began burning down the hootches on our right flank. I don't think an order was given to do so. I think it was spontaneous revenge, the pent-up release of frustrated, scared, and angry grunts. The hamlet was deserted, except for one old gray-headed Vietnamese man in humble clothes who reminded me of the lone holdout you hear about who won't leave his home despite an impending natural disaster. This old man wasn't going anywhere, either, and he sat staring at us, his face a mask of pure hate as his home and the homes of his neighbors went up in flames. He didn't say a word. The grunts ignored him, but worse was yet to come for them this day, and I've always wondered if that stubborn old man survived their wrath.

We attacked across the clearing on line. Our tanks and tracks were well spread out, and the grunts advanced behind and between our vehicles. There was no enemy fire. Twenty-five meters from the edge of the woods, we got the word to commence firing, and doing so we rolled on into the trees amid much smoke and noise. The enemy suddenly responded in kind. Everyone stopped, and Sergeant Truxel began pumping away with the .50-cal MG, then reached around for a bottle of vodka he kept in a pack stuffed in the bustle rack. "It's good for the nerves," he smiled, taking a swig. Before Truxel put his .50 back in action, this easygoing, soft-spoken, but slightly crazy lifer offered me the bottle. Riding shotgun on the bustle rack, I was firing my AK-47 like my life depended on it—it did—and given all the stuff hitting the trees around us and ricocheting off our armor, I just wasn't interested. Truxel's eyes, however, got hot, so what the hell, I took a fast swig and shoved the bottle back in his hands. Satisfied, Truxel passed the bottle to Harding, who was crouched beside me behind the turret, busily firing his M79 grenade launcher into the trees.

As we fought it out toe to toe with the enemy bunker line, Sergeant Truxel kept nipping at that bottle of vodka between bursts, and I kept thumping fresh magazines into my AK-47. I had previously picked out a beautiful one from the stack at Tan Son Nhut and had filled a U.S. rucksack with captured ammo magazines. Our new M16 was a superb weapon, but it still didn't compare to the AK-47. For one thing, the M16 magazine was designed for twenty rounds, but because of its weak spring it could handle only sixteen to eighteen without jamming. The enemy weapon, which never seemed to jam no matter how dirty, had a thirty-round banana magazine, and when you put it to your shoulder and squeezed the trigger, it gave you an incredible surge of power. There was just something about an AK-47.

The only drawback was that the AK-47 fired with a bone-chilling *crack-crack-crack* that was all its own, and as I blasted away I was startling the hell out of the Wolfhounds leapfrogging past us. Their attack bogged down, and within minutes the grunts started pulling back. Two Wolfhounds rushed rearward past our tank, dragging a third Wolfhound whose right hand had been blown off and whose right leg was hanging on by only a few strands of bloody muscle.

"It's a fucking slaughter pen!" one of the grunts shouted furiously. "The gooks are dug in deep. We can't get in there!"

Captain Patterson ordered us to fall back with the infantry. We backed up to the hamlet, firing all the way. When our fire finally stuttered out, there was only silence. Nothing moved in the woods. Two USAF fighter-jets made repeated passes—this was the first time we had ever received close air support—one dropping bombs, the other napalm canisters that sent flames leaping a hundred feet in the air. There was no ground fire. We weren't surprised. We couldn't imagine that the enemy could survive such an inferno.

We attacked again. Unbelievably, the enemy was still in position, and our line of M48s and M113s again halted amid the hornet's nest of fire and blasted back against bunkers we couldn't see. Truxel fired Beehive rounds, blowing swaths through the brush like a giant shotgun. The roar was overwhelming. Smoke and dust filled the air. Amid this chaos I finally spotted an enemy soldier—I saw a face in the bushes and realized that an NVA with a rocket launcher over his shoulder was pushing up the cover over his spiderhole—but before I could even swing my AK-47 on him, the bastard fired his RPG.

His target was the track to my right. It was the command vehicle of Lieutenant Hardies of the 1st Platoon, who at that moment was sitting on the open cargo hatch cover, one foot braced against the forward edge of the hatch. Hardies was talking on his CVC radio mike, controlling his platoon, and his track commander, Sgt. Kenneth L. Devor, his machine gun either jammed or burned out, was standing in the cargo hatch, firing an M79 instead. The RPG hit the front of their track—Wham!—and I watched Hardies and the artillery sergeant sitting beside him go flying off the back deck. The rocket had penetrated the engine compartment and exploded inside the vehicle so that Hardies was peppered with forty or fifty little pieces of shrap-metal in the back of his legs and buttocks and up his lower back.

His commo helmet still clamped on, Lieutenant Hardies, who had a Colt .45 shoulder rig strapped on over his flak jacket, climbed aboard the APC to his right and began firing the .50-cal MG to cover his wounded artillery sergeant and his driver, who had jumped from his hatch with burst eardrums as they scrambled out of the kill zone.

The only crewman who hadn't gotten out was Kenny Devor. After the war, Hardies told me that Kenny had been killed instantly— standing in the cargo hatch, he took the brunt of the explosion when the RPG penetrated the front of the vehicle—but at the time I thought he might be wounded and lying unconscious inside the APC. I couldn't stand the thought. Kenny was a great guy—a hometown sports hero from Walnut Bottom, Pennsylvania, he was one of those solid, uncomplaining draftee GIs who wins wars—and jumping down from my tank, I frantically ran over to his APC. It was no use. The RPG had started a fire in the fuel compartment and as quick as I got there, the track's ammo load was already cooking off. The entire vehicle was consumed in flames, and as I tried to dart in and open the back hatch—I couldn't, the heat was too intense— sparks bounced off me and a hot round that must have zinged up through the cargo hatch went down my shirt, burning my neck and back. I beat a retreat back to my tank, and when we finally recovered that track at a later date all that remained was a charred and gutted and stinking hulk in a silvery pool of melted aluminum armor.

The battle ended in chaos. Unable to silence the well-camouflaged, well-entrenched enemy, demoralized infantrymen began taking cover behind our tanks and tracks. More and more rockets were slamming in, and Captain Patterson ordered us to pull back thirty feet to get reorganized. We did so, but then Patterson or the infantry officer in command of the operation decided to withdraw completely—"Break it off, break it off!"—and as we started back, emboldened enemy soldiers rushed forward from position to position to keep firing at us. It was smoky and getting dark as dusk approached, and everything seemed to be spinning out of control. Mobbed by a dozen frantic Wolfhounds who were afraid they'd be left behind, Truxel's tank ended up coming out last, and he kept up the fire as we plowed backward out of the trees and into that clearing. We made it safely across thanks to Truxel's blazing .50 and the Beehive rounds he was punching off, and no thanks to the track crews who turned around to make a beeline for the ville instead of working as a unit and providing covering fire for one another. It was almost every man for himself at that point.

Truxel notwithstanding, we probably wouldn't have survived if not for the air force. The jets were swooping in again, strafing the edge of the woods with 20mm automatic cannons, pinning the enemy down and allowing us to make good our retreat. The jets came in so close that empty shell casings falling from them bounced off our tank.

Continuing backward, we were flush with a big thatch-roofed hootch in the ville when the tank suddenly stopped.

Harding and I scrambled to jerk open the grills over the engine: As happened on occasion, two metal collars, about eight inches across, had slipped loose from the final drive that imparted power from the engine to the transmission.

I easily got one back in place, but the other was jammed and Harding grappled furiously with it. Some of the Wolfhounds piled up on the turret and back deck were throwing a little fire back the way we had come—enemy muzzle flashes were blinking at the edge of the woods—and all of them were screaming at us to hurry up and get the fuck out of there, worried as much about the enemy as the jets, which were making their strafing runs one at a time from south to north and coming in closer to us at each pass. They were methodically saturating the area with cannon fire, unable to see our straggling tank in the gathering darkness. There was no doubt in my mind that we were dead. The next pass would tear right through us, but Harding was so physically strong that he was able to force the popped collar back into place, and as soon as the tank regained power, the driver took off with a lurch. We hadn't gone twenty feet when a jet strafed the area precisely where we had been sitting.

Chapter Twelve

We caught up with the rest of the unit in an open field where it was hurriedly trying to set up for the night before the enemy could counterattack. Captain Patterson was standing there at a distance from everyone else. He was totally at a loss, and as we rumbled past he looked up at us without seeing us. His helmet was missing. He seemed dazed. He disappeared a few days later, yanked out by the squadron commander and sent where he could do no harm.

The troops also blamed Patterson, but more violently: "He doesn't know what the fuck he's doing. Let's kill the sonofabitch. . . ."

We weren't a unit that night. We were just all that was left. The entire troop was down to three tanks, twelve personnel carriers, and about eighty men. We had lost most of our experienced leaders. Expecting the worst, we hurriedly unloaded the resupply Hueys that landed in the dark inside our joint infantry-cavalry perimeter. We got stacks of metal machine-gun ammo cans and 90mm rounds, which were packed two apiece in wooden boxes with rope handles. We grabbed the boxes, one guy at either end—they were heavy, each projectile must have weighed almost fifty pounds—hustled them over to our tank, and cracked them open, then I spent the rest of the night atop the turret, sleeplessly scanning the area with a Starlight Scope.

Nothing happened. . . .

Charlie Troop swept the battlefield for the next two days but found nothing of value. The enemy had evaporated again, and we returned to Cu Chi. Our sandbagged hootches were dark even when the lights were on, and we sat around in little groups in the gloom, somberly talking and drinking beer. There was none of the usual laughter and horsing around. We knew we were going back out. We knew many more of us were going to be killed and maimed.

The Hoc Mon operation terminated on February 12. Troop B had three KIA, and hard-luck Charlie Troop eleven; the Wolf-hounds lost twenty-nine KIA, and between us we had 177 WIA.

Hoc Mon was a victory—the claimed body count was 623 VC and NVA—and to cap it, Troop B displayed two captured .51-caliber antiaircraft guns outside its orderly room in Cu Chi.

Big fucking deal. Lieutenant Colonel Otis must have sensed our mood; we were in the motor pool working on our vehicles when the squadron commander arrived unannounced, and we stopped what we were doing and gathered around him in a circle. Otis had come down by himself. "I appreciate what you've been through, and I wanted to thank you for serving so well," he said with simple and ut-ter sincerity, holding his helmet in the crook of his arm. Otis was short and pugnacious looking. He had been shot down again dur-ing the Hoc Mon operation, scratched along his right arm by a metal fragment in the process. He said that there were probably go-ing to be some rougher days ahead, but if we functioned as a team nobody could beat us. Otis knew us as individuals, even the privates and spec fours, and as he spoke about our comrades who had been killed, tears ran down his face. Tears ran down many of our faces too. "God bless you all," Otis said as he left.

Charlie Troop was rebuilt with replacement troops and replace-ment vehicles, and to shake everything out we ran reconnaissance-in-force patrols outside Cu Chi. We checked out various tree lines and paddy areas, but made no contact and always returned before dark. This lasted for three or four days. Then we went back to the field for real.

Dwight W. Birdwell, Class of 1966, Stilwell (Oklahoma) High School.

Dwight Birdwell (far right) in Korea shortly before shipping out for Vietnam. July 1967.

Capt. Leo B. Virant II, commander of Troop C, 3d Squadron, 4th Cavalry (25th Division). The time is sunset, the location Highway 1 ten kilometers north of Cu Chi. A night of patrolling the main supply route is about to begin. (Courtesy Leo Virant)

Charlie Troop pauses while a dud artillery round, or Viet Cong mine, is blown during a Reconnaissance in Force (RIF) operation. (Courtesy Leo Virant)

An M48 tank and an M113 armored personnel carrier cover dismounted troops checking out a tree line. Note the runway matting rigged up to the tank as protection from rocket-propelled grenades. (Courtesy Leo Virant)

Dwight Birdwell (center) and other tank crewmen listen to a message on the C/3/4th Cav tactical net during a RIF operation. (Courtesy Leo Virant)

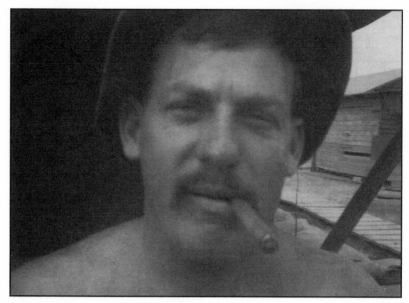

SSgt. Gary D. Brewer took command of C/3/4th Cav when all the officers were wounded or incapacitated at Tan Son Nhut on the first day of the Tet Offensive. This great NCO was awarded the Distinguished Service Cross. (Courtesy Gary Brewer)

Kenny Devor with a pet monkey in Cu Chi base camp shortly before Tet. (Courtesy the family of Kenneth L. Devor)

Frank Cuff, better known as "Fighting Frank," was one of the best soldiers in Charlie Troop. (Courtesy Frank Cuff)

Russell "Cowboy" Boehm really had been a cowboy before being drafted. He is next to a bunker built between two Charlie Troop barracks in Cu Chi. (Courtesy Frank Cuff)

On the move on Highway 1. Note the sandbagged outpost beside the road; it was manned by a militia squad from a local village. November 1967. (Courtesy Ted Hardies)

Two tanks from C/3/4th Cav roll out of the Boi Loi Woods in an unusual fog the day after Christmas, 1967. (Courtesy Leo Virant).

Charlie Troop operated in a densely populated area. Whenever the unit stopped, Vietnamese mamasans would show up selling soda and beer. (Courtesy the family of Kenneth L. Devor)

A Charlie Troop laager in a rubber plantation during the deceptively tranquil days before the Tet Offensive. (Courtesy the family of Kenneth L. Devor)

An M577 command track roars past a group of Vietnamese children. (Courtesy Leo Virant)

Tank C-35 after the Battle of Hoc Mon. The tank was overrun by the enemy, and napalmed by the Air Force. February 1968. (Courtesy Bob Wolford)

An APC maneuvers down a muddy road between two flooded rice paddies. (Courtesy the family of Kenneth L. Devor)

SSgt. George S. Breeding was wounded three times during his first three months with C/3/4th Cav. (Courtesy George Breeding)

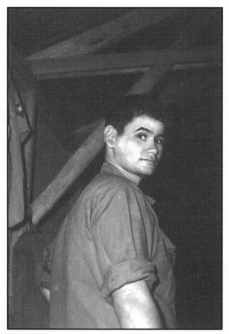

Dwight Birdwell some weeks after the Tet Offensive. (Courtesy John Rourke)

Birdwell's tank, C-36, in the motor pool at Cu Chi. Note the 25th Division insignia on the searchlight cover. (Courtesy Tony Adamo)

Jack Donnelly, shown here at Cu Chi base camp, served as a loader on Birdwell's tank. (Courtesy Jack Donnelly)

Bob Wolford reading *The Valley of the Dolls*. April 1968. (Courtesy Bob Wolford)

Russ Gearhart, shown here as a new guy, went on to win the Silver Star and two Purple Hearts. (Courtesy Russ Gearhart)

Steve Uram behind a .50-caliber machine gun mounted on the back of an APC. (Courtesy Steve Uram)

Lieutenants Tony Adamo (left, under orderly room roof) and Jack Hubbell. (Courtesy Tony Adamo)

The 2d Platoon of C/3/4th Cavalry around June 1968. Frank Cuff is standing on the far left, and Steve Cook is kneeling in front of him, holding up his four-fingered left hand. Russ Gearhart is standing on the far right. Lucio Herrera is sitting in the middle with a bush hat on. (Photo by Russ Boehm/Courtesy Russ Gearhart)

Doc Gearhart poses with an enemy flag captured on May 27, 1968 after the 3/4th Cav destroyed the 271st VC Regiment. (Courtesy Frank Cuff)

Dean Foss, the fighting mechanic of 3d Platoon, C/3/4th Cav. (Courtesy Dean Foss)

The rainy season, which began in mid-May, limited armor operations for one obvious reason: the fifty-two ton M48 tanks sank into the mud when they left the main roads. (Courtesy Bob Wolford)

Looking forlorn, a tank sits in a rice paddy during a monsoon rain. (Courtesy Leo Virant)

Dwight Birdwell (right) hooked up with hometown buddy Larry Crittenden during his R&R in Taipei, Taiwan. July 1968.

Bob Wolford, Mike Christie, Dwight Birdwell, Ed Delaney, Jack Donnelly, and John Rourke (left to right), at The Wall. 1985.

Part Five

AROUND AND AROUND

(FEBRUARY–JULY 1968)

Chapter Thirteen

The first contact we made after returning to the field lasted only seconds. It was devastating nonetheless. The unit was on the move that grey and overcast morning. The lead tank was commanded by our new platoon sergeant, Sfc. William Jenkins, a sharp and gentlemenly NCO from South Carolina whom some of the guys remembered from Fort Knox, where he had been their drill instructor. Our tank was a replacement vehicle, and the driver and loader on this factory-fresh C-35 were also new guys. Assigned as gunner, I was sitting on the back deck with Jack Donnelly, yet another replacement in bright green fatigues, as the well-spaced column followed us north on one elevated road, then east on another that cut in a straight line across a huge field that was neatly furrowed and planted with beans or tapioca. We were four klicks due west of Tan Son Nhut.

The area appeared deserted. To my amazement, we took fire from a tree line on our far left flank. We later reckoned that the enemy had set up an ambush where the north-south road bisected the tree line and, dismayed when we turned east, had opened fire in a frustrated attempt to hit *something* despite the extreme range involved.

Sergeant Jenkins instantly began returning fire with the .50 but was still traversing the main gun when two RPGs suddenly flashed from the tree line. They were aimed right at our lead tank and seemed to float in slow motion toward us across that huge field.

They looked like two orange balls of fire. I had rolled flat alongside the turret to put a dismounted M60 into action on its bipod. Uselessly, frantically, I fired at the RPGs. In the next instant, both scored direct hits on our tank, blowing me off the back. I crash-landed to the right of the road, losing my rarely worn steel pot in the process. I was stunned and numb, barely aware that my right eardrum was ruptured, or that I was bleeding from my ears and nose, or that I had been peppered with fragments in my back and the right side of my face.

My head was throbbing. I didn't know what was going on—yes, I did, but I couldn't fathom it, I couldn't make my body respond and was only vaguely aware that Donnelly was lying next to me. He had been kneeling on the back deck when the rockets hit, preparing to fire his M79, and was now sprawled in the dirt, moaning in pain.

I found out only afterward that one of the rockets had caught Sergeant Jenkins in the chest, blowing him in half as he fired the .50-cal MG. The other had slammed into the loader's hatch cover, and Pfc. Larry R. Moore of Hampton, Virginia, standing in the open hatch with just his head exposed, had been decapitated by the blast.

The smell of burnt meat hung in the air. Our tank sat dead on the road, on fire, the ammo stored in the bustle rack having been set off by the rockets. Meanwhile, the rest of the unit, under the command of brand-new Capt. Robert Shafer, hastily backed out of the kill zone and right out of view. Left behind in the confusion, Donnelly and I were too shaken and banged up to have defended ourselves had we had weapons—and we didn't, his grenade launcher and my machine gun were missing in action, and my prized AK-47 was in the flaming bustle rack—and would have been killed or captured except for the fact that the enemy probably didn't know that we were stranded there behind the raised road. They would have been unwilling to cross that large field in any event for fear of being caught in the open and chopped up by the gunships they could assume were en route.

At least that's what I wanted to believe. The outcome might actually have been pretty grim, but little First Sergeant Delacerda—hard-assed, hated, but dedicated Old Army NCO that he was—came to the rescue, hugging the side of the raised road as he crawled forward on all fours, dragging a stretcher. Since the unit had withdrawn many hundreds of meters back down the north-south road, it took him at least fifteen minutes to reach us. He was all by himself.

Delacerda knelt beside Donnelly. Both his ears were bleeding, and it was later determined that he had one tiny metal fragment in his right eye and another lodged in the back of his head that had sliced through his nose and nasal passages. He had a multitude more in his head and upper chest and shoulders. He looked like raw hamburger.

"Birdwell, you've *got* to help me," Delacerda implored, snapping me out of my stupor. "We've got to get him back!"

Rolling Donnelly onto the stretcher, we moved out, bent low behind the road as a little small-arms fire snapped overhead from the distant tree line. In the rush, we left someone behind ourselves. We had assumed the driver of our burning tank had been killed. He hadn't. The new guy was actually buttoned up inside his hatch, dazed, confused, but unhurt, and when he finally realized that he was out there all alone on the road, he belatedly put the tank in reverse too.

The troop had circled its wagons in a field off to one side of the north-south road. Delacerda had just gotten Donnelly and me back there when our tank showed up, trailing flames. Horrified that I had left a fellow crewman behind, I pulled away from the medic who was starting to check my wounds, hauled the semicoherent driver out of his hatch, and rushed him to cover as ammo continued to cook off in the bustle rack, then, grabbing a fire extinguisher from a nearby personnel carrier, scrambled aboard the tank to put the fire out.

The situation secured, I sat beside Jack's litter, one medic bandaging me while another thumped a morphine Syrette into Donnelly.

In short order, a Huey landed for us. "You've been through a lot," Delacerda told me. "Go on back and get those injuries checked out."

I didn't argue like I had at Tan Son Nhut. I was too shaken, physically and emotionally. It might have been logical for the unit to pull back since, as I was later told, .51s had opened up from the tree line and Charlie Troop needed to put some distance between itself and the enemy before calling in artillery support, but in my gut I couldn't believe that my friends had deserted me out there on the road. It was scary. Something had gone very wrong with the outfit, and it finally sank in that it might not always be the other fellow who got killed, it could very well be me who ended up in a body bag.

I gladly climbed aboard the medevac. The evac hospital was overflowing, so after a quick cleanup of my wounds, a busy doctor told me that they would get back to me when they could. Sore all over but in little real pain, I simply hiked back to the troop headquarters. Along the way, I thought about Delacerda, who had really put it on the line for me and Donnelly. He probably would have taken the same chance for any of his troops, but I had the impression that our previous confrontations had left Delacerda with a certain grudging respect for me. He was brown, I was brown, and I think he saw in my aggressive, go-for-broke attitude a bit of himself as a young soldier. Whatever his motivation, I know that I had a tremendous amount of admiration for the first sergeant from that day forward and realized that he had a heart of gold under his cold and macho exterior.

When I walked into the orderly room that evening, Sgt. Richard Travato, a short-timer recently pulled out of the field to help run the troop rear, looked at me in shock. His mouth dropped open, and he literally turned white as a ghost even though he was a dark, olive-skinned Italian-American. He ran up and hugged me, exclaiming that I wasn't really dead. I asked him what the hell was going on, and he explained that the unit had initially reported the gunner of C-35 as having been killed. I'd been the gunner, and Travato showed me where he had racked my name up on the KIA board behind his desk. Smiling broadly through the tears in his eyes, he crossed it out.

I received a Purple Heart for Tan Son Nhut. I didn't get one for my second wound—it occurred on February 19—but I did end up deaf in my right ear. I was unconcerned. Being a kid, I guess I thought I'd grow a new eardrum, but it doesn't work that way.

I wasn't very aggressive this time about getting back out to the field and spent over a week in Cu Chi. I've always felt guilty about that, but maybe in fairness to myself I should note that my head was still ringing and my balance was still out of whack when I rejoined Charlie Troop.

Sergeant Kampe got ahold of me almost as soon as I climbed off the resupply helicopter and implored me to rejoin his commo section. Everybody was getting slaughtered, he said. I had already done my part. I owed it to myself to get out alive. I must have still been rattled, because I agreed. Luckily for my conscience, I immediately had a change of heart and reported to my old platoon. I didn't tell Kampe, and he found out that I was headed back to the field only when we rumbled past his commo setup and there I was waving to him from the back of a personnel carrier. He looked at me like I was a fool, but I felt it was my duty. I had already missed one major firefight as it was.

On February 28, 1968, Captain Shafer and C/3/4th Cav, acting on information from a prisoner who claimed to know the location of a weapons cache—the VC defector was choppered out to the unit, along with an interpreter—conducted a search of the deserted village just south of Highway 1 some six kilometers northwest of Tan Son Nhut that they had been led to. No cache was found, and after breaking for chow, the unit, violating a cardinal rule of war, turned around to leave on the same dirt road it had originally taken into the area.

Sergeant Harding commanded the lead tank, C-35, which stopped upon reaching a T-shaped intersection inside the village—the column would have to turn left or right at that point—because an old Vietnamese man with an oxcart was in the middle of the road.

Harding and his loader, Cpl. Robert W. Hunt, climbed off their tank to check the old man's ID card and get his oxcart out of the way so the column could pass. "That's when we got ambushed," remembers Sergeant Breeding of the 2d Platoon. "The lead tank got hit with something like six RPGs. They never had a chance. . . ."

Harding and Hunt were actually still alive, though pinned down. No one remembers what happened to the old man, and opinions are divided as to whether he was an enemy lure, or if he had actually been trying to warn the GIs and thus forced the enemy to initiate their ambush before the whole unit was in their kill zone.

Whatever the case, everyone immediately retreated. The driver of the lead tank bailed out and ran back to climb aboard another vehicle. "They were shooting down onto us from the roofs of the houses along both sides of the road," notes Private First Class Cuff, a track driver in the 2d Platoon. "I dropped my seat down so my head was below the top of my hatch—everybody did—there was very little return fire—and we just backed up blind in a straight line. We kept banging into each other. The track in front of me kept banging into me, and then I'd give it some gas and I'd bang into the track behind me. . . ."

Captain Shafer got the unit reorganized, and C/3/4th Cav commenced an on-line assault against the village. Almost immediately, Lieutenant Ware's 3d Platoon ran into a wall of fire. Ware was brand-new. Russin had originally been replaced by a Lieutenant Fetner, who lasted only a week or so before being shot in the leg when the platoon bumped into a hit-and-run squad of NVA.

Ware replaced Fetner, but lasted less than two weeks himself. "We were on a little incline, trying to get up over something, and we took an RPG," recalls Bob Wolford, the sole M60 gunner on the platoon command track. The rocket hit the top of the gun shield behind which Sgt. Klaus D. Egolf was firing the .50-cal MG. Egolf was killed instantly, and Ware was hit in the face, as well as the chest and arm. The maimed lieutenant stumbled rearward. The driver, though uninjured, deserted the vehicle. "The explosion kind of dazed me, and when I regained my senses I realized that Ware was gone. The driver was gone. The medic was there, but he had shrapnel in his ankle and leg," recalls Wolford. The medic opened the door built into the rear ramp of the personnel carrier, "and we could see the rest of the platoon moving back, leaving our track in there. The medic took off running to catch up with them. . . ."

Unaware that the track commander was dead, Wolford hesitated to leave the APC. "Egolf had dropped down inside from the cupola, and I didn't know if he was alive or dead, or what was going on, or what I should do. The track was filled with smoke, and I couldn't really tell what was going on. I tried to talk to him, but I wasn't getting any response from him. I dragged Egolf to the back door. I got him out, but then I just had to assume he was dead because he wouldn't move and I couldn't move him, and the enemy fire was still heavy. I just ran right back toward our vehicles. They were probably fifty yards back. They were still returning fire even as they backed up, and my biggest fear then was getting shot by my own people. . . ."

● ● ●

Charlie Troop proceeded to blow the village off the map. Gunships and artillery were employed, and when the troop went back in on February 29, it was behind a wall of fire of its own. "The place was totally chewed up," says Cuff. "After about fifty million rounds of .50-caliber machine-gun fire, there's not going to be much left, and there wasn't anything over six inches tall in that village. . . ."

There was no contact. The enemy had pulled out during the night, taking their casualties with them. Charlie Troop recovered C-35 and found its missing commander, Sergeant Harding, lying inside a thatch-roofed hootch that had survived the onslaught. Harding had apparently been hit in the crossfire and had bled to death. "He was still warm, so he must have died just before we got there," reflects Cuff. Harding's missing loader was nowhere to be found despite repeated sweeps back and forth through the flattened village.

"The VC were gone, and Hunt was gone too. . . ."

Corporal Robert Hunt had been captured. I went back out to the field around the first of March, and we learned of Hunt's fate probably that night or the next when his voice suddenly echoed eerily out of the darkness through a bullhorn. "All Troop C members should surrender," he said in a monotone. "Go back to your homes. Leave the people of the Democratic Republic of Vietnam alone. . . ."

The broadcast stopped, then the bullhorn crackled back to life some time later at a new position outside our laager. "You need to surrender," Hunt continued. "Surrender, surrender . . ."

The enemy took Hunt around our whole perimeter and repeated the performance at new laager sites for the next few nights. It was unreal. In this war, we captured them. They didn't capture us!

I liked Hunt, who was a twenty-eight-year-old Regular Army NCO from Beckley, West Virginia. Unfortunately, as I understood it, he'd recently gotten divorced and, his job performance suffering as a result, had been busted from sergeant to corporal before being shipped to Vietnam. Hunt joined the unit shortly after Tan Son Nhut. He wasn't a buddy-buddy kind of guy, but he was a fine field soldier.

During the course of our operations, we did what we could to locate Hunt. Assuming the worst, we dug up every fresh grave we came across for the first couple weeks of March. The guerrillas did not mark their graves. They were simply earthen humps soon to be overgrown. The bodies were wrapped in ponchos or thatch mats. Peeling them open and grimacing at the stench, we found only decomposing enemy soldiers. Hunt had completely disappeared. He did not come home with the other prisoners when the cease-fire was signed and was simply declared dead ten years and five months after his capture.

Chapter Fourteen

arch 1968 was another bad month. I was on a scout track
then, and the days all run together in my memory in a
sweat-blurred montage of monotonous sweeps across
scrubby fields under a relentless sun. The land was flat, the sky vast
above us. Dust rose in a languid haze as our tanks and tracks moved
forward on line. Each was manned only by a commander and driver. The rest of us took turns dismounting, and the vehicles slowly
followed as we plodded and plodded and plodded along—the mission was reconnaissance in force, search and destroy, whatever the
command was calling it then—looking in wells, going through tree
lines, checking for any sign of enemy activity. We never found them.
They always found us. Three or four RPGs would suddenly whoosh
from a hedgerow as an enemy squad—we were fighting regulars
now uniformed in fatigues, web gear, and green pith helmets—covered the withdrawal of the NVA platoon or company we had unknowingly been approaching. The result was always instant pande-
monium. Black smoke would belch from the tracks that had been
hit. Fire would be returned at a frenzied rate, heedless of the dismounted troops—the unit was wound so tight, one AK burst would
start a Mad Minute—and because our officers were green, the unit
filled with replacements, and most of the rest of us shaky and battle
rattled, we didn't aggressively pursue the contacts, but would instead back off to call in air and arty and gunships and to bring in
medevacs for our wounded, who were often the same new guys who
had come out aboard the evening resupply ship just a few days before. Many went back with an arm or leg blown off.

Each contact hung us up for hours. With our overwhelming firepower we usually managed to kill a few NVA for our troubles—guys
were starting to do weird things like putting cigarettes in the

mouths of dead enemy soldiers and taking photos—but we never had a chance to catch our breath, and we weren't meshing together as a unit. We were really just a big fucking mob out there.

The tempo of operations was relentless. It was search and destroy during the day, ambushes and LPs—listening posts—at night. Each of us wondered when our number was coming up. It was just a matter of time. We were taking the heaviest casualties in the squadron— a third more than Alpha Troop, three times as many as Bravo Troop. There was a believable rumor that an NVA battalion had been assigned to shadow Charlie Troop and hit us at every opportunity.

I stopped writing to the woman I had met on leave before shipping out for Vietnam. She pleaded to me in letter after letter to explain what was wrong. She finally sent a desperate ultimatum: If I didn't answer her in two weeks, she was going to consider us through. That's what I wanted. Move on. Forget about me. I was dead. . . .

Everything was fucked up. Morale had bottomed out, and there was a lot of heavy drinking and heavy pot-smoking when we laagered in at night. During watches atop my track, I'd turn my Starlight Scope around, and in the fuzzy green glow, I could see guys—not all of them or most of them, but more than ever before— huddled around the lowered back ramps of personnel carriers, getting high, getting numb, escaping for the moment. The moment was all that mattered.

I had been made track commander of my scout track. My crew were potheads too, but I left them alone, having come down several notches in the expectations I'd had when I first got to Vietnam. There were some bare minimums I still held them to, but I had the impression that the guys were so angry and stressed out that if you messed with them too much, you might turn your back and get your head blown off.

Refusing to be intimidated, Sfc. Alva A. Cooper, our new platoon sergeant, came on strong. Cooper was an old Georgia boy with reddish skin and balding, close-cropped reddish hair. I believe he had a German wife. Cooper joined C/3/4th Cavalry in early March fresh from a tour as a cadre at the legendary NCO academy in Bad Tolz, Germany. Still imbued with the spit-and-polish standards of that institution, he viewed us with narrow eyes and a fierce, critical scowl, and my initial impression was that this by-the-book superlifer was going to get a lot of people killed, himself included.

"Why aren't you shaved?" Cooper would snap at some bedraggled trooper. "Why don't you have that .50 cleaned? Get your ass in gear, young soldier, or I'm going to nail you with an Article 15. . . ."

Cooper was applying shock treatment, and it worked. It didn't take me long to realize that the man was an outstanding leader: a brave, hardnosed disciplinarian, he also took care of his troops.

Though Cooper alone could not replace all the Deans, Brewers, Breedens, and Danylchuks we had lost—that the professional NCO corps had been mostly used up by that stage in the war was a primary factor in the decline in morale and performance—and though the constant turnover in personnel due to casualties meant that we never regained the cohesiveness we had had before Tet, Cooper did as much as any one man could to hold us together and keep us going. I think the platoon would have fallen apart completely if not for Cooper.

The war ground on. It was another hot day when we picked up an old Vietnamese man in an otherwise deserted farm area west of An Duc. The fact that he was out in the middle of nowhere by himself cast him as a possible Viet Cong sympathizer—his ID card checked out, but it could have been fake—and even as the old man tried to explain why he was there, a captain and a defector-turned-scout who we called Chieu Hoi Charlie threw him up against the side of an APC.

The captain fired off a question. Chieu Hoi Charlie translated. The old man mumbled that he knew nothing about the enemy, and the captain slammed the butt of his CAR15 submachine gun into his face.

The questioning continued, accompanied by more thumps to the head and chest and hard-fisted punches to the stomach. "I don't care if this guy's a hard-core NVA. This is bullshit," I muttered angrily to Cooper, who looked pained, but said nothing. I finally screwed my courage up—"That's it, I'm going to stop it," I blurted, having little rank to worry about—but as I started forward, Cooper jerked me back by my collar and snapped, "Let it go, let it go—it's not yours."

The captain finally turned the old man loose.
We saddled up and continued on.

The unit was laagered in for the day, cleaning weapons and catching up on our vehicle maintenance. Helicopters brought in mermite cans of hot food and cases of beer. Mamasans and children showed up to sell soda and blocks of melting ice plastered with straw, and the whores—that was the word we used—spread poncho liners out behind some bushes. Prostitutes were everywhere, frequently delivered to us on mopeds and three-wheeled Lambrettas by ARVN pimps wearing sunglasses with mirrored lenses. Some guys would make a game of banging another one every mile along the highway. Banging a whore on the fly was like lighting up a cigarette.

The round-faced Indian medic who had performed so magnificently at Tan Son Nhut, and who I had come to like very much—he was a damn good soldier and a decent, honorable, soft-spoken man—did not share the general attitude. He carried in his wallet a photograph of a beautiful Indian girl. He said he was going to marry her when he got home to Washington State. He loved her. He was faithful to her.

That day in the laager, however, the medic took a turn with one of the girls. It wasn't like him at all, but, anyway, it happened. I think it was the very next day that his penis swelled up so badly that he was limping. The second day he couldn't walk. The third day he couldn't see—syphilis can affect the optic nerve—and he was medevacked out, his eyes crusted over. I don't know if his condition was permanent, but it was bad enough that he was sent back to the United States. For all the champion whoremongers in the unit, I thought the fate of this fine man who had slipped once in the two or three months he'd been there was tragic, and I was terribly upset by the image of my friend having to explain to his family and his girl what had happened. If I could, I would have told them that he was as much a casualty of the war as the bloody men we loaded on the Hueys.

Chapter Fifteen

Every time I bumped into Sergeant Kampe, he worked on me to get out of the field. He told me he could get me a job as a radio repairman at squadron headquarters. "Get out while you can, Dwight. You're too smart a guy just to wind up being a piece of sausage in a blown-up track," he would tell me. I don't know why Kampe took a liking to me, but he treated me like a son—he was only ten years older than me, but with his gray hair and his hard-drinking, chain-smoking ways, he looked like he was ninety—and was determined to save my life. "You're gonna get killed," he'd argue. "What a waste. You don't need that to happen. You're a bright fella. You can do better than this. You've got a good career and a good life ahead of you."

I was ready to listen. I was out of steam. I had not fully recovered from my injuries of February 19 and would get viselike sun headaches, especially during our dismounted operations. They were so ferocious that sometimes I thought I was going to black out.

More than that, I was still mentally shook up. Given all the men we had lost to head shots, I had become terrified of snipers and kept waiting for the bullet through the brain that was going to snap the lights off, or worse, leave me a mumbling vegetable hooked to machines.

Kampe must have been combat fatigued himself because he once hugged me—sergeants do not *hug* enlisted men—as he pleaded with me to take him up on his offer. He was a tough old NCO again a moment later. "You're going to get your fucking ass blown away," he barked. "You're going to go home in an aluminum casket, and you're just going to be just another goddamn dead hero. *For what?!*"

I asked some of my buddies what they thought I should do. "Get the hell out," they said. "What the hell's wrong with you?"

I finally told Sergeant Cooper that Kampe had lined me up with a rear job, and that I was going to take it. "You're one of our most experienced men, and I want you to stay, but I understand," Cooper said with a look that said he was very, very disappointed in me.

Feeling like a deserter, I left Charlie Troop at the end of March and reported to the squadron communications section in Cu Chi. Base camp was not paradise. This being the dry season, it was incredibly hot and a truck rumbling past would leave you coated with dust as fine as flour. But we had showers, fans, and cold beer. Life would have been just grand, in fact, if not for Sfc. Adrian Meckles—another pseudonym—who ran the Commo Shack up at squadron. There were just the two of us in there, and we got along like two scorpions in a bottle. Meckles was a tall, handsome, dark-skinned black man from Jamaica—he had a Caribbean accent—with the physique of an Olympic track star. He was serious and efficient and hardworking. He was also an authoritarian asshole who constantly took me to task about my hair being a little long, or not buttoning the top button of my shirt while working, or not shining my boots to the proper luster, or drinking in the NCO Club until closing time when I was off duty.

I did not shape up. I wasn't in the mood to take any shit off some rear-echelon lifer who had never been in combat. Meckles didn't feel like taking any shit himself. The more sullen I became when he dressed me down, the more make-work projects he came up with for me when we finished with our normal duties. He had me going sixteen hours a day sometimes. I cleaned the Commo Shack. I cleaned the jeep. I dug enough trenches and bunkers to put a mole to shame—we needed them, Cu Chi was being rocketed on a regular basis as of Tet—and I can remember leaning exhausted on my foldout entrenching tool in some half-finished position one day as I tried to tell Meckles that I couldn't excavate the size bunker he wanted in the time he had given me unless I got some help.

Meckles looked down at me contemptuously. "The only help you get in this world is when you're born and the doctor slaps you on your ass and gives you that first breath," he said. "That's the only help you're ever going to get. You're not going to get any here."

It got pretty personal at times. When I first met Meckles, I had made some guilty comment about having seen a lot of my friends killed, adding lamely that I had read somewhere that the good always die young. "Remember what you said about how the good die young?" Meckles would taunt me. "Well, Specialist Birdwell, it seems to me that *you're* still alive and well. Why is that now?"

Meckles was implying that I was a coward. I wasn't sure anymore that I wasn't, and when I finally exploded— *"Fuck you, get off my back!"*—he went into a rage, his face an inch from mine as he chewed me out. The whites of his eyes turned red, and he almost vibrated as he tried to restrain himself from pounding me through the floor.

I didn't want to get beat up, but I couldn't let the bastard get away with fuckin' with me like he was. I considered Meckles as much a foe as the Viet Cong, and declaring war, I started doing sneaky shit like letting the air out of his jeep tires, or gingerly loosening the screw-in handles of whatever radio he had just repaired so that when someone from the line troop that had turned it in came to pick it up the handles would pop off in his hands, making Meckles look like an idiot. Then there was the time I lobbed a tear gas grenade into his hootch at about two o'clock one morning. He came awake thrashing and coughing, and I beat feet out of there before he could spot me. He was mad as a hornet the next day, but, unable to put the finger on me even after much investigation, he didn't press the issue. The bad blood continued to boil, but thankfully another sergeant first class, one with a very reserved attitude, was assigned to our area, and he functioned as something of a middleman between me and Meckles.

Except that they always occurred at night, there was no pattern to the rocket and mortar attacks on Cu Chi. Perhaps a week would go by without an incident, then we'd get hit two or three nights in a row. Sometimes three or four rockets would slam in, followed by another salvo after a lull of an hour or two. Sometimes they would come in one after the other after the other for several intense minutes.

Mortar shells descend with a sharp teakettle whistle. Usually they whistled all the way in, but if the whistling suddenly stopped you were in trouble. It meant the shells weren't going to land somewhere else in the sprawling base camp. It meant you were in the target area, and the rounds were only seconds away from impact.

The mortars messed with your mind, but it was the rockets that did the real damage. The enemy used Soviet-made 122mm rockets, which were nine feet long and left craters as big as rooms. Helicopters orbited Cu Chi at night, watching for flashes—at a word from these airborne spotters, the base alert siren would start wailing—and counterbattery fire from our artillery pounded the launch sites with such speed that the enemy had to move out as soon as they fired their rockets. These defensive measures usually restricted the enemy to short barrages.

They were bad enough. The situation was such that in April, the division engineers placed office-sized metal shipping containers known as conexes into entrenchments dug almost fifteen feet deep next to our barracks—our troop tents had earlier been replaced with single-story, wood-frame barracks—and bulldozers then pushed the earth back over the top. These instant bunkers would have survived a direct hit, but nothing else did—not the trucks turned into Swiss cheese when our motor pool got hit, not the new tank engine that was left overnight on the back of a truck only to be blown to smithereens by a million-to-one shot, and not the barracks that took a rocket through the roof in the middle of a card game. . . .

There was always something going on in the barracks, and even after I had been reassigned to squadron I spent a lot of nights over in the one my old platoon occupied. They were rectangular, tin-roofed structures with low, pitched ceilings, bare light fixtures, and concrete floors. The upper half of each wall was one long screened-in window. Cots were lined up in two rows with footlockers in front of each, but nothing was really organized—I mean, this was Vietnam, not a base in the United States—and when the troop was in from the field, there were beer cans and ammo and weapons and junk strewn everywhere. We built a little bar with an electric fan just inside the front door and had photos from home and *Playboy* centerfolds tacked up on the walls. There were several overlapping circles of activity on any given night. Some guys would be watching the Armed Forces Vietnam Television Network. Others would be drinking or talking or playing cards in little groups, chests bare or shirts unbuttoned in the heat. The groups tended to shake out along musical lines. Johnny Cash and Buck Owens would be playing in one huddle, the Beatles, the Boxtops, and Tommy James and the Shondells in another. Motown was big too. The potheads would be doing their thing in the back of the barracks with the Doors and Jefferson Airplane.

Things sometimes got out-of-hand. Throwing smoke grenades into barracks was not uncommon. It wasn't unknown, either, for some boozed-up GI to grab a .45-caliber grease gun—they were still issued to tankers—and let out a whoop and a holler as he stitched the ceiling. That would always scare the shit out of you because you couldn't be sure that the trigger-happy fool wouldn't lose control of his weapon or accidentally swing his fuzzy sights in your direction.

Drunken fistfights were another way of letting off steam. I did some serious drinking myself in the rear, as did Richard Johns, a buddy of mine who was an Ottawa Indian from Northport, Michigan. We shared a certain demented sense of humor and used to have some heavy conversations in our native tongue—or at least that's what the guys thought. If the truth be told, I wouldn't have known Ottawa from Chinese, and Richard sure as hell couldn't understand my fractured Cherokee. We were just jabbering at each other, but it impressed our buddies who thought we were communicating in some universal Indian language. There is no such thing.

Another favorite trick was to tie together the bootlaces of some poor passed-out GI, and then scream *"Incoming!"* We also thought it was great fun to blast someone's cot with shaving cream when they were out drinking at the EM Club, so that when they stumbled back to the barracks and threw back their camouflaged poncho liner to climb into bed there would just be a sea of white foam underneath.

Richard and I were always messing with Bob Wolford. Bob would take a lot of crap, but he was sly and patient, and he would always get you back better than you got him. I hate chicken, so one night when I passed out myself, Bob shoved one drumstick in my mouth and another in my hand, then took several Polaroid photos that he embarrassed me with the next morning. Very, very slick!

On May 9, the unit was out in the field, and the barracks were relatively empty. Several men were writing letters, and someone was strumming on a guitar. One of our short-timers, Sp5 Charles R.

Rosenbusch—a good-looking guy from Worcester, Massachusetts, who had a strong, magnetic, hustler-type personality and was always a good time—had a loud card game going with some headquarters troops, and guys who were in the rear with VD, guys who were leaving for R&R, and guys who were coming back from R&R.

I pulled up a chair. They had some Motown going on a big reel-to-reel Sony tape player and were stacking up empty Ballantines. I was drinking bourbon whiskey myself, but I wasn't really enjoying the party—I was in a perpetual bad mood thanks to Sergeant Meckles—and around midnight I thought, to hell with it, time to fold up. I was a little wobbly anyway, and figured that if I didn't leave then and there, I might not be able to make it back to my hootch at squadron.

Only seconds after I hit the road, the alert siren went off. I didn't dive for cover, but simply kept walking, a little too drunk, depressed, and frustrated to give a shit. The rockets came in like thunder, but it didn't matter, and upon reaching my hootch, I just crashed.

I went back over to the troop area the next day and ran into Jim Lancey, the tank driver who was now working in the orderly room. "Dwight, you won't guess what happened," he said ruefully. "Where we were playing cards—a rocket hit and killed five guys."

I was stunned and went down to look at the barracks. It was a shambles, the 122 having come right through the roof. Everything inside was torn and bloody and splattered with flesh—the dead included Rosenbusch and Barry Lewis from my old infantry squad, who was only days away from going home—and people were upset, people were crying, people were just crazy with outraged grief.

Numerous men had been wounded, including my buddy Sergeant Breeding, a hard-muscled, tough-minded career NCO who had a magnificent tattoo of a dark blue panther drawing red streaks as it stalked up his left bicep with its claws out. Breeding had only recently been medevacked from the field with his second combat wound—rocket fragments in his left forearm—and released from the hospital that very day, when the rocket attack began he was asleep in the troop's senior NCO hootch, a sandbagged tent supported by a wood frame that was located behind the platoon barracks.

There was a slit trench alongside the hootch, and a mad scramble erupted for the screen door to get to it. Breeding was the last man in the pile, right behind SSgt. Frank E. Williams, the popular 2d Platoon sergeant who had been sent back a day or two earlier on an empty supply chopper to have a dentist attend to a toothache. Breeding had just reached the door when it slammed shut in his face. He jerked it open to follow Williams out, and at that instant the rocket hit the adjacent barracks. The concussion violently blew Breeding backward across the hootch, and he crashed down dazed and bleeding among the cots, little fragments burning in his face and scalp.

Breeding had gotten off lightly. The sandbags stacked up around the hootch had absorbed much of the blast. It was instead Sergeant Williams who, having just made it outside, caught the brunt of the explosion blowing out the side of the barracks, and amid the chaos—guys were screaming hysterically, tracks were being brought up to illuminate the scene with their headlights—Breeding picked up one end of the stretcher onto which Williams had been placed and lifted him onto the back of one of the jeeps from troop headquarters being used to run the casualties over to the evac hospital. Williams had gaping holes in his back—his lungs were exposed— and a gaping hole in his side, but for reasons we never understood, he was not medevacked to a larger medical facility. He simply lingered in the evac hospital until dying of pneumonia three weeks after being wounded. Breeding visited him several times, and Williams kept asking why he hadn't been shipped to Japan yet, and, suffering terribly—his morphine drip wasn't enough, he could only be given a limited amount because a full dose would depress his damaged respiratory system—he kept begging Breeding to bring him some Darvon, something he was afraid to do because he had been warned by the nurses he spoke with that the pain pills might counteract their treatment of Williams. In the end, their treatment didn't work, and Breeding would forever bludgeon himself with the thought that if only he had done what his friend asked he could have given him a little peace before he died.

Chapter Sixteen

First Lieutenant Anthony R. Adamo, for whom I had much respect as a brave and modest man who always took care of his troops and never pulled rank—and with whom I would become very close on a personal basis late in my tour—had originally taken over the 2d Platoon of Charlie Troop in March 1968. I met him, however, only after I'd been reassigned to the squadron communications section. I had dropped by the troop area that day to visit with the guys when an E7 tank commander in Adamo's platoon sneered, "Birdwell, when are you going to be ready to go back to the field with some *men?*"

Lieutenant Adamo must have heard about Tan Son Nhut from some of his troops, because he jumped right in that E7's face. "If I ever hear you talk to Dwight Birdwell like that again, I'll take those stripes right off your arm," he barked. "This man's a hero, and you're talking to him like that? He's seen more than you'll probably ever see!"

Man, I thought, I *like* this guy! The E7 had hit a nerve, though. I was troubled about sitting out the war in the rear—while I fixed radios and fought with my sergeant, Charlie Troop made heavy contact all through April and May—and to assuage my guilty conscience, I sometimes went AWOL to hitchhike along with my old platoon during combat operations, if only for a day or two here and there.

It was not enough. I knew I had to get out of Cu Chi once and for all—it was a matter of duty, pride, and self-respect—so I caught a Troop D resupply ship out to the field to talk with Sergeant Cooper, the 3d Platoon sergeant, about transferring back into Charlie Troop.

Having made my decision, I felt revitalized. I felt downright cocky, in fact, and came on strong with Cooper: "I'm *thinking* about coming back out. What will you do for me to get me back in the platoon?"

Ol' Coop cracked a grin. "I want you back, Birdwell," he said. "I'll give you a tank, and a little bit down the road I'll make you an E6."

Thus, I became a real soldier again. I think Meckles was planning to file charges against me for insubordination and being absent without leave, but Sergeant Cooper ramrodded my transfer through one step ahead of this potential trouble and, true to his word, immediately assigned me as the proud commander of tank C-36.

I was right where I wanted to be. I was pumped up. I was back in the saddle and ready to win the war all by myself. Wanting my tank to stand out from the others in Charlie Troop, I made sure it was the cleanest and best maintained, and emulating the guys I'd grown up with who decorated their trucks and hot-rodders with flames, I had some kids take the cover of my tank searchlight down to a little shop in Cu Chi village where a Vietnamese artisan painted the front of it with a big red-and-gold 25th Division emblem.

It was dumb to go so conspicuously into battle, but my tank was my hot rod, and I had to play it up. Our fifty-two-ton M48s really were the kings of the road. I remember driving through Cu Chi village one day behind a bunch of ARVN in a troop truck, when they abruptly stopped to talk to some women along the side of the road. I sat idling behind them for five or ten minutes—no sweat, I could appreciate them wanting to talk to some pretty females—but they were blocking the way, and I finally motioned them to move aside. The ARVN got terribly indignant, and perhaps showing off for the girls pointed their little carbines at me. In response, I dropped the main gun down into the truck bed and, traversing my turret, started pushing the truck off the road. The driver got out of there real quick at that point, and, needless to say, not a carbine shot was fired.

I had a three-man crew. The loader and gunner were two solid citizen-soldiers, and they became two of the closest friends I had in Vietnam. However, my driver, Pfc. Thomas T. Ferris—and this is not his real name—was a hard-faced, hate-filled country boy who disliked me from the moment he laid eyes on me, and that was before I had even moved into the command cupola of C-36.

I was still with squadron then. That particular evening, I had made it down to the barracks, and when I walked in, some of the old guys greeted me warmly: "Hey! Dwight Birdwell, how ya doin'?!"

There was a new guy sitting among them. "So you're Birdwell," he said. "I've heard of you. You think you're something, don't you?"

"No," I mumbled, astonished.

That new guy was Ferris, and little did I know that he would be my driver when I rejoined the platoon. He soon came to despise me, and I him. It was a miserable situation—for one thing he wouldn't follow my orders—and we were headed for a major confrontation when he abruptly became a casualty.

My loader was Jack Donnelly—the same Jack Donnelly who had been wounded with me on February 19. He'd virtually been shredded that day, his first in combat, and I never expected to see him again, but after one week in the 12th Evac and three weeks recuperating in the troop rear, he had been tagged fit for duty and sent back out. That's how badly we needed warm bodies.

Jack was a farmer's son who had been drafted upon graduating with a degree in forestry from Virginia Tech. Twenty-five years old, he was quiet, considerate, and dependable, and, raised as a Primitive Baptist—they made us Southern Baptists look like a bunch of heathens—he was the only complete and absolute no-swearing, no-drinking, no-whoring, read-his-Bible-every-night trooper in all of Charlie Troop.

My gunner was Pfc. William E. Watts of Fort Worth, Texas. He was a tall, slender, and upbeat guy. Bill spoke very proudly about his dad, who had recently retired from the army as a colonel or general, and he possessed a decidedly mature, well-rounded outlook on life from having been raised around the world. Bill would talk about the beauty of the land and the people of Vietnam—no one else seemed to notice—and whenever we stopped on the highway and the pimps showed up with whores sitting sidesaddle on their mopeds, Bill would ignore them, and instead spin stories for the children who also flocked around us. They made him smile, and he made them laugh.

Bill and Jack were also to become casualties.

I would lose Ferris, Watts, and Donnelly—one maimed, two of them dead—in little meaningless contacts of the kind that wore us down in body and spirit during the summer of 1968. For all my bravado, my timing was terrible, for what turned out to be Charlie Troop's last big battle with the NVA had actually been fought just a day or two before I got back out there. It had been a completely successful action, probably the unit's only total, flat-out, hands-down, kick-ass-and-take-names victory of the entire Vietnam War. . . .

Having moved into the capital area in response to a second wave of urban attacks known as Mini-Tet that began early in the month, the troop was still laagered near Saigon on the night of May 26–27, 1968. "In the middle of the night, somebody got into a fight in the distance. You could hear it, and it continued all night," remembers Lieutenant Adamo. "We knew what was going to happen in the morning—what always happened—we were going to go in there because we were mobile and we packed a lot of firepower."

The battle involved the 4/23d Mechanized Infantry, 25th Division, repelling repeated attacks by the 271st VC Regiment of Tan Son Nhut fame on its laager in a rice paddy three kilometers west of Saigon.

Though unable to breach the position, the enemy did not disengage as dawn approached. Inexplicably, the bloodied, bogged-down 271st dug hasty spiderholes in the open paddies and held its ground even as the inevitable air strikes began at first light.

Lieutenant Colonel Otis arrived shortly with the entire 3d Squadron, 4th Cavalry. "We were all on line, pouring fire into the enemy. They were completely stuck, the jerks!" exults Adamo. Having gotten his elements into position from his helicopter, Otis transferred to his command track as he orchestrated for the second time the destruction of the 271st VC Regiment. Notes Adamo: "The jets were taking off from Tan Son Nhut. We were so close to the air base, they had to loop back around in a big circle before coming in to drop their napalm and bombs. It was the first time I ever saw high-drag bombs. They released them behind us, and the fins would pop out so they just floated over us into the enemy. . . ."

Meanwhile, a lucky RPG hit near Lieutenant Colonel Otis's track, and the squadron commander caught a fragment in his left hand, which was on the radio-intercom switch on the side of his communications helmet. He was also hit in the neck, back, and arm.

Infuriated, Captain Shafer got Adamo on the horn: "Charlie two-zero, this is Charlie six. Be advised that Saber six just got hit, and is being dusted off. Now, get 'em!"

Charlie Troop advanced like rolling thunder. "We had complete fire superiority, and it wasn't much of a fight. It was a slaughter," notes Adamo. There were dead VC and NVA sprawled everywhere. "It was exciting. It's a pathetic thing, but when the guys are winning, they enjoy it. That's just the way it is. Guys were jumping off the tracks and running around, shooting in holes and throwing grenades. It was a moment of high passion, and there probably was not much quarter given to the enemy soldiers who were still alive. . . . "

The day I rejoined the unit, it was still working around Saigon. To celebrate the victory, Captain Shafer had authorized some passes into the capital, and Cooper, just back from one such excursion when I arrived, excitedly described to me not only the battle—"It was like shooting fish in a barrel!"—but also his adventures in a steam bath during his mini-R&R. The old platoon sergeant already had a ruddy tint to his skin, and after being scrubbed, massaged, and otherwise worked over, he was as bright as a lobster. He was almost glowing.

The whole unit was in good spirits. Charlie Troop had seized a big red hammer-and-sickle flag and had stacked up so many enemy weapons that the two-star division commander had choppered in for a look. The price had been one KIA in Troop A—there were none in B and C/3/4th Cavalry—and a grand total of only thirteen WIA.

The enemy body count was in the neighborhood of three hundred. The only explanation for their poor showing was that they had lost a crippling number of their veteran cadre during Tet and Mini-Tet.

Afterward, many guys triumphantly flew captured enemy battle flags from the radio masts of their tanks and tracks. The perfect victory was marred, however, because Lieutenant Colonel Otis's injuries were severe enough—his left hand was permanently disabled—that he was unable to return to his beloved Three-Quarter Cav. His loss was traumatic to us all. Shot down seven times during his command of the squadron, Otis was the kind of officer who wouldn't ask his men to do anything he wasn't willing to do himself. When we were on line kicking NVA ass, or getting our asses kicked as the case might be, Otis would be just overhead in his command ship, or lo and behold, he might suddenly appear next to you on his track, directing fire, moving back and forth, working to secure the objective. He was replaced by just another faceless light colonel.

The war continued. It was too much for us. Captain Shafer was a good officer, and there were many good men in the unit, but having seen Charlie Troop in action before Tan Son Nhut, I have to say that by those standards we came completely unraveled during the summer of '68. There were many reasons why. We had inflicted crushing losses on the enemy during Tet and Mini-Tet, but they refused to admit defeat. Realizing their error in facing us in open battle, they pecked at us from the shadows. It was the kind of frustrating guerrilla warfare that we had encountered before Tet, only many times worse. As we again spent much time escorting convoys and outposting the MSR—the rainy season having started in mid-May, we were generally restricted from operating off-road, it being too easy to get a tank bogged down in the mud—we constantly came under sniper fire, we constantly hit mines, and we constantly ran into quick little ambushes while running the road at night. We had never taken fire during convoy runs before Tet. Now it was common. I had never been on a vehicle that hit a mine before Tet, but there were several incidents that summer in which I would be backing my tank up or making a turn, and suddenly my ears would be ringing, the tank would be tilted at an odd angle in a cloud of smoke and dust, and we'd have to spend several hours replacing damaged road wheels and tread sections. We took a lot of rocket fire, so in addition to the perforated runway matting already rigged on our tanks, one sheet to each side, we hung extra tread sections around the turrets, stacked sandbags around the command cupolas, and filled the bustle racks with ammo boxes and cartons of canned rations, and when we laagered in at night we staked a section of cyclone fencing in front of each vehicle, all of which would hopefully slow down an incoming RPG.

There were no more big battles, just bullshit hassle after bullshit hassle that kept us constantly on edge. Charlie Troop was working out of a small artillery firebase up the road at Trang Bang—this was in June—and each night I'd pull my tank into a prepared position on the perimeter so that my 90mm main gun pointed over the earthen berm toward a tree line out beyond the wire. For several nights in a row, I took small-arms fire from those woods, but I never cut loose in return, concerned that I might accidentally blow away some of our own men positioned out there in the dark on LPs.

Perhaps emboldened by this nonresponse, an enemy rocket team slipped in close the next night—they walked right past our listening posts—and, under the cover of a quick mortar barrage, proceeded to RPG the shit out of that berm position. Luckily, I was not there. My tank had been outposted on the highway just outside the firebase.

Unfortunately, the tank that had taken my place took three direct hits. We had seven WIA—the entire tank crew, plus the guys on an adjacent personnel carrier that was also blasted with an RPG.

We lost First Sergeant Delacerda that morning. It was his own damn fault, but none of us were thinking right anymore. Delacerda was so anxious to catch up with the bastards who had stung us that instead of waiting for the combat engineers who were clearing the MSR with mine sweepers—it was a daily ritual, and no traffic was allowed to pass until they were finished—he snapped at his driver to cut around them and get the damn show on the road. Delacerda's track roared past the startled engineers and ran over a mine fifty feet farther down the highway. The driver was killed, the vehicle junked, and the last time I saw Delacerda he was lying in a ward in the 12th Evac in intense pain, his back broken or at least terribly wrenched, and concerned because word was that he was going to be court-martialed for his lack of judgment. It was a sad end to a brave man.

These losses ate at our morale like acid. They could not be justified. They contributed nothing to the war effort. It didn't matter that we found three dead Charlies and a bush hat smeared with

brains after we medevacked Delacerda—they had either been hit by
the return fire from the berm the night before or the gunships we
had called in to blast the darkness—because we weren't even trying
to win the damn war anymore. GIs like myself who'd come in-country before Tet had always been waiting for LBJ to crank up the B-52s
and take the war to Hanoi. I had hoped our squadron would lead a
Patton-style blitzkrieg into the communist sanctuaries just across
the border in Cambodia. We were never unleashed, however, and
already sapped by the antiwar protests back home, our sense of purpose had ultimately been shattered when Johnson declined to seek
or accept the nomination of his party for another term as our president, halted the already limited bombing of North Vietnam, and
entered into the Paris Peace Talks.

The guys may never have fully understood what we were fighting
for, but we actually thought we'd been fighting to win. Replacements who joined Troop C that summer understood the new mood.
"Nobody back in the States wants this war," they told us. "What the
hell are we doing here? We're just getting killed for nothing!"

We had been abandoned. We hated the rich kids going to college
while the blacks, the browns, the farm boys, and the sons of the working class went to Vietnam. We hated the politicians who had left us
mired in this no-win war, but mostly in our bitterness we turned
against ourselves. You would have needed a machete to chop
through the hate and tension as the unit fractured between blacks
and whites, hawks and doves—we were as split as the people back
home about Nixon, Humphrey, Wallace, and Bobby Kennedy—
rednecks and potheads, good soldiers and the fuck-offs who didn't
care about cleaning their weapons, taking care of their equipment,
staying awake on ambush, or anything else except getting their asses
out in one piece. Nerves were frayed and tempers short. Best friends
snapped at each other, and arguments and fistfights suddenly flared
over little things that wouldn't have mattered before.

The stress level was so high because there seemed to be no end
to the carnage. The enemy were not supermen, but they were committed to their cause. The average GI just wanted to take his Freedom Bird back to the World. Our minds were on Mom, Dad, the
girl back home, a good job, and getting behind the wheel of a new

Mustang or Pontiac Firebird. In comparison, that little NVA out there had nothing to look forward to but his next handful of rice, and either death or victory. They were in for the long haul. We killed enemy soldiers who had fatalistically tattooed *Born in the North, Die in the South* on their chests, and I once souvenired a pith helmet from a dead North Vietnamese, one of several we'd piled up that day, who had decorated the underside of the plastic brim with brave little etchings of U.S. Air Force jets going down in flames.

It seemed almost pointless killing NVA. The whole thing seemed pointless. We weren't winning, the enemy wasn't quitting, and the ARVN weren't interested in fighting their own war. When I joined the army, I'd been marching in tune with Barry Sadler's "Ballad of the Green Berets." Times had changed. In July or August '68, a bunch of us were down at the NCO Club in Cu Chi. There was a little Filipino band onstage, and when they segued into "We Gotta Get Out of This Place" by Eric Burdon and the Animals, our new national anthem, everyone went crazy, screaming, yelling, throwing tables and chairs—we're talking about E5s and E6s here—and some guys just cried and sang along for all they were worth: *"We gotta get out of this place, if it's the last thing we ever do. . . ."*

We had a scout-dog handler attached to us from the 25th Division. Instead of doing his job, that sorry motherfucker rubbed sand in his German Shepherd's ears, stomped on its paws, then reported the dog as injured and rode out with it on a resupply Huey.

Malingering became epidemic. If a guy got jungle rot on his feet so bad that he had to be pulled off the line, he'd trade his contaminated socks and boots with a buddy also looking for a ticket out. These same troopers also took to banging whores without rubbers, hoping to catch VD, which was good for a week of treatments back in Cu Chi.

We were getting slaughtered, and that week in the rear might just save your life. Every day counted toward the magic 365. . . .

The situation got so out of hand that the new squadron commander put out the word to Captain Shafer to keep the troops away from the whores—the problem wasn't only venereal disease, but that the guys, whether they used rubbers or not, weren't staying fo-

cused on the task at hand, especially vehicle maintenance—and I
was sitting atop C-36 one afternoon, a little amused and a little sad-
dened at the state into which we had sunk as the colonel hovered
over us in his helicopter, so low you could see his furious face as he
threw smoke grenades into the bushes off to one side of our perimeter where the whores had half the damn unit standing in line. That
broke things up, and Shafer, taking his cue, jumped down from his
track with his CAR15 submachine gun whenever the kids and the
girls showed up after that and fired a few rounds into the air to scare
them away. He also used a defused grenade, which really put them
to flight, but he soon grew sick of dealing with this mess, and things
went right back to the way they had been. Orders didn't mean much
anymore in Vietnam.

People also got real loose with dope that summer. They smoked
it day and night, in the rear and in the field, and it was no longer a
matter of buying little baggies of weed and rolling your own. De-
mand being what it was, the mamasans along the road now sold
what appeared to be factory-sealed cartons of Salems and Winstons,
but they were counterfeit—cannabis instead of tobacco—and when
a guy tore the cellophane off a pack and lit up a perfectly normal
looking cigarette, that pungent marijuana smell would hit you.

I saw a lot of replacements get fucked up on pot. These All-Amer-
ican guys would come in, they'd start messing around with marijuana because it was the thing to do, and in thirty days—you could
mark your calendar by them—they'd be chain-smoking dope and
walking around like nervous cats. They were paranoid. They were
freaked out. They were not taking care of business.

Lieutenant Adamo almost killed a careless pothead during a
night attack on Charlie Troop. Asleep in his track when the shooting started, Adamo instantly snapped awake, grabbed the detonator
to the claymore mines arranged in front of his personnel carrier—
the firing cord from each one ran down through the open cargo
hatch—and squeezed them off with blinding flashes. Moments
later, a trooper clambered into the track through the back hatch.
The kid was soot-faced and begrimed from the backblast of the claymores, and, amazed that he was still alive, he excitedly confessed
that "we were smokin' some shit, and I fell asleep on the ground out

in front of the track, and then the next thing I know the claymores are going off. Goddamn, another ten feet and I'd have been in *front* of 'em! . . ."

One of my high school teachers had fought with a tank battalion in World War II, and he warned me when I joined the army to stay out of Armor. The biggest problem was the neverending maintenance required to keep a tank in fighting condition. I used to envy the infantry. During stand-downs, they just had a personal weapon to clean, and then their time was theirs. Tankers not only had to clean an M16 and .45, but we also had a .50-caliber MG and 7.62mm coaxial to worry about, and then it took the entire crew to push the big ramrod through the 90mm main gun to swab it out.

Weapons cleaned, we had to work on the tank next, a chore that included pulling the four large batteries that powered the tank— they were just barely accessible under a metal floorboard in the cramped turret—then passing each heavy, cumbersome, acid-dripping battery up through the loader's hatch and cleaning out the battery carriages.

Maintenance was a constant bitch in the field, too, and a lot of guys grew complacent about it, especially after we lost so many of our old taskmaster NCOs. I did what I had been trained to do in Korea, and every time we stopped, I'd check the weapons, I'd check the oil, I'd check the transmission fluid, and I'd check the individual tread sections, which were known as blocs and were joined together by links, which in turn were held in place by bolts. The bolts tended to vibrate loose, and with one tread being made up of 79 blocs, 158 links, and 474 bolts, for a grand total of 948 bolts when both treads were taken into account, there were always at least a few that needed to be tightened up. It was a little maddening.

Race was another big issue. There being strength in numbers, the white guys tended to walk softly around the sensibilities of the black guys. Richard Johns and I, however, were a minority of two in the platoon, which meant that we had to put up with a certain amount of grief about our Indian blood. Most of it was in the nature of ignorant but essentially innocent remarks and jokes. Some of it was intentionally hurtful. "Hide the firewater, hide the firewater, those Indians can get drunk just *smellin'* that shit!" a certain Staff Sergeant Harry Rabinowitz—who was a wiseass career guy from New Jersey—said with exaggerated urgency when my tank pulled up next to his APC as he and his crew were drinking a few beers. Rabinowitz thought he was being real funny. I wasn't amused, but short of pitching a fit or starting a fight, there wasn't much to be done. Rabinowitz rode me a lot that summer, calling me a "redskin" or "blanket-ass" with this c'mon-can't-you-take-a-joke sneer, and there was a night in the barracks when he used me as the butt of one of his witticisms: "Boy, when I get home, the big thing's not going to be that I was in Vietnam. It's not going to be that I was in a line outfit, or that I saw a lot of combat. The big thing is going to be that I slept next to a *goddamn worthless Indian!* They're not going to believe it!"

Rabinowitz said that in front of everybody. I smoldered inside, shamed and furious. I know I'm being thin-skinned. Hell, we all treated each other pretty rough in the U.S. Army. Just ask the unpopular soul in Charlie Troop who was called "Fuckhead" so many times he actually started to respond to that insult like it was his name. *"Hey, Fuckhead, get your ass over here. . . . "*

That I was part Cherokee was a complete nonissue for most of the guys—I don't want to paint a distorted picture, I didn't serve with a bunch of bigots—but there were always a few like Rabinowitz who felt the need to level you, to keep you in your place. In Korea, I'd known a GI I'll call Harper, who joined our tank battalion after being shot in Vietnam with the 1st Infantry Division. Harper used to talk about how he hated blacks and longhairs, and how he and his buddies had bashed Freedom Riders when they came through his native Georgia.

Still, we were fellow soldiers, and I thought we were friends. I was wrong. "Birdwell, you're nothing but a damned Indian," Harper finally felt compelled to inform me, total redneck that he was. "That's all you'll ever be, and you'll never be as good as a white man."

Most of the friction that existed—and, again, it wasn't rampant, but it was real—was between blacks and whites. We had an incident when I was in AIT at Fort Knox that involved an Arkansas boy named Gifford getting in a shoving match in the barracks with a buddy of mine named Cefus who walked that black walk and talked that black talk. I don't remember who threw the first punch, but Cefus was a giant, and Gifford quickly ended up on his butt with a bloody nose. Embarrassed, he spat, "You goddamn nigger!" That was it. Cefus went crazy, running outside to grab a big stone marker that sat in front of the barracks. Before he could smash Gifford with it, I and an urbane, college-educated black draftee named Hennington intervened, and after things simmered down I had a long talk with Hennington and an overwrought Cefus who started crying as they told me about all the obstacles and discrimination that black men faced in the United States of America. They said things needed to change.

I remember one bitter subzero night on the DMZ in Korea when I threw back the flap of a big tent to get in out of the cold and realized that there were twenty-five or thirty black GIs from my tank unit in there. They were in the middle of an animated discussion, but they stopped as soon as they saw me and stared with stony faces.

"Aw, hell, that's Dwight Birdwell," the leader of the group finally said, breaking the tension. "He's a fuckin' Indian. He's one of us."

It was thus that I sat in on a Black Power meeting. Hennington and Cefus had made sense to me, and the grievances laid out by the guys in that tent—failure to advance in rank, harsher punishments than white GIs received from our mostly white NCOs—also carried weight, but black disaffection with the system seemed to take on a life of its own in Vietnam. It became an excuse for not doing your job. We had actually all gotten along pretty well early in my tour, but the Martin Luther King assassination had been an ugly turning point, and many black replacements who joined us thereafter murmured bitterly about being cannon fodder in the White Man's War. They said Muhammad Ali had been right when he refused to be inducted, and some came up with any excuse they could to get out of the field. Even a lot of blacks who refused to take the easy way out and stayed on line were tinged with this new anger, but it must be added that however quickly we broke up into our own little groups whenever we returned to base camp, we were at least united in the field, each one of us carrying his load and depending on the man to his right and left regardless of color because we knew that we were all truly and completely equal in the rifle sights of the Viet Cong and North Vietnamese.

The jungle rot some of the guys were trying to catch in order to kiss the field good-bye was nothing to mess with. That stuff would eat you alive. I can attest to that because shortly after taking command of my tank, I developed a fungus on my feet that refused treatment, and which eventually spread up my legs and across my lower stomach. I was not overly concerned at first. The infection was most aggravating when it rained, but it didn't actually rain all the time during the monsoon season. There would be short, violent downpours each day that soaked everything as you sat under your poncho—you could see the clouds rolling in, low and leaden—then the sun would come out again, the heat and humidity as bad as the rains. Healing scabs began to form one day, but I was out on LP that night and a drenching cloudburst left us lying in muck and mud. The scabs melted away into raw, mushy, oozing flesh, and the pain was so intense I clenched my teeth as I literally cried to myself in the dark. There was no stopping the fungus after that, and despite repeated antibiotic injections from the squadron surgeon, I ended up looking like a leper from the waist down, thankful only that the festering rash had not engulfed my male parts along with everything else. The chafing was so bad that sometimes I had difficulty walking, and I went barefoot whenever I could—not only because I needed to air my feet out, but also because they were so cracked, red, pussy, and inflamed, especially between the toes, on top, and around my ankles, that I couldn't bear to pull my boots on. The raging infection dogged me until I rotated home, and then, just as the base camp doctors predicted, it completely cleared up within a few days. It was grand. It was wonderful. I had almost forgotten what it was like not to live in pain.

Sergeant Cooper asked me several times if I wanted a new job in the rear because of the jungle rot, but I toughed it out because I figured I owed it to him and Lieutenant Jack Hubbell—our newest platoon leader was a solid officer, and a fine, mature, self-possessed man—and to my buddies who were still out in the field with poor, beat-up, out-of-luck Troop C, 3d Squadron, 4th Cavalry, 25th Infantry Division.

I wasn't the only one who stayed in the field with jungle rot. For all the morale problems of that hard summer, there were still those, like my tank crewmen Bill Watts and Jack Donnelly, who hung in there despite various pains and afflictions and homesickness and the gut-churning anticipation of the next mine, the next ambush, the next firefight. They had been raised to always do their best. This they did, and there was a certain nobility to the quiet bravery and devotion of such men who remained true to themselves and to their friends while doing some thankless damn thing like serving in Vietnam.

These were the good soldiers. There were Bill and Jack, and Bob Wolford, Dean Foss, and Ted Bagley, a black buddy of mine who was just a prince of a guy—I remember getting choked up and crying when we said our good-byes at the end of his tour—and Steve Uram of the 1st Platoon, the son of an up-from-the-ranks air force warrant officer, who was not only smart, nice, and dependable, but who was also one of the most purely professional troopers in Charlie Troop.

There was Dan Czepiel, also of the 1st Platoon, an outgoing man, tough soldier, and loyal buddy: After being reassigned to the Troop D motor pool, where he had access to whiskey and other hard-to-find items, he always remembered us thirsty guys in Charlie Troop.

There was Steve Cook of Tahlequah, Oklahoma, who had been maimed in a freak accident: Jumping from the top of his track while under fire, he'd snagged his wedding ring on a bolt securing the radio mast in place, and the weight of his body popped his finger right off. Nine fingered now, Steve wore that ring on a chain around his neck, and guys kidded him that the next thing he'd lose was his head.

At the top of the list there were "Fighting Frank" Cuff and "Cowboy" Boehm, the kind of solid God-and-Country boys I was proud to count as among my best friends in Vietnam. Cuff and Boehm were veterans of Tan Son Nhut and Hoc Mon, and, battlewise and level-headed, they could quickly size up a combat situation and react the right way without being told. In fact, they showed green lieutenants the way things were done and also pointed our replacements in the right direction. They were the cornerstone to Charlie Troop.

Frank was from rural Ohio—his dad worked in a sawmill—and his nickname was a straightforward acknowledgment of his aggressive, let's-go-kick-their-ass brand of soldiering. He was hard as nails about taking care of business. You either cut it with Frank or you didn't.

Quiet, mature, twenty-six-year-old Cowboy Boehm actually had been a ranch hand in Montana before being drafted, and constantly practiced his roping to keep in form. I admired the fact that instead of hovering around the latest issue of *Playboy* like most of us, he was content with his subscription from *Western Horseman* magazine. Our camp followers left Frank and Cowboy a little cold. In fact, if a whore wouldn't take no for an answer, they'd grab her by her wrists and ankles, swing her back and forth a couple times to build up some momentum, and pitch her into a mud puddle.

There was also Lucio Herrera, an even-tempered, salt-of-the-earth Mexican-American, one of ten children who grew up working on their immigrant father's little farm in Hebbronville, Texas. His was a strong family of devout Roman Catholics. Lucio was a tank loader in the 2d Platoon. He'd caught shrapnel in the knee at Tan Son Nhut and another fragment had grazed his head at Hoc Mon, but at a time when guys were reporting every nick and scratch as a combat wound, whatever the actual circumstances—three Purple Hearts got you reassigned to the rear—Lucio didn't make a big deal of either injury, and after getting stitched up, he just went back on the line without complaint. He finished his time as a tank commander and went home with no awards for his wounds, no awards for his valor, nothing but a routine end-of-tour Bronze Star. He deserved better.

Specialist Four Russell A. Gearhart, the new 2d Platoon medic, was a peppery character who used to collect bottles of Jack Daniels from officers in the squadron for treating their VD without making any entries in their medical records. In the field, Doc Gearhart was a madman. When the lead vehicle of a road-bound column hit a mine, sending a piece of tread up into the air, he jumped off his APC—the fourth vehicle in the line—dashed forward, and was already pulling the unconscious and banged-up driver out of his hatch before that tread hit the ground. Russ was also a lifesaver. He once performed an emergency tracheostomy, using a 5cc syringe as an airway—he turned it into a tube by discarding the plunger and cutting off the little teat at the needle end with his scalpel—for a trooper who was choking on blood in his nose and throat after being blasted in the face by a booby trap. Russ steadied himself, made his incision, inserted the improvised airway—and the dude took a breath. Russ immediately taped the tube in place and got his wounded man out on a Huey.

Frank Cuff had been a hero at Tan Son Nhut. Along with Gearhart, he was again a hero when the squadron pushed into War Zone C and established a giant laager position amid the low brush and skinny trees of a rain forest on the Cambodian border. The enemy attacked during the night. I was still back at headquarters at the time, but I heard about what happened. Our listening posts pulled back as ordered. However, a GI from the 2d Platoon LP was hit in the crossfire—as usual, the casualty was a new guy, only two weeks with the unit—and was left out in front of the line. The other members of the LP made it back to Adamo's track and told the platoon leader that they didn't know if the GI was alive or dead. All they knew was that the kid's head had been split open, apparently by one of our own .50-cal MGs. Impulsively deciding to go after the missing man, Cuff got everyone to cease fire on the part of the line facing the LP—he physically jerked one machine gunner off the back of a track to get him to cool it and bellowed at the rest that he would kill any sonofabitch who opened up while he was out there—then ran right toward the enemy, accompanied by Gearhart and a trooper named Rodriguez who constantly shadowed the medic, playing the role of guardian angel because Gearhart usually didn't bother to bring his weapon with him. It got in his way when he was treating casualties. They found their man about a hundred meters into the trees—he was already dead—loaded his body onto the stretcher they had grabbed on the way out, then ran back among the flares and tracers, at which point the platoon resumed firing. The enemy faded back into the night, taking their casualties with them.

Despite it all, there were some light moments. There was the evening when, quite by accident, a bit of manna from heaven dropped into our laps courtesy of the Philippine engineer battalion stationed up the road at Tay Ninh. It happened like this. The platoon was outposted along the highway. As the last convoy of the day went high-balling past—the truckers had taken to hauling ass since Tet and the increase in ambush incidents—a case of San Miguel beer bounced off the rear of a Philippine supply truck that was tucked in among the U.S. Army vehicles. The bands holding together the pallets of beer in the back of the truck had come loose, and more cases started tumbling overboard as the convoy sped on. It was getting dark, however, and the truckers weren't stopping for anything, let alone spilled beer. I don't know if San Miguel is really as good as we thought it was, but reality doesn't matter. It's the illusion that counts, so we—and I mean everyone, the *whole* platoon—neglected our duty, deserted our posts, and abandoned military equipment to chase that truck and scoop up the gold glittering in its wake. We were yelling and screaming like kids as we ran down the shoulder of the road. Truckers bringing up the rear looked at us like we were nuts as they went past, and we must have run a mile, but we didn't care. We walked back to where we had left our tanks and tracks with twenty or thirty cases of beer, feeling blessed. The peace accords had been signed in Paris, the war was over, we were all going home. We had *San Miguel,* man!

We used to have some kind of cheap beer delivered to us in the field in seven-foot-high stacks on shipping pallets—they slingloaded them in under Chinooks—and I would imagine that on those nights very few of us were actually awake on our watches. I also don't think there was a fire extinguisher in all of Vietnam that actually worked; whenever they were recharged, the guys would immediately blast their cans of beer with them. It really got 'em cold.

My buddy Richard Johns used to buy extra beer from the mamasans, and it wasn't unknown for him to pass right out atop his APC. I saw him blissfully zonked out several times when we were under fire.

Soldier humor could be pretty rough. We had a good trooper in the platoon, a stocky, curly headed guy from Delaware who the whores—and it seemed like all the girls who worked the highway knew him—called L. D. for Long Dick. They were not exaggerating.

L. D. was a nice guy, but he was a character. He'd climb atop his personnel carrier, break out his equipment, and start swinging it in circles for the girls. The drunker he got, the more swinging he would do, and one night to everyone's amusement, he swung himself right off the top of his track. He wrecked his knee, which must have amused him, too, because he was evacuated back to his wife in the United States.

I came in from LP one morning that summer and saw that our medic was over with two guys who were sitting on the lowered back ramp of an APC, trembling and shaking and just generally looking out of whack. They reminded me of some hogs we had when I was a kid that got into some bags of cement. They were acting really stupid when we found them. Those two GIs were kind of acting the same way, and it turned out that they'd also eaten something they shouldn't have, namely a chunk of C4 plastic explosives. I started laughing my ass off when they admitted what they had done and asked them what in the hell they'd been thinking about. I never got an answer but could imagine they had either heard the stuff made you high or made you sick enough to get out of the field for a while. Despite their pain, the guys started laughing, too, and, in fact, they were medevacked and never came back. I don't know if they went home or went straight from the 12th Evac to Long Binh Jail.

Another day the platoon was herringboned on the highway south of An Duc, waiting for the afternoon convoy. We were taking a little fire from the ville, and returning a little, when a middle-aged Vietnamese man wearing a sun helmet, a white shirt, and black pants came bicycling up the road toward us from the other direction. We wondered if he was going to suddenly unlimber an RPG launcher when he got close, but that wasn't his intention at all. He was there to make some money. The big wire basket attached to his handlebars was stuffed with tomatoes and loaves of bread, plus a jar of Miracle Whip and a big ol' five-pound block of government cheese. He also had a little ice chest filled with Coca-Cola strapped to the back of his bike. I couldn't believe it. I had grown up on mayo-tomato-and-government-cheese sandwiches, and I must have bought five from this daring entrepreneur. The sandwiches were a dollar and a half, the Cokes a buck a bottle, and after the sandwich man worked his way down the platoon line, making sure to stay on the safe side of our vehicles as the sniper fire continued to snap and buzz overhead, he turned around and pedaled back the way he had come.

There was another incident that summer that was funny the way a sick joke is funny. It was also revealing. We had some type of special recon platoon temporarily attached to us, and I wouldn't have been surprised if its Vietnamese members—there were also Thai, Lao, and Cambodian mercenaries—had been recruited right out of the jails in Saigon. They were thugs. They sported bush hats and tight-fitting, tiger-stripe camouflage suits, and when we pulled into villages, these strutting punks would slap the old men around—the young men were nowhere to be seen—as they shouted questions and checked ID cards and stuffed whatever caught their eye into the sacks they carried. They really knew how to win the old hearts and minds.

These heroes were doing their usual slapping and looting bit in one particular village one particular day when several of them began chasing some chickens around with a pistol. They didn't have any luck shooting the zigzagging fowl, but they did manage to physically grab a few, which they then sealed in a metal can. Lighting a big pile of rice stalks on fire, they proceeded to toss the can into the flames. It was terrible, but you could hear the chickens squawking and their feet furiously scratching inside the can as they roasted alive. Lunch had not yet been served when we suddenly got the word to move out, so they quickly pushed the can out of the fire with a stick, pulled the half-cooked chickens apart, feathers and all, hustled up some plates and steamed rice out of the hootches, and pulled themselves up onto our tracks, where they sat giggling and jabbering and shoveling the mess into their mouths with their fingers as we moved out. Who's kidding who, I thought, these guys are never going to beat the NVA.

Chapter Seventeen

Some of the guys hated the Vietnamese. They hated the way they looked and they hated the way they talked. They hated the whole damn country and every man, woman, child, and water buffalo in it. Most of the others didn't hate the Vietnamese but merely viewed them as some lesser form of human being. They treated them with an utter lack of respect, and after the war when I heard people bemoan the fact that the United States was so unpopular around the world despite its massive foreign aid programs, I would think of these American boys and some of the things they did in Vietnam.

It was the middle of June 1968. One link in the convoy security chain my tank, was outposted by itself at a bridge where a marshy creek intersected the main supply route south of An Duc. It was a bad spot. There had been so many mining incidents that the little concrete bridge was mostly demolished—it was now reinforced with culverts—and we used to muse that the enemy used the site as a training area for new sappers. It was mined practically every night. The unpaved highway was a mess. We had spent the better part of this particular morning, in fact, towing bogged-down civilian buses off the road. Four of those big, dilapidated, overcrowded, low-riding rigs coming up from the capital broke their axles when they hit the soft dirt where the multiple mine craters had been filled in, and after getting the people off, we'd attach towing cables, drag them off to the side of the road, and wait for the next one to try its luck navigating the obstacle course. I finally decided to pull every damn bus off the road before they hit that rough stretch and hold them there until the passage of the morning supply convoy coming up past Cu Chi from Saigon.

In short order, I had three or four more buses strung out along the shoulder of the highway. Apparently a helicopter pilot screening the convoy route described this scene to our acting troop commander, a Captain Lodge—Shafer was in the rear with a kidney problem—who in turn radioed me for an explanation: "I've got a report that there's a concentration of vehicles at your checkpoint. What's going on?"

I told him, but Lodge was less than impressed. "That's the stupidest thing I've ever heard of," he snapped. "You're going to have total blockage. The convoy won't be able to get through!"

I tried to explain again about the broken axles, but Lodge had an explosive temper, and he cut me off, screaming that "You *will* get those buses moving again, or I will personally move down to your location and relieve you of command of your tank!"

Lodge added that he had half a mind to bust me back to E4. My driver, Ferris, who hated me, gloated, "You think you're hot shit, Birdwell, but you don't know what the fuck you're doing."

Fuming, I waved at the bus drivers to hit the road—"Let's go, let's go!"—then got Lodge on the horn a moment later to report that the first bus to move out had broken its axle and was blocking the MSR.

"Charlie three-six, I owe you an apology," the captain radioed back. "You had the right idea. You keep those buses off the road. . . ."

The convoy went past shortly thereafter, led by the bulk of the 3d Platoon. When it cleared our area, Captain Lodge and the other two platoons of Charlie Troop started south from their own security positions to the north of mine to conduct a cordon-and-search in An Duc. They had just crossed the Trang Bang Bridge on Highway 1 when they were ambushed, and two troops from an attached ARVN platoon were killed, and four more were wounded, along with a GI, when the personnel carrier on which they were riding took an RPG.

We monitored the radio as a medevac came in, and the operation proceeded: Troop C surrounded An Duc, and the ARVN moved in, rounding up enemy suspects and firing up a fourteen year old who tried to run away. He had no weapon, but body count was the name of the game and he was duly reported to squadron as a Viet Cong.

Finally, dusk approached. Lodge came up on the radio to inform me that the evening convoy was headed south from Tay Ninh and that there was a civilian traffic jam at the southern edge of An Duc. He was sending a track to relieve me at my checkpoint, and I was to proceed north and clear the road so the convoy could pass quickly and safely through our area. No problem, except that Ferris decided he was going to show me how a real soldier handled these people when they got in the way. As soon as we arrived, he jumped off our tank, stormed into the snarled traffic—I think a truck had stopped to unload something at a market and was blocking half of the two-lane highway—and started yelling and screaming and kicking people who were walking or riding bicycles. Ferris hollered at them to move their asses out of the way. He cuffed them on their heads. Not sure how crazy this enraged trooper might get, they hurried past as meekly as possible, bowing, their hands held together in the Buddhist prayer position. I shouted at Ferris to knock it off, but he punched a moped driver right in his face as he tried to putter past, sending him into a tailspin. I climbed off the tank myself at that point. . . .

Ferris and I had gotten into it before over this kind of crap. An immature punk, he used to play chicken with civilians on mopeds and Lambrettas, taking up the whole road with our monster-sized tank and forcing them to swerve off into the muddy paddies. He also used to come up behind them, pushing and bumping them off the road. He thought the resulting crashes were a riot. I'd bark at Ferris to cool it, but he'd keep the pedal to the metal as he zoomed up on his next hapless victim—I'd be screaming the whole time, and he'd be chanting back over the intercom, "Fuck you, fuck you, fuck you!"—and the only one way to get him to stop was literally to beat him. Since the main gun was directly over Ferris's hatch when it was facing forward, I'd have to turn the turret all the way to the rear to get to him. If I traversed it to the right, the gun tube would slam into the roadside hootches, to the left and I'd be clipping people too. I'd then slide down onto the front of the tank, stomp on Ferris's head, and sit on his shoulders, punching him as hard as I could until he brought the tank to a halt. He couldn't fight back very well when pinned under me in his hatch, but as soon as he stopped, he'd spring out, seething, ready to throw down. I didn't have the time or interest. I'd shout at him that I was giving him a direct order to get back into his hatch and move out, and muttering curses and threats he would.

And then the next day he'd bash another civilian into a ditch. I finally reported this to Sergeant Cooper, who called Ferris over and ate his ass out: "If I ever hear of you giving your tank commander trouble again, I'll have you in Long Binh Jail before the day is over."

Ferris was a tall, lanky, stoop-shouldered country boy who wore his bush hat pinned up in front. That was his trademark. He was cocky, and evil eyed as a rattlesnake. "Your kind don't get out of the woods back home," he told me after Cooper chewed him out. "My day's comin', you sonofabitch. I am going to kill you."

The way he said it, I believed him. I was extremely leery of Ferris from then on, and when I'd leave him on the tank at night and go off-road to set up our LP, I'd always wonder if he was going to stage some kind of incident and open up in my direction with the .50-cal MG.

As far as Ferris was concerned, I was the one with the problem. He had a point. I wasn't the only one in the unit who tried to treat the innocent bystanders with some compassion—and I noticed that it was the good soldiers like Frank Cuff and older guys like Lucio Herrera and Russell Boehm who fought the war, not the civilians—but to many of the GIs in Charlie Troop the Vietnamese were all just gooks, dinks, slopes, and slant-eyes, and the GIs had more feeling for their pet dogs and monkeys. Having been discriminated against themselves, I had expected the black troops to have a certain amount of empathy for the impoverished Vietnamese. Some did, others didn't. White and black alike, a lot of the guys—maybe a third—would throw C-rations at the kids who ran alongside our columns begging for food, pitching the cans like baseballs and aiming for their heads. They would bully vehicles off the road and lob tear gas grenades into the crowd as we tore through towns and villages. They would zap a water buffalo hitched up to a cart in the hind end with a slingshot as we rumbled past, sending the animal into panicked flight, or laughingly jump down from a personnel carrier onto the back of a three-wheeled Lambretta, popping the front wheel into the air and scaring the living shit out of the driver. Sorry, Charlie!

I never saw it, but you always heard stories about some tank driver accidentally running over a moped he'd been harassing, grinding up driver and Vespa alike under his treads.

Some buddies from another platoon told me how their E6 tank commander had a few beers one morning, jumped into the driver's hatch on a lark, and was merrily hot-rodding it down the highway when he rear-ended a bus near Trang Bang. They said he killed or at least badly injured several people on the bus, but nothing ever came of it. The tank commander was a good NCO, and it had been an accident after all.

There were uglier incidents. There was nothing systematic about them. Things just seemed to happen in the heat of the moment like at Tan Son Nhut, and guys could count on their buddies to turn a blind eye. Most of the prisoners we took made it safely back to the rear, but more than a few were roughed up before being loaded on the Hueys, and one buddy confided in me that he had seen a man in our unit furiously slamming a captive VC's head against his tank until the man's skull split open, splattering his brains.

Tony Adamo's guys were moved to tears when they discovered a dead baby in a hootch that one of their tanks had blasted during a night attack on the Phu Coung Bridge. Likewise, even though my buddy Steve Uram barely missed becoming a casualty on several occasions at Hoc Mon, when a noncombatant was injured during the action he rushed to her aid. "The Wolfhounds were firing the hootches next to our laager by forming a ball of C4 on a stick, lighting it, then tossing it on the thatch roofs," Steve told me. The grunts were denying the enemy possible firing positions, but had not checked to see if the homes were occupied. "Me and another guy saw a female trying to crawl out of a burning hootch. We ran to get her and grabbed a hand each to pull her away. As we pulled, her skin was so badly burned that it sloughed off in our hands. We finally managed to get her away, and she went out on a dust-off later that night, but she was so badly burned I don't see how she could have survived."

There was that side of it. I remember also how some of the guys, bored with the whores, would try to cajole the mamasans who peddled soda and beer into a five-dollar roll on a poncho liner. These were peasant women in peasant black, conical hats secured under their chins, and they always said no. That was usually the end of it. Once, however, when we were stopped on a dirt road off the highway, a track driver, a real bully, started hassling a mamasan, who smiled stiffly that she was too old for what he wanted—she looked about thirty—and tried to ignore him. I thought the dude was just joking, but a short time later I saw that mamasan hurriedly packing her wares up and rushing off while that trooper joked with his buddies about what a great piece of ass she'd been. I don't know if he was just talking big, or if he had really violated that woman. My feeling was that he had.

I have no doubt in my mind what happened the time I saw an E7 lead a fifteen- or sixteen-year-old soda girl by her arm into the trees. She emerged disheveled and crying hysterically. . . .

These guys didn't get it. *They just didn't get it.* My God, you don't treat women like they're there for the picking. You don't get your kicks abusing the innocent; you don't take your anger out on the defenseless. My mother had always impressed upon me to do unto others as you would have them do unto you. I believed in that and in the Bible; I still wanted to believe in the war—these so-called gooks were the people we were fighting for!—and blended in with all that was the thought of old cruelties inflicted upon the American Indians at the hands of the U.S. Army. Being of Cherokee heritage, I didn't want to turn around three or four generations later and perpetuate the same sort of abuse myself, especially with people who were poor farmers just like my people were poor farmers, and who in some cases looked almost exactly like Indians I knew back in Oklahoma.

Ferris had cleared the traffic jam. He had also gotten completely out-of-hand. Having jumped down from the tank, I was arguing with him when a two-and-a-half-ton Dodge truck came our way through An Duc, headed south with a load of grain sacks. The truck was light-blue, with side boards and a canvas tarp over the back. Ferris stood in the middle of the road, shouting and motioning the driver to pull off to the side. He was intent on keeping the road totally clear until the evening convoy came through, but the driver—who was accompanied by a woman and child in the truck cab—merely slowed down a bit, smiling and shrugging his shoulders like he didn't understand English. He wanted to get his cargo on down the road and thought he could bullshit his way through our checkpoint.

Infuriated, Ferris slapped leather—he had a holster on his hip—and he leveled his .45 on that driver, who immediately jerked to a halt and started pleading for his life. The woman was shrieking.

Unwilling to grab the pistol for fear it might go off, I shouted, "Ferris, god*dammit*—put that gun up! Put it up; *put it up!*"

Ferris thumbed the hammer back, and answered in a voice of casual, don't-tread-on-me menace: "Fuck you, Birdwell."

"Ferris, if you hurt those people, *I'll kill ya.*"

I meant it. Ferris was in front of the truck, aiming through the windshield. I was to his left. The driver started pulling off the road. The truck was rolling past us on our left—and the next thing I knew, I was sprawled on my back maybe twenty feet from where I had been standing. The big dual-mounted rear wheels on the left side of the truck had hit a mine buried in the shoulder of the highway.

I'd been peppered with little fragments and was bleeding heavily from a bad slice on my right hand. The truck was a wreck. The dual wheels had been blown completely off, hub and all, and grain was pouring out the back onto the ground. The driver had gotten the woman and child out of the truck, and in a flash they were *gone.*

Ferris was lying unconscious in the road. Donnelly and Watts ran over from the tank. There was nothing we could do: Ferris had caught a big fragment under his chin that came out the back of his head at the base of his skull. He was alive, but clearly fading fast.

The assistant division commander happened to be airborne in the area, and his Huey landed on the road almost before the dust had settled. The one-star general hopped out, along with the equally spit-shined division surgeon, a lieutenant colonel, who bent quickly over Ferris, checked his wounds, and then to my shock opened his chest up with the scalpel he produced from his medical bag and began massaging the exposed heart. The surgeon finally stopped and looked up at the general. "He's gone. There's nothing I can do for him."

We wrapped Ferris's body in a poncho and loaded it aboard the general's helicopter, which took off, leaving behind a big pool of blood on the road. Tracks from other security positions had raced to our location by then, and the evening convoy came rumbling on through about that time. Lodge called me on the radio later that night. "I know you've lost your driver," he said. "That has to have been a tragic personal loss for you, but you did an excellent job today."

"Thank you" was all I said.

Chapter Eighteen

Charlie Troop made it up to Tay Ninh around noon and laagered in a shady holding area astride the highway just outside the main base camp gate. When it got dark, we were supposed to spend the night running the road back and forth between Tay Ninh and Cu Chi. "We are going to own the night," Captain Shafer had sarcastically informed his platoon leaders when originally assigned this antimining mission. Shafer had been wary of putting the whole troop on the road like ducks in a row: "The first night they don't know. The second night they're watching you. Be careful the third night."

This was the third night. Unfortunately, we weren't thinking in those terms down at the vehicle crewman level. We hadn't gotten the word. We thought we were there to simply escort a convoy back to Cu Chi, and, not expecting any trouble, many of the guys got real funky as the afternoon wore on and we waited and waited and waited for a convoy that wasn't even coming. There was a lot of drinking, a lot of pot smoking, and there were whores everywhere. Some of the business was being carried out in the trees around the holding area. Other girls set up shop under little poncho lean-tos rigged up beside some of the personnel carriers or were inside the tracks themselves on air mattresses, the guys waiting their turn idly watching the action from where they sat around the open cargo hatches.

It was a flaky situation. I don't know where the hell our heads were, but by the time we finally hit the road late that night we were not exactly at our best. We had some listless, hungover crewmen on the tanks and tracks, and I don't think the run would have turned out the way it did had so many guys not been so out of sorts and had not all of us been just plain tired from being up three nights in a row.

Lieutenant Adamo later told me that he fell asleep while sitting on the back of his track when his platoon, which was in the lead, stopped to move aside a cart that was blocking the highway. He came awake with a start when the column started moving again.

Charlie Troop was going through Go Dau Ha at that time. Adamo had a tank on point and was himself on the fourth vehicle in line. Shafer's command track was the sixth, and following the last vehicle of the 2d Platoon, my tank was leading the 3d Platoon. The 1st Platoon was bringing up the rear. We didn't know it then, but one of the drivers behind me had also dozed off while that cart was being pushed out of the way. Since no one else on his track saw the vehicle ahead of them start off again—it was a pitch-black night—the column split, half of us speeding on, the rest of the unit idling behind the zonked-out driver. It was only shortly thereafter that those of us back on the move drove right into a well-planned, ferociously executed ambush, and those elements accidentally left behind raced to catch up with us, including a mortar track that fired illumination rounds on the run, putting some light over our desperate and chaotic melee.

We got nailed where we least expected it. Once we had cleared the town of Go Dau Ha, the next landmark along our route was the then-unoccupied Go Dau Ha fire support base, which was built on the site of an old French fort on the east side of Highway 1. The position was reopened at intervals by artillery units, and when it was not being used by the redlegs we would pull in there to rest and recuperate. The Go Dau Ha fire support base was a place to get mail, write letters, clean weapons, and get resupplied. It was in our backyard.

Adding to our false sense of security was the fact that this stretch of the MSR was presently outposted by Alpha Troop. There were M48s and M113s parked on the left shoulder of the highway at perhaps one-hundred-meter intervals. Charlie Troop sped on by them.

Our lead elements had just passed another Alpha Troop outpost—a lonely looking tank and track—and were about five hundred feet short of the Go Dau Ha fire support base when ambushed. It was 0130, July 3, 1968. Though my tank took some small-arms fire from a little row of deserted, shot-to-hell hootches on the right flank, most of the ambushers were actually on the left side of the

highway where the terrain was flat and open—they had dug spiderholes along the shoulder of the road—and they concentrated their
fire on the lead platoon. One moment, everything was rolling along
nice and quiet, and the next all kinds of hell had broken loose up
ahead, rocket-propelled grenades trailing rooster tails of fire and
exploding against vehicle after vehicle, almost every vehicle in the
platoon, with brilliant flashes and sprays of white-hot sparks in the
night.

*The lead tank was hit first. Spotting something on the road, the com-
mander of C-27 flipped on his searchlight for a second and saw that there
was an NVA standing in the middle of the highway aiming an RPG at them.
It was a glancing shot, however, and C-27 never slowed down. The tank
passed completely through the kill zone, at which point it turned around on
the road and began returning fire. Six more rockets slammed into it, killing
two crewmen and wounding the commander in the face.*

*The ambush was fast and furious. Captain Shafer's track took its first
rocket just as the driver, Frank Cuff, stopped and pivoted a quarter turn to
the left so Ralph Ball, the TC, could start pumping back with the .50-cal
MG. Rocket number two hit the command track fifteen seconds into the ambush, penetrating the aluminum armor, and Shafer—who had just jumped
down inside from where he had been sitting on the back in a little metal
chair—let out a pained grunt on the radio as a big chunk of metal ripped
into his thigh. Ball was also wounded, and the .50 went silent. Shafer was
hollering for help, so Cuff, unaware in the heat of the moment that his back
had been peppered with fragments, dropped his seat, rolled backward into the
hull section, and tried to find the door built into the back ramp so he could
pull the disabled troop commander outside to cover.*
*Cuff was not only half deaf, but also half blind from the bedazzling flash-
bulb-like rocket explosions, and he was still groping for the door when a third
RPG punched through the left side of the APC.*
*Finding the hatch handle, Cuff dragged Shafer onto the road. Shafer
stood up, intent on hobbling back down the line to find a vehicle with an in-
tact radio—he thought that last rocket had demolished those inside his command track—but Cuff pushed the captain to cover in the ditch on the right
side of the road.*

The fight was only at the minute mark now, but Lieutenant Adamo was already in the ditch—several rockets had slashed through the air past his head, and one had blown a hole through his track's engine compartment— along with Ralph Ball and several other semidazed troopers from the lead APCs, all of which had been blasted. Their crews had been forced to unass the exploding vehicles so quickly that many had grabbed neither weapons nor ammunition on their way to cover. Shafer told Cuff to crawl down the ditch to the platoon sergeant, who was on one of the rearward vehicles that were returning fire, and explain that the lead element was totally out of action, virtually defenseless, and needed help. Cuff did so, and though unarmed himself, he then crawled back up the ditch to rejoin the group huddled alongside Shafer and Adamo.

Under only light fire from either side of the road, my platoon took no hits, and we immediately herringboned to return it. I couldn't actually see anything, but I had tracers ricocheting off my tank—not to mention several RPGs that overshot our column—so I put the main gun in the general direction of those hootches on the right where I thought the crap was coming from, and laid down some HE and Beehive. I also swept the darkness with the .50, while a trooper on a personnel carrier behind me who was a gung-ho fanatic about the LAW rocket furiously fired off a stack of them.

My buddy Doc Gearhart used to mellow out at night with this little pot pipe of his, arguing that even if we did come under attack that the first AK-47 burst would instantly clear your head and leave you stone-cold sober to do your job. His opinion was validated when he ended up with a Silver Star for the ambush outside Go Dau Ha. . . .

Gearhart was driving the personnel carrier directly behind the command track, and the first rocket to hit that vehicle splattered his left hand with fragments as soon as he stopped and turned to face the ambush. Gearhart grabbed his medic's bag and jumped out of the track, and while he bandaged his badly bleeding hand, Sergeant Nichols, the track commander, started laying down a base of fire with the .50, rhythmically pumping off three-round bursts until he had emptied thirty or thirty-five ammo boxes by the end of the action.

Under this cover, Gearhart ran up the line of APCs to attend to the wounded, discovering only afterward that three bullets had passed through his baggy jungle trousers without touching him.

The most seriously wounded man whom Doc Gearhart encountered was 1st Lt. Richard A. Thomas—call sign Vindicator 33—who had served as the troop's artillery forward observer since Tan Son Nhut. Thomas had been blown off the back of the command track by the first rocket to slam into it. However, in an act of daring for which he was subsequently awarded the Distinguished Service Cross, the FO rushed back to it when he saw Shafer being dragged out —he thought the captain was dead—climbed inside by himself, donned a headset and steel pot, and, making contact with squadron headquarters, urgently requested gunships and a fire mission.

Lieutenant Thomas was giving directions to the first gunship to reach the scene when another direct hit rocked the already battered APC. Punching through the armored hull, the RPG tore through Thomas's right arm just below the shoulder, spinning him around so that he was facing the right-rear bulkhead as the rocket crashed on into the smoke and white phosphorus grenades stored there.

The inside of the track exploded in a brilliant white flash. As Thomas dived out the rear hatch, Doc Gearhart grabbed him, threw him to the ground, and put out his burning fatigues. Gearhart then helped Thomas to cover in the roadside ditch as the track went up in flames and, ignoring the FO's relatively minor injuries—Thomas had bad burns on his arms and face, but his flak jacket had otherwise protected him—secured a tourniquet around his shattered arm and thumped a morphine Syrette into his leg. When Gearhart moved on to help someone else, Thomas, too pumped up to lie still as the medic had told him to, walked up the road, his arm flopping grotesquely at his side, held in place by only a few strands of muscle. The troops in the ditch shouted at him to get down, which he did long enough to ask them how they were doing and assure them that help was on the way before continuing forward even as the gunships began making their runs, using the burning command track as a marking point.

Thomas's arm was later amputated in the 12th Evac.

The action sputtered out as quickly as it had flared, the ambushers fading back into the darkness after only a few minutes of intense firing. Adamo leapfrogged his way forward, getting the unit reorganized while ducking the fire of a lone NVA who was popping up from a spiderhole with an AK-47 to cover the withdrawal of his comrades. Adamo's troops threw hand grenades across the road whenever the diehard dropped down to change magazines.

The stalemate was not broken, however, until the Alpha Troop element reacting to the ambush came up from the south—having left behind a burning APC that hit a mine—led by a tank that pulled off onto the east shoulder of the highway to roll up the enemy's flank even as Adamo shouted a warning to the tank commander about the NVA in the spiderhole. Unable to hear anything over his engine, the tank commander was caught by surprise when the enemy soldier suddenly lit up the side of his turret with a full magazine. Sparks flew everywhere, but the tank commander was unscathed, and grabbing an M16, he rose up when that North Vietnamese ceased firing and blew him away with a burst of his own. There were blood trails leading out of the area, but that solitary enemy soldier in the spiderhole was the only actual body count of the battle.

If we said we were in trouble, Delta Troop always scrambled to our aid with lightning urgency. This night, however, as quick as our gunship support got there, the fight was already all but over, and when the Cobras began laying in the rockets and minigun fire—they were working both sides of the road, parallel to our column and getting closer with each pass—we were concerned about catching some stray stuff from our own side. The dirt we could see flying up in the light of the flares bursting overhead seemed too close for comfort, but the pilots knew their business. There were no mishaps.

The only enemy fire at this point was from a distance—some AK-47, plus a few rounds from a captured M79 grenade launcher—and ignoring it, Doc Gearhart stood on the road with a strobe light and brought in four Hueys for our casualties, directing each to land in its turn behind Nichols, who was still putting down suppressive fire from his APC.

We had three dead and thirteen wounded, and almost every vehicle in the lead platoon had been disabled. Captain Shafer was among those medevacked. Gearhart went out on the last Huey, a fifth of whiskey in his good hand, and polishing it off he hurled the bottle out into the night sky en route to the 12th Evac. Incidentally, those Hueys were also from Delta Troop. I have all the respect in the world for the regular dust-off medevacs, but the bond between the squadron's ground units and our Delta pilots and crews was such that they took chances for us that the dust-offs wouldn't and probably shouldn't have. Delta was fantastic. They just didn't give a damn about enemy fire. They would let it all hang out, coming right on in no matter how hot the situation.

It was almost dawn before the flareships and gunships headed for home, and Charlie Troop, leaving behind a small element to secure all the disabled vehicles strewn along the highway until they could be towed in, straggled into Trang Bang. The troop XO choppered in from Cu Chi to take command, and we moved out later that same afternoon in response to a convoy ambush south of An Duc.

The action was over by the time we arrived. The convoy had pushed on, leaving behind a shot-up truck. We herringboned in place for the night. There being no rest for the weary, we swept our section of the highway in the morning, which was the Fourth of July 1968—the day I was to win my second Silver Star—and, leaving the 1st Platoon outposted along the MSR below An Duc, continued into Cu Chi for resupply, headed back up to Trang Bang to get reorganized and do a little patrolling, then picked up a straight-leg infantry platoon and began rolling south after dark for a night sweep of An Duc.

The grunts rode in aboard our personnel carriers. My tank was the last vehicle in the column, and I was seriously uptight as we cleared the ramshackle gate at the north edge of town because if you were looking for trouble you were going to get it in An Duc. It seemed like we got hit every time we went near the place. There had been so many incidents that though the villagers used the little buildings along the road as marketplaces during the day—at least those few that had not been gutted in previous firefights—they abandoned them at night to sleep in hootches built farther back from the road. Every hootch had its own family bunker. The contact this time erupted just after we'd stopped and the grunts dismounted to begin the sweep. It was more of the same—rocket explosions up front, green tracers zipping past—and we blindly laid down suppressive fire to both flanks, reinforced in short order by gunships and an orbiting flareship, until the word came to back out so we could call in artillery on the ambushers. I did so gladly and easily, since my tank was farthest removed from the fireworks at the head of the column.

We withdrew some three hundred meters. Everything was proceeding smoothly—the artillery would begin firing as soon as the Cobras expended their ammo—until someone began whispering on the radio, and we realized that the crew of an APC, disabled when an RPG hit its engine compartment, was still back in An Duc.

The stragglers were in the roadside ditch, and since they had not been detected, and since a rescue effort would probably result in a lot of vehicles burning in the night, the decision was made to leave them where they were until the enemy pulled out. It was prudent, it was logical, but it smacked of abandoning our own, and somebody—I think it was the XO—came up on the net to ask in a doubtful voice, "Do we have anybody who would volunteer to go in?"

No one said a word, and I don't blame them. "This is three-six," I finally chimed in. "Let me have a shot at it. Let me give it a try."

"Cool it, cool it," someone else blurted on the radio. "You're too big. They'll blow your ass away. We need to wait!"

"Do you really think you want to try it?" the XO asked.

"Yeah, let's go for it," I said as coolly as I could.

Bill Watts had replaced Ferris as my driver—Jack Donnelly was still my loader—and I told him over our intercom, "You hold that pedal to the floor, Bill. I don't care what you see, you keep going, and don't stop for *anything* until you get to that track."

We went in straight and fast, parachute flares from the orbiting Huey lighting the way. Wearing a radio headset and sitting on the opened cupola hatch cover, I began firing the .50-cal MG even before we shot through the north gate of An Duc. The enemy let us have it once we were inside. More green tracers. One or two more RPGs, which were poorly aimed and flew harmlessly past. I guess we startled them, one lone tank barreling in like we were. I was a barefoot tank commander, my feet too swollen with jungle rot that night to wear boots, so I had hot brass bouncing painfully off my dangling feet as I raked to the left and raked to the right, pitching empty ammo boxes overboard and frantically grabbing fresh ones from behind me in the bustle rack. I didn't dare fire the main gun. It would have been too reckless given the men stranded inside the ville and our outposts along the highway on the other side of An Duc.

The disabled personnel carrier was off on the left shoulder of the road, and as soon as we stopped behind it, the guys materialized out of the dark—five or six of them, track crewmen and straight-leg grunts, all of them scared to death—running toward us and scrambling up the front of the tank as I shouted, "Is that everybody?"

One of the guys screamed that it was. "Let's get the hell out of here," he implored, hanging onto the turret. "Go, go, go!"

At that point, we should have turned around and roared back the way we had come. However, during the lull following Charlie Troop's initial withdrawal out of the ambush, the enemy had scraped together mounds of dirt and brush about every twenty feet along the edge of the highway. I had to assume the damn things were mined, which meant we couldn't just back up and pivot around—if we hit a mine and got stuck, we were all dead—so I told Watts, "We're *backin'* out of here. Stay in the tracks in the road. I can't guide you all the time, so you're going to have to do the best you can."

Bill put the tank in reverse and floored it, staying right in the groove, even though he couldn't see the way we were going from his forward-facing hatch, and even though our tanks had cross-drive transmissions. The transmission required that he keep a clear head as I gave him quick directions between .50-cal bursts, because if I barked, "Driver, left a hair!" it really meant he had to turn the steering wheel to the right. That sounds simple, but under fire it could get pretty confusing, and the faster we were going the more dramatic the effect of a slight turn of the wheel. For all that, we glided safely past the mounds. I was praying that the enemy hadn't gotten real slick and dashed in behind us to plant a mine in the road itself, which they hadn't, and with the hitchhikers who were hanging on for dear life firing their M16s one-handed from the turret, we made it all the way back, taking only a smattering of small-arms fire along the way, and no more RPGs.

We rejoined Charlie Troop. Everyone was going wild as we shut down, but the cheering was short lived. "We've got another track in there," the XO ruefully reported on the radio. "Three-six, you want to try it again?"

I immediately answered in the affirmative, but I was furious. We had already tempted fate once. The NVA would surely be ready for us if we tried that stunt again. I couldn't believe that we had gone through all that for nothing. We could have picked up both crews in one trip! They're trying to kill me, I thought—and I meant the bad guys and our side—they're doing everything they can!

Okay, once more into the breach, motherfucker. We went through the gate again, and everything started popping heavier than before. I was blasting away with the .50, the muzzle flash a big ball of orange that silhouetted me against the night sky like the perfect target—or so my buddy Bob Wolford, who was one of those we were going in to rescue, later told me—as tracers zipped all around our fast-moving tank, some of them ricocheting off the turret. Hugging the right side of the road, Watts squeezed past the first of the disabled tracks, just brushing the mounds along the shoulder, and we roared on up to where the second one was conked out. Wolford and several grunts sprang from the roadside ditch. Bob was bareheaded, his intense curly hair standing straight up in front like it had been electrified. His face was stark white, his eyes wide—I had never seen such terror—and he rushed toward the tank in an animalistic lope, looking like someone I didn't know. The old Bob was gone. This one had been deserted, discarded, left in a ditch to die. The situation was totally out of control, and he was totally freaked out. He was just running. They were all just running, and as soon as they clambered aboard, we immediately started backward.

In the shifting light of the flares floating down, I thought I could see shadows darting toward the road to cut us off. There were undefinable movement and muzzle flashes, and I was so preoccupied returning fire with the .50 that I told Watts, "You're on your own. You're going to have to do this yourself this time without any help from me."

It was a straight road, and though once again facing the wrong way to steer by sight, Watts kept us on track and got us out of there.

We made it back to the platoon, and there was a lot of backslapping and way-to-go's from the guys as we climbed off the tank. Fuck that, I thought, just don't tell me there's a third one in there.

Bob sat down in the middle of the road and proceeded to get shit-faced as beer after beer was handed to him. I thought I was okay, but realized that my knees were shaking uncontrollably.

Movement was detected around the abandoned tracks, and one of our tanks trained its 90 down the highway, alerted the elements on the other side of the ville—"Button up, it's on the way"—and fired an HE round right through the back of one of the APCs. There was a big boom, then the fuel caught fire and the stuff inside—claymores, grenades, LAWs, box on top of box of machine-gun ammunition—began cooking off, exploding at intervals throughout the night. We pounded the ville with arty, too, then swept in at daybreak, finding no sign of the enemy, living or dead, and discovering that those piles of brush contained not a single mine.

Clever fucking bastards.

Part Six

THE END OF THE ROAD

(JULY–AUGUST 1968)

Chapter Nineteen

Three nights after the ambush, the platoon set up along either side of the main supply route where it ran through the hamlet of Phuoc My about ten klicks up the road from Cu Chi. We hated being in villages at night. The brush and hootches restricted our fields of fire—we weren't totally blind, but there were too many concealed approaches an enemy could use to slip in close—and we always hunkered in tight behind claymores and trip flares and RPG screens, the chain-link fencing we carried rolled up on our vehicles during the day and then stretched in front of us between engineer stakes at night to detonate rockets in midair on their way to their targets.

There was a little berm-enclosed militia outpost about a hundred meters from where we were set up, and we caught some stray tracers from that location at dusk when those sad-sack PFs began blasting away for some unknown reason with a .50-caliber machine gun.

The troop exec got on the radio. The firing was soon secured. That mishap was infuriating enough, but even more disturbing to me was the Vietnamese man who had earlier come down from this supposedly friendly outpost. He was unarmed and naked except for sandals and a loincloth. He walked around my tank, studying it, sizing it up. He appeared to be looking for a vulnerable spot amid the sandbags, the runway matting, and the tread sections arranged around the turret, the better to slam an RPG up our ass, and alarmed, I demanded his identification card, which he produced and which I stared at blankly, not sure what a forged one would have looked like anyway. The card appeared to be legitimate. I handed it back and watched as this strange figure returned to the militia compound.

Two hours before midnight, I was scanning to my front with the Starlight Scope when some water buffaloes penned up beside a hootch on the other side of the road behind me—the tank was facing west—began milling around. I scanned the area but couldn't see anything because of all the huts back in there. I knew from back home, however, that livestock didn't move around at night unless something was disturbing them, so after ten or fifteen minutes of this I finally woke up Bill Watts to take my place atop the turret, radioed the lieutenant that I was going to check the disturbance out—"Don't shoot me when I'm over there" I intoned—and walked across the highway with my flashlight and M16. I worked the whole area. I checked around the water buffalo stall, treaded quietly through the brush along the far side of the ville, and finally went house to house, shining the flashlight over people who would sit up from their bamboo sleeping platforms, smiling warily, trying to look innocent. They probably were.

I found nothing. I finally walked back to Watts and told him to report that I'd come up empty handed, then, feeling restless, started back across the road to talk to some buddies of mine on an APC.

At that instant three or four rocket-propelled grenades were fired at my tank from the exact area I had just checked. They flashed past with rushing hisses—*whoosh-whoosh-whoosh*—and I turned to see Bill Watts being launched from the command cupola like a fiery comet, one of the well-aimed RPGs having penetrated an uncovered spot on the left rear of the turret, setting off several WP rounds inside.

The other two men on the tank were also messed up bad. Jack Donnelly had been sleeping on the back deck when the RPG slammed in. He was wrapped in a poncho and curled up on his side, hands between his thighs and something under his head—he had his boots on, but had unfortunately removed his flak jacket—along with a sergeant from the grunt unit attached to us. We had been working together for a few days now, and I and this sergeant had really hit it off. We clicked perfectly. He had talked that afternoon about his upcoming R&R to Hawaii with his wife—and now as I ran back toward the tank he was sprawled beside it with so much flesh and muscle blown off one leg you could see the bone gleaming from his knee to his foot.

Jack was down on the ground, too, his legs shredded almost as badly as the sergeant's, screaming, "Dwight, help me, help me!"

Not realizing how grievously injured Donnelly was as I urgently rushed toward Bill, I snapped, "Shut up, Jack—be a *goddamn man*— I gotta take care of somebody that's hurt a lot worse than you!"

Bill Watts was splattered all over with white phosphorus. He was smoking, burning up—in agony—and when I picked him up to carry him back to the road, his skin stuck to me. Turning him over to our medic, I went back for Donnelly. Meanwhile, the rest of the unit was blasting away into the night. That was the drill—when you took fire, you just fired your ass off in return until you could sort out what was going on—but there were no more RPGs, and only a few bursts of AK-47 fire as the enemy covered their disappearing act. This was a hit-and-run ambush, not a major attack, and when our suppressive fire petered out the only body count was five villagers and three water buffaloes. Ten other civilians, including three small children, were wounded in the crossfire and medevacked.

That came later. The immediate concern was to get a chopper in for our own wounded. The Huey got there fast, landed right on the road, and quickly departed with Watts and the sergeant— whose leg was amputated in the evac hospital—and poor Jack Donnelly, who had again been torn up on my tank. He wouldn't be back this time, such were his injuries, and I felt a sick knot of guilt in my guts for having failed to ferret out those RPG teams. I hoped Jack didn't hate me. He had every right. He had been peppered in the top of his head, slashed across his forearms, and had terrible gashes in his legs from below his knees all the way up to his inner left thigh in the groin area. He also had a bad wound in his knee that became infected, and by the time the doctors had finished scraping away the affected flesh and bone, trying to clean the infection out, it looked like a rat had been gnawing at his leg. He spent eleven months in hospitals.

After the medevac, I was sitting alone in the dark when a personnel carrier pulled up to plug the hole left by the loss of my tank. It was still drivable, but the inside of the turret was a shambles and the main gun was out of action. One of the track crewmen, a replacement who hated my guts—there was a lot of animosity between the old guys and some of the loudmouthed, jerkass new guys like him—remarked cuttingly, "Well, somebody else took it for you again."

Talk like that was giving me a bad reputation: "You don't want to get around Birdwell. People get killed around him. . . ."

I don't know how many times I had missed death by mere fractions of time and space. I was virtually shoulder to shoulder with my tank commander at Tan Son Nhut when he was shot in the face. I got away with relatively minor injuries when my new tank commander and loader were blown to pieces by direct hits. I left the barracks and a rocket went through the roof, turning the place into a slaughterhouse. Another tank replaced mine behind the berm at Trang Bang and immediately got knocked out of commission. My driver got blown away next to me at An Duc and I merely suffered some flesh wounds. I walked away from my tank and fifteen seconds later an RPG took out my new friend and the rest of my fine crew, including the man who had just taken my place in the command cupola. . . .

Perhaps I really was a jinx.

I also felt like my time was coming. Captain Shafer told me as much when I happened past his bed in the 12th Evac on my way to visit Donnelly and Watts after driving my disabled tank to Cu Chi. Though obviously in bad shape, Shafer retained his forceful persona. "I understand that you've lost another tank," he said. "Since I've been with the unit, what is that, four or five that you've lost?"

"I think that's the fourth one, sir."

"I know this is a particularly tough one on you because of what happened to your crew," Shafer continued. "I want to wish you the best, but I'm going to tell you it's time for you to get off the line and stay off the line because your luck is gone. The next one's on you."

I know, I thought, I know. . . .

I felt bad about Jack getting wounded again so severely when he should never have been sent back out to the field after being blasted the first time. I felt bad about barking at him when he called to me for help. I felt bad seeing him in the hospital, sliced up, stitched up, and hurting, and I felt even worse when I saw Bill Watts. I had been walking through the wards, unable to find him when he saw me and called my name. I looked, but he wasn't there. "Dwight, don't you know me?" he said. I looked again, and I realized that the man talking to me with Bill's voice was unrecognizable as Bill Watts. His hair was burned off. His skin was burned off. He was all red and raw and blistered, clear fluid oozing from the cracks, and his charred body had swelled up like some grotesque pink sausage. I could barely look at him, but I didn't break. I couldn't let Bill see me choke up because he would have known then how badly he looked, and I forced myself to be cheerful as Bill, who seemed happy to just be alive and determined to do his best despite all, told me about how wonderfully the nurse who was there with him during my visit was taking care of him, and how he was soon going to be evacuated to Japan.

Bill had wanted to be a tank commander, so I said something like "When you get back, buddy, we'll give you your own tank."

Bill grinned a brave grin, but all I could think was that it should have been me, it should have been me—I should have prevented this—and after I said good-bye, I sat on a bench outside the hospital and just cried and cried and cried, hiding my face in my hands.

Getting ahold of myself, I noticed a little girl, maybe ten years old, sitting to my right, talking animatedly with her parents. She was an incredibly pretty thing. She was obviously going to grow up and be a world beauty, and then she turned toward me—and her right eye, the whole right side of her face, was gone. It was just a mass of scar tissue. I presumed she was there to be treated by our doctors, which was all well and good, but the way we laid down the firepower it was likely we had inflicted her injuries to begin with. I had to get up and leave, thinking about how much Bill had loved these children, and despairing that for everything we had poured into this war, all we had managed to accomplish over here was to mangle little kids and tear up good men like Jack Donnelly and Bill Watts.

Private First Class William E. Watts, age twenty-one, died on July 12, 1968, five days after being hit by white phosphorus. His name, engraved on a metal plate, was thus added to the board in the little squadron chapel at Cu Chi—the names were arranged by troop, and Troop C's columns were the longest—and some guys who found a spare dog tag of Bill's while cleaning up his personal effects asked if I wanted it, since we had been so tight. I said that I did.

I'd had a bellyful. I was worn out and used up, and what remained of my spirit was ultimately extinguished by our new troop commander, whose real name I'll shield behind the pseudonym Captain Harris because he was the worst officer I served under in Vietnam. I had been hopeful when Harris took over—lean, tall, and darkly handsome, he at least looked the part of a hard-charging cavalry officer—but soon came to regard him as a barely competent ticket-puncher whose primary concern was his career. He was there to make a name for himself. Too bad he didn't know what he was doing. Harris had an aggressive, overbearing, I'm-going-to-show-you-how-it's-done demeanor, but was forever doing stupid things like getting tanks stuck in muddy fields that their veteran commanders had argued were impassable. Harris was a hateful prick to boot, quick to belittle people and snappish under pressure, and he didn't seem to give a damn about his troops. It was a small matter, but I remember how he decreed that when the troop stood down, one man was to be on duty all night long in the radio shack beside the orderly room to monitor the squadron net. If another unit made contact, that man could alert Harris a step ahead of squadron headquarters. If nothing of consequence developed, the troop commander still expected a detailed report of all the radio traffic in the morning. We came in from the field to rest, recuperate, and maintain our vehicles, not monitor radios, and the new duty station was not only grossly unfair to the individual expected to forfeit his first good night's sleep after however many days or weeks of combat operations, but also a tremendous waste of time. If squadron needed us, they would call.

In a moment that said it all for me, I walked past Captain Harris's tent late one night and overheard the troop commander and a couple of his lieutenants cynically talking about writing each other up for Silver Stars. It was you-scratch-my-back-I'll-scratch-your-back time. They were not fabricating exploits out of whole cloth, but as I eavesdropped, outraged, they laid it on thick, using grand and dazzling phrases to transform quick firefights into major actions and their own nominal roles into the stuff of Patton and Rommel.

I had totally lost faith in our leadership. During Captain Lodge's temporary command of Charlie Troop, for example, the unit spread itself so thinly in an effort to catch the enemy sappers who were disrupting the MSR that my tank, and my tank alone, was assigned to run the road all night between An Duc and Trang Bang. In fairness to Lodge, I think this mission originated with squadron headquarters, but in any event, I couldn't imagine what good my lone tank was doing cruising up and down the highway other than presenting itself as an easy target for an RPG team or detecting a mine by running right over it in the dark. It was insane, and secretly hoping that the squadron commander was listening, I raged on the platoon net that the colonel was an idiot unfit to command a combat unit; I demanded to know why I shouldn't just sit and wait in place because, hell, the enemy was going to watch me go by, slip out to plant a mine in our tracks, and wait for me to come back through, and the engineers were going to have to sweep the road in the morning anyway, and we were going to lose my tank for no reason.

"That's it. No more," Lieutenant Hubbell finally snapped. "Young soldier, your job is not to reason why. It's to do or die."

Hubbell was right, of course, and I shut my mouth at that point, having pushed it to the limit—but his remark set me on fire. I was frustrated with all of them, from our own officers on up to General Westmoreland, who seemed unable to look beyond his attrition strategy even though it wasn't working, and the politicians back home who didn't have the backbone to hit Hanoi and the communist sanctuaries in Cambodia. We were fighting with one hand tied behind our back, and we weren't accomplishing much that I could see. We just operated in circles, never taking and holding anything—at the end of my tour, we were exactly where we had been when I first got there—destroying villages instead of protecting them, always reacting to the enemy instead of forcing them to fight on our terms, and paying an intolerably high price for our all-important body counts.

Incidentally, the enemy ignored my lone tank during that long night on the road. In fact, having stopped for a moment to scan with the Starlight Scope, I actually caught three of them walking with slung AK-47s along the outer edge of a tree line toward An Duc. Instead of using the trees for cover, these overconfident smart-asses were in the open. It was at least two hundred meters from the highway to the tree line, and they must have imagined themselves invisible at that range. Getting Lodge on the horn, I explained the situation, and prepared to hit those suckers with the searchlight and cut them down with the .50 in the same second as they froze like deer in headlights. Unfortunately, the only time I ever really needed the searchlight was the one time it wouldn't work. "Oh, shit, the Xenon's down!" I reported to Lodge. The captain had our mortar track fire illum over the area, but by then the trio had vanished back into the night, and though I thoroughly plastered the tree line with machine-gun and main-gun fire, and we brought in arty, I doubt that we hit anything.

After my tank was battle damaged, I took over as Sergeant Cooper's driver on C-35, which was a choice assignment because he liked me and treated me well, and I in turn respected Cooper as one of the last of the old breed of hard-core Regular Army NCOs. At that time, Cooper's was the only tank left in the platoon—his own being down with maintenance trouble, cool, sharp, funny Sergeant Thomas served as our gunner—and we had no more than two or three APCs still up and running. However understrength we may have been, higher command continued to use us like we were a real platoon, and as we ran the road night after night—taking AK fire and RPGs, getting little sleep—all of us got a little shaky, a little rattled, a little uptight. Tanks were big-ass targets, and going up and down the highway was like being in a shooting gallery. Someone was always taking potshots at us, even in broad daylight, but over the steady hum of the engine we wouldn't even know we were being sniped at sometimes until rounds ricocheted off the armor or went buzzing past our heads with the high-pitched whines of near misses. Serving on a tank was like being on death row, certain that your time was coming, but not knowing when, the anticipation of death darkening every moment.

Every day I thought, Is this going to be the day?

Adding to the stress were the large number of civilians in our area. They were always in the way. I remember moving north through An Duc one evening just at dusk—I was still a tank commander then, and C-36 was bringing up the rear of the column—and as I passed the last house in the ville, a shuttered window suddenly popped open and I instantly lowered my 90 on it. I knew an RPG would be shrieking at me from the window any second, but I held my fire given our strict rules of engagement, concerned that if I went ahead and blew the hootch away without permission and the only occupants turned out to be innocent Vietnamese, I might end up in Long Binh Jail.

The tension was terrific, and even when a young woman appeared at the window, I didn't relax—a female guerrilla, if that is what she was, could handle an RPG launcher as easily as a male—but instead traversed the turret to keep the main gun on that hootch until we cleared the ville. The woman just stared at me with utter hatred.

For all their bravery, I hated the Viet Cong. I hated the National Liberation Front, and I hated the North Vietnamese Army. They were bigger assholes than we were when it came to the civilians. They knew what would happen when they ambushed us inside towns and villages, and though we really poured it on in return to protect ourselves, they ultimately bear most of the responsibility for the innocent bystanders killed and maimed by Charlie Troop.

In addition, we still found the occasional assassinated government official, hands bound behind his back, shot in the head, and dumped along the side of Highway 1. The VC needed a good ass kicking for the way they made war. I just wish we had given it to them. . . .

Trying to clear his head, Sergeant Cooper would tell me to haul ass whenever we hit good open sections of road during the day. "Is that the best you can do?" he'd challenge, and I'd really put it in gear, leaving the personnel carriers in our dust as I maxed it out, moving so fast that the tank vibrated violently and fishtailed back and forth so badly that a less experienced driver would have lost control. We were rockin', just flat-out rockin', Cooper flush with adrenaline and laughing on the radio, "This is just like being in Germany!"

The platoon sergeant was a little too cranked up. The truth was that after six straight months in the field, Sergeant Cooper—who was granite, who led by example, who took care of his men—had been worn down. God knows it was a matter of who was shakiest at that point, me or Cooper, but I knew he was cracking when, after we'd run the gauntlet once again in good old An Duc and lost our radio mast along the way to small-arms fire, he walked around the next morning, exclaiming, "Damn, an RPG cut my antenna off!"

We humored him—"No shit?!" I said, "I'll be damned, boy, you're one lucky sonofabitch"—but we knew Cooper was seeing things. If an RPG had hit his radio mast, which was next to the command cupola, he would have been scattered in little pieces all over An Duc.

Lieutenant Hubbell talked to me soon thereafter, and said sadly, "You know, I'm going to have to get Cooper out of here."

Cooper was eventually transferred up to squadron. I hated to see him go. Without him, we were in a black hole. Meanwhile, my last action with Cooper before his reassignment occurred when our three-track platoon was moving down a freshly paved road past a complex of magnificent French-built villas used as an ARVN training facility south of Cu Chi. We had two lanes of smooth asphalt with wide shoulders and were barreling along at a good clip without a care in the world—come on, this was a paved road right next to an ARVN base, we didn't have to worry about mines, right?—when a huge explosion suddenly sent our tank swerving off the road and into a water-filled rice paddy through which we spun as if on ice. We were totally out of control—several road wheels had been blown off, and we'd thrown a track—but luckily did not roll over. I thought we had been blasted by a recoilless rifle, but upon getting reorganized and examining the big crater in the road we determined that the enemy had carved out a section of the six-inch-deep blacktop, placed their mine, the biggest I had ever encountered, then returned the asphalt lid, mindful to fill the seams in, all while under the watchful eyes of the ARVN, who we always suspected of being infiltrated with Viet Cong.

Our tank had to be towed back to Cu Chi.

• • •

My ears still ringing from the blast, I left for R&R a few days later and spent the last week of July in Taipei, Taiwan. I did the tour-bus thing by day and partied all night. I'd like to say that I was never once tempted by the females in Vietnam—sin or not, these were some good looking women—and I'd like to say that I didn't connect with a local lovely in Taipei, but I did. However, my jungle rot got in the way, and we ended up sitting out on the balcony of my hotel room until six that morning, telling each other about our families, and our hopes and dreams and plans. We were about the same age. She spoke English well, too, and was as intoxicating as the Coke and Kentucky bourbon I was sipping. It was a nice night.

I never did get laid, which was supposed to be the main event on R&R. I was too depressed to care. Although it would have appeared to a casual observer that I was having a great time—I even ran into a hometown buddy, Larry Crittenden, who was stationed with the U.S. Navy in Taiwan, and we hit the bars together in our civvies— there was in reality a desperate undertone to my nonstop partying. I was trying to squeeze as much living as I could into those seven days. After all, I might not have seven days of life left when I returned to Nam. I don't think I hit the bed once that whole week. I couldn't afford to sleep. I felt that my time left on earth was short. I felt like I had used up all my luck in the war. I had survived five pulls on the trigger of the big revolver pressed against my temple, and the next time it was going to go bang. Death was waiting for me back there.

When we originally disembarked at Taipei, we were told that any-one who showed up drunk at the end of R&R would be held over until he sobered up, the threat being, I guess, that we would be listed as AWOL by our parent units. For the hell of it, everybody showed up half in the bag, but surprise, surprise, no one was ex-cluded from the flight back to Vietnam.

Actually, I was so worn out by the end of R&R that I found myself looking forward to going back to Vietnam so I could get some rest.

While we were waiting in the terminal at Tan Son Nhut for the transport plane to Cu Chi, a big Hispanic sergeant from the

Wolfhounds noticed what unit I belonged to—in our traveling khakis, we wore our regimental crest on our epaulets, and our division patch in a plastic sleeve hanging from the button of our right breast pocket—and stormed up to me, screaming furiously that "the Three-Quarter Cav isn't worth a shit. You're nothing but a bunch of killers. We've lost more to you trigger-happy idiots than we have to the NVA!"

The sergeant was so mad I thought he was going to stomp my head, but some of his buddies pulled him away, which was lucky for me because I was in no condition for a fight. I was still shaky from that mine. I was exhausted. I was hungover. I was hurting. And I couldn't muster much anger at the sergeant because I'd heard talk on several occasions of cav units taking light fire in their night laagers and returning it with everything they had, only to accidentally waste straight-leg grunts who were out in the dark on ambushes and listening posts. It wasn't a common occurrence, but it happened enough that I was convinced the enemy calculated our uncoordinated overreaction into their tactics and tried to get us to shoot at each other.

They really were clever bastards.

My morale was already low. It dropped even lower when I got back to my platoon, back to my tank—Cooper shortly departed, which was the worst thing that could have happened—and back to Captain Harris, who picked me for that ridiculous radio-watch assignment of his the next time we went into Cu Chi. I was in no mood for such bullshit. I told Harris as much when I reported to him in the orderly room—in fact, I undiplomatically announced that the idea of sitting by a radio all night was as "dumb as hell, because if anything big goes down they're going to call you on the telephone"—and the situation escalated accordingly, the captain finally shouting at me that "You're not fit to be an E5. Maybe you need to start at the bottom again."

I told Harris that maybe he did too. Our new top, First Sergeant Munshowers, chewed my ass and threw me out of the orderly room at that. Munshowers liked me, however, and though in the heat of the moment I was shouting abuse at him, too, over my shoulder as

I left, I think he was really just trying to get me away from Harris before my back talk got so reckless that the troop commander would have no choice but to go ahead and actually bust me for insubordination. Munshowers was trying to save me from myself.

It was a temporary reprieve. The very next time we were in base camp, Captain Harris again singled me out for radio watch. Okay, fuck you, I thought, I know what you're doing. I brought my poncho liner with me and, curling up in it, mutinously went right to sleep in the radio shack. Harris came in to check on me during the night and, finding me snoozing away on duty, went absolutely berserk, winding up his tirade with a disgusted "Get out of here!"

I did, remarking arrogantly as I grabbed my poncho liner, "Well, that's what I think about your goddamn radio watch."

I suppose I should be glad that Harris didn't slam me with an Article 15, but he did make sure that I never got the E6 stripes Cooper had put me in for. I felt I had earned them as a tank commander, and it burned me that even my conversion from specialist fifth class to sergeant E5 somehow failed to go through at troop headquarters.

We got a new division commander not long after I rejoined the troop. Who am I to talk about generals, but this one made an extremely negative impression, not only for his personal style—whenever he visited the unit, or happened past us in his jeep in base camp, he always had his chest out and his face set in the faultfinding glare of a petty tyrant—but also for a pair of asinine directives he issued before inspecting our unit upon assuming command. One was that he would court-martial any man he found who did not have all his assigned equipment, or who had extra unauthorized equipment, which resulted in a mad scramble to bury in the troop rear all the spare weapons, tools, and gear we had accumulated. Using a bulldozer, we even buried an armored personnel carrier that had been declared a combat loss, replaced with a new track, then brought back to life by our mechanics. What a waste.

The second directive was in regard to our tanks. This new spit-shined general ordered us to remove all the sandbags, tread sections, and runway matting we used to protect ourselves from rocket-propelled grenades on the grounds that the additional weight caused undue maintenance problems, and then on top of that to shine the turrets for the inspection with diesel fuel like we were a Stateside unit. It was stupid. It was crazy. It absolutely stunned me. I couldn't believe how disconnected our officers were from what we were facing in the field. I couldn't believe all the stupid things I had seen that had gotten people killed, and when we went back out with our naked, stripped-down tanks, that was it for me. I had been pushed over the edge. I didn't want any more. I was just going to survive this fucked-up situation and get the hell out of there.

Part Seven

ROTTING IN THE REAR
(AUGUST–DECEMBER 1968)

Chapter Twenty

I was through with the war, or at least with the way it was being run, and I was through with the army. My only problem was that when my tour ended, I still had nine months remaining on my enlistment. I was especially unenthusiastic about pulling that kind of time because I'd been slated to join a support unit attached to the Armor School at Fort Knox. I talked to guys who knew about the outfit, and they said you worked sixteen or eighteen hours a day keeping the vehicles going for the Armor School, and that virtually every Vietnam returnee assigned there ended up getting busted. I guess we were a rebellious lot, and I heard stories of guys showing up with E5 combat stripes, and three weeks later they were E3s with a pair of Article 15s.

I didn't need that. Fortunately, the army had a program for disenchanted guys like me: sign up for four more months in-country and qualify for a five-month early out. In other words, I would be discharged from the army immediately upon returning from the Republic of Vietnam.

Thus, I extended my tour. I didn't go about it the right way, though. I had always prided myself on being a good soldier, and a good soldier did his duty. In this war, that meant twelve months on line. However, between my communications section assignments at troop and squadron headquarters, and the time I'd spent in the rear recuperating from wounds, I had put only eight good solid months in the field, and that included the relatively quiet period before Tet.

As far as I was concerned, I hadn't done my duty. I was thoroughly fed up with the people running the show in Charlie Troop and wasn't about to go back to war with them, but I could have transferred to a different unit—I had been very impressed with what I'd seen and heard of the 11th Armored Cavalry Regiment—and, having made a fresh start, gone on to serve my four-month extension in the field. At least then I could say that I'd pulled a full combat tour. Instead, feeling battle-rattled and out of luck, I opted for a job at troop headquarters, a reward for extending, and drifted through those last four months as a burned-out rear-echelon motherfucker in Cu Chi.

Looking back, I wish I had done the right thing at that moment in my life. I would give anything in the world to be able to do it all over again because there isn't a day that has gone by since that I haven't hated myself for taking the easy way out.

I have heard it called survivor's guilt. It is my cross to bear because, even though I've been told many times that I am holding myself to unrealistic standard, and reminded that had I reported my third wound I would have automatically been reassigned to the rear anyway, it has not eased the burden. In my heart, I know the truth.

In any event, the first sergeant, to whose orderly room I had been assigned, pulled me out of the field during the third week of August. My duties were driving the jeep, monitoring the radio, and passing messages between squadron and troop headquarters. In other words, I didn't do much of anything. There were ten or twelve of us who worked for the top—misfits, screwballs, short-timers, combat-fatigue and jungle-rot cases, guys awaiting court-martial—and we lived in a shack down out of the way by the motor pool where nobody bothered us. If I wasn't on radio watch at night, I'd either join the party at our shack—the place was a regular Animal House—or, if in a black mood, I'd take a bottle out to the perimeter and, sitting alone atop a bunker, drink myself numb, trying to ease the pain, while the flares popping overhead cast the miles and miles of concertina wire in a sickly white light, and red tracers bip-bip-bipped out into the great void, the perimeter guards firing perfunctorily as a precaution against possible ground attack. I had never felt so worthless.

Sometimes it would rain. Sometimes we would be rocketed, though not as heavily as before. Sometimes we could see thick black smoke rolling up from B-52 strikes, and I'd remember how in the field those raids looked like summer storms—the giant bombers, which flew too high to be seen, were always coming in after Tet—and how the concussive booming would swell the air around us and make the ground tremble under our tanks and tracks. I would remember and hope that the guys I'd left behind were hanging in there, taking some solace in the fact that our casualties dropped off dramatically that fall. The war had finally lulled in our area.

Not completely, though. I happened to be floating through the headquarters area one day shortly after my reassignment when the first sergeant informed me that a helicopter was inbound with some prisoners. "How about going over and getting them and taking them to the MPs?" he asked. I strapped on my pistol belt and was sitting in our jeep beside the Delta Troop helipad when the Huey landed, and the door gunner and an escorting cavalryman unloaded five bound and blindfolded North Vietnamese soldiers. The prisoners wore only black shorts and had matching NVA-style short-on-the-sides-long-on-the-top haircuts. They were all young and looked lean and mean. We packed them in my jeep, and I drove over to the military police compound, stopping next to a little building and announcing to the trooper on duty that "I've got some prisoners here for you guys."

The next thing I knew, a half-dozen military policemen roughly jerked the prisoners out of the jeep—these tough guys were suited up in MP brassards and polished MP helmet liners, crisp jungle fatigues and spit-shined jungle boots, the whole nine yards—and with much kicking, slapping, and shouting hustled them into that little plywood building. They were pumped up and really enjoying themselves.

Cocksuckers! Those NVA have probably done more and seen more, and are better soldiers, than you asshole MPs will ever be, I thought, and I followed them into the building, trying to break it up.

"C'mon, man," I implored one big, cocky-looking NCO who seemed to be in charge. "Just leave 'em alone."

The sergeant wheeled toward me, insulted. "Nobody tells us what to do," he snapped. "We're MPs. We're the cream of the army."

With that, the sergeant started thumping the prisoners in the back of their heads with the butt of his M16. Enough was enough. I shoved the sergeant backward with both hands, shouting, "You fucking MPs aren't anything but a bunch of lowlife sons of bitches!"

I had taken the sergeant by surprise. He was mad as hell and knocked me right down on my ass with a solid punch to my face. I sprang back up, and the other MPs immediately intervened. They weren't breaking the fight up. They were piling on me. "I told you nobody fucks with MPs," the sergeant barked as I screamed more abuse and struggled against them, getting my arms cranked up even higher behind my back for my efforts. One of them held up a field phone for me to see. "You sonofabitch," he shouted, "if you keep this up, we'll hook it up to *your* dick instead of theirs!" Instead they threw me out the door. I made a good face-first landing, and feeling humiliated, my nose bloody and my lip split, I just climbed in my jeep and left. I had gotten my ass whipped, and I hadn't accomplished a damn thing. If anything, I'd probably gotten those sadistic pricks even more fired up for their interrogation of those North Vietnamese soldiers.

Sergeant Dean, our grand old daddy of a platoon sergeant during my first few months in the field, had been reassigned to troop headquarters after recuperating from his wounds, and it was good to hook up with him again in Cu Chi. For one thing, I was having second thoughts about my decision to get out and asked him his advice about staying in the army. "Don't be a damn fool," Dean snorted. He had made a home in the army because he was a poor boy with few options, "But there's no future in it for someone like you. You can do better than this. Get an education and make something of that bundle of talent that God gave you."

Dean also warned me that "the army's changing, and not for the better. Leadership, discipline—it's all going downhill. . . ."

Like me, Dean was just killing time. His twenty years in, he was going to retire the day his plane landed in the United States. In the meantime, he wasn't about to go back out to the field and get his ass shot off again, especially for an institution that had shamed him like the army did shortly before he rotated out of Vietnam.

It was a complicated situation. Although Dean had come out of the Korean War with five stripes, a subsequent restructuring of the army's enlisted pay and grade system converted E7s like him to E6s. For pride's sake, those thus reduced were allowed to continue wearing their E7 stripes for a set number of years on the assumption that they would be promoted back to sergeant first class during that time.

Dean was a great combat soldier, but he didn't make E7 again, and near the end of his Vietnam tour he had to replace his sergeant first class stripes with staff sergeant stripes, which gave the impression he had been busted and really embarrassed him.

Sergeant Dean had another reason for staying in the rear. One no-win political war was enough for him. More specifically, he thought this one was going to end any day now. I was sitting near him in our eight-seat latrine one morning when Art Parsons stuck his head in—transferred off the line, too, he was now on the shit-burning detail—and Dean exclaimed, "Hey, forget about burning shit. You get your ass back up there to the orderly room and stay glued to the radio, and let me know what comes out of those Paris Peace Talks!"

In retrospect, maybe I know why Dean didn't get his stripe back. He was in the New Army, but played by the rules of the old Brown Shoe Army where senior NCOs had a finger in every pot. The division had an ice plant at Cu Chi, and Dean told me to take a truck over there for our allotment. "Just tell 'em you're there to pick up the Three-Quarter Cav's ice," he instructed. I did so. No problem the first day. No problem the second day. On the third day, plain-clothesmen from the Criminal Investigation Division were waiting for me, and I ended up handcuffed and told that I could make one call. I called Dean, and when he showed up they arrested him too. He made his one call—he had NCO contacts all over the division and knew just who to reach out to—and ten minutes later we were released with a mild warning not to ask for so much ice next time. It turned out that I should have been picking up ice for only the troop, not the whole squadron, and that Dean had been using the extra in a little club he was running. He must also have had access to cheap booze because when he was packing up to go home, he told me that he hadn't forgotten that he'd earlier borrowed a hundred dollars from me: "I can't pay you back. I don't have the money, but I'll give you a case of whiskey, and you can sell it off bottle by bottle and make three times what I owe you."

That proved to be absolutely true.

Dean was also right about the slide in discipline. The most obvious sign of the problem was the flowering of the marijuana culture in Cu Chi, and, based on what I saw at other big bases, probably every major installation in Vietnam. There had been some dope around in '67, but there was no comparison to the situation as it existed as my tour wound down. In the old days, the one night Sergeant Dean found a trooper getting smoked up inside his tank turret when he should have been on watch, he simply hauled the kid up through the hatch, bashed him over the head a few times with the butt of his .45, and the word got around. Dean would have worn his arm out during the latter half of 1968. Marijuana was everywhere. Guys were quietly smoking it in the bunkers those nights I sat out on the perimeter, and on any given day around Cu Chi, you'd encounter scores of red-eyed dudes, each with his personal pot pipe—the country boys favored corncobs—in his lapel or sticking up from one of his slanted breast pockets. It was a symbol. It was a badge of honor. It was an act of defiance, a way for a trooper to tell the world that he was a marijuana man, a very serious marijuana man, and that he didn't have any use for Nam or the Green Machine—the United States Army.

It frustrated me that our officers turned a blind eye to all the pot smoking, especially in the field where it had no place. Perhaps they thought the guys needed a release valve. Perhaps with so many other things to worry about—like fighting a war—it just wasn't a priority, or perhaps, at least for some of them, it was none of the above: One night in base camp while I was still a tank commander, I walked past a hootch occupied by several lieutenants and realized, disillusioned, that marijuana smoke was rolling thickly out of it at the top where the walls were ventilated. It looked like a smokehouse.

There probably wasn't much the officers could have done. Marijuana was simply part of the landscape by mid-'68. We had elements of the 101st Airborne base camped with us at Cu Chi, and I was stunned by the number of paratroopers from this supposedly elite unit who sported pot pipes in their breast pockets. They were as bad as the scruffy old draftee-filled 25th Infantry Division.

I am aware that there were other ways of looking at this issue. Had I had a less conservative outlook on life, I might not have been so uptight about the dreaded weed. I might have accepted it as something no better or worse than booze, which bothered me very little even though I had seen the devastating effects of alcoholism back home. Hell, John Wayne drank, he didn't smoke dope like the people tearing down the country did, and to me, getting smashed in the rear was as much a part of soldiering as keeping your weapon clean in the field. It was tough; it was macho; it was American.

It could also get you in trouble. I had acquired after getting off line a shirt with lieutenant bars that I wore to get into the officers club of an engineer unit across a dirt street from the 3/4th Cav area. They served bourbon and Coke on ice and never asked for identification. One afternoon, however, as I came back across the street, listing to one side, one of our tough ex-NCO lieutenants noticed my shirt and took me to task: "Birdwell, when did you make lieutenant?"

"I make lieutenant every fucking time I want to go across the street and get a drink," I snapped back, in no mood to be hassled.

Getting hot himself, the lieutenant barked at me to hand over my shirt, then told me to get my ass into a new one with the proper rank on it and take Lieutenant Hubbell up to division. This I did, but while waiting for Hubbell to tend to business inside the headquarters building, I saw an E7 who had been one of my drill instructors in Basic—he was in the Wolfhounds now, it turned out—and producing a bottle of whiskey from the sack he was carrying, he climbed into the jeep with me. I spilled some booze on my shirt before my old buddy continued on his way, and peeling it off, was sitting there barechested and smelling of alcohol when Hubbell reappeared. "You better let me drive," he said.

We were about to leave when the division sergeant major spotted a trooper out of uniform—me—and walked briskly toward us, demanding names. Ignoring him, Hubbell started to pull away, and I stood up, hanging on to the windshield with one hand and grabbing my nuts with the other as I shouted, "Eat this, you lifer sonofabitch!"

The sergeant major bellowed red faced to stop that jeep, but Hubbell, anonymous behind his sunglasses, bush hat pulled low, stomped on the gas—I went bouncing into the back—and we made a clean getaway because our jeep happened to be new and had yet to be numbered and marked with unit ID. Short-timers, 1. Lifers, 0.

Given my own propensity for getting blasted, I guess my real problem with marijuana was that it represented cultural changes that I could not abide and led almost inexorably to harder stuff. Heroin and acid and speed were just making it on the scene in the rear about the time I rotated out—some guys were getting real screwed in the head—and even before that, we had a handful who had graduated from grass to opium. I bumped into these heavy-duty heads through my buddy Mike Christie, who was then assigned to the squadron ammo dump. Mike was a serious man on duty. I can remember pulling into the ammo dump when I was a tank commander to resupply with main-gun rounds, and there was Mike, stripped to the waist, deeply tanned, and gleaming with sweat as he humped those heavy, rope-handed 90mm ammo boxes, his tattooed arms as taut and hard as cables. He was ready to go home, God, he was so ready to go home, he told me when we got a chance to talk—he seemed as forlorn as I—but until then he had a job to do, and he was really busting his ass.

Mike was like a brother to me, so after I got my job in the rear, too, I tagged along when he dropped in on a little hidden-away pot party in the Bravo Troop area—except that it wasn't just pot, these bead-wearing, peace-sign-flashing troopies were also passing a big opium pipe around. It got worse. Feeling good, they started laughing about how the last CO of B/3/4th Cavalry—an aggressive, abrasive, hard-nosed, by-the-book captain—had been KIA in late August 1968. They told me that they did it. Their story was that they'd made a pact to waste the troop commander the next time they made contact, and that the one who'd been selected—I guess they drew straws or some damn thing, but they wouldn't say who among them had been picked—had actually gone ahead with the plan.

"Sorry 'bout that," one of them giggled, "but that fuckin' idiot was too Stateside. He was going to get everybody killed."

Meanwhile, someone noticed that as the pipe went around, I kept handing it on without taking a hit, and objected suspiciously, "What the hell's your problem, man? Who *is* this guy?"

It was time to go. I was extremely disturbed by what I'd heard. Those stoned-out fuck-ups had probably been bullshitting me, but, unfortunately, their story was not utterly fantastic. Things had changed that summer. There was, for example, an arrogant, much-hated lieutenant colonel who commanded some type of 25th Division supply unit at Cu Chi, and one night, person or persons unknown—word was that they were "brothers"—rolled three hand grenades under his air-conditioned trailer. The colonel survived unscathed, either because he was sleeping at the other end of the trailer or because he wasn't even home at the time of the attack.

The dead troop commander had also been a hated figure known for his abusive tirades. It is impossible to say what really happened to him, but I did pick up other hints here and there that he'd caught some friendly fire. The details of the captain's last firefight leave the whole question up in the air. There had been a major convoy ambush, complete with trucks burning on the road, where the main supply route cut through a rubber-plantation village in Bravo Troop's sector below Go Dau Ha. While two platoons deployed on the flanks and laid down suppressive fire, the captain accompanied the assault platoon that pushed into the rubber, engaging the NVA, at least until several personnel carriers were stopped in their tracks by RPGs. The captain was killed at that chaotic moment—he was shot in the back, the only KIA at that stage in the action—and while his body was brought back, along with several troopers wounded by rocket fragments, a platoon leader took command and kept the assault going. The firefight turned into a pitched battle, and when darkness approached, Bravo Troop, low on ammo, backed out of the rubber, set up blocking positions on the highway in a heavy thunderstorm, brought in the artillery, then went back in at daybreak to find the place deserted, except for villagers who explained that the enemy had used their oxcarts to slip away with their casualties during the night.

• • •

The dead captain's predecessor and successor were excellent officers, and despite whatever may or may not have happened out in the rubber, Bravo Troop was the sharpest in the squadron—low casualties, high morale, high body counts, and all that good stuff—something I hate to admit because sometimes they really strutted around Charlie Troop for having come to our rescue when we got the shit kicked out of us at Tan Son Nhut. I didn't want to hear it. What happened to us would have happened to whomever went in there first that morning, and if it hadn't been Charlie Troop that got mauled so badly down there, which set in motion everything that happened to us afterward, then maybe we wouldn't have become such a dispirited outfit and maybe I wouldn't have given up on a career in the army.

Chapter Twenty-One

I was brooding too much and drinking too much. Frustrated with my circumstances and disappointed in myself, I was turning into a real jerk. I didn't have many friends left—they were dead; they were wounded; they had rotated home—but managed to piss off those that were still around. George Breeding, for one. George had been reassigned to Headquarters Platoon after picking up three Purple Hearts but was still so gung-ho that he went back out on operations whenever possible, delivering chow from the first sergeant or temporarily filling in wherever needed on undermanned tank crews.

When George wasn't in the field, we'd jog along the base perimeter road in shorts and jungle boots—I had started putting on weight in the rear—until the evening when some sniper fire kicked up dust around us and sent us diving for cover. That was the end of the running for me, but George chalked the incident up as a freak and kept after me to PT with him again.

"No way," I said arrogantly. "Hell, George, I'm not like you—I got a life. You don't. You're just Regular Army. You're expendable!"

That didn't go over too well. In October, I took a second R&R to Taipei, another reward for extending, but being down, I mostly squabbled with George, who went with me. I didn't want to hear his drinking stories and his girl-chasing stories, and he didn't want to hear about how I was going to go to college after I got out of the army.

"Shit, Dwight, you don't need to go to college," he'd say over his beer. "Just get a job. You're not college material."

That was the kind of crap I had put up with back home, and it burned. "What do you know about college, George?" I snapped back a little too harshly. "Hell, you didn't even get out of high school!"

George could be a mean, flinty-eyed rooster if he wanted to, and I had an ornery side, too, and our friendship cooled off after any number of these stupid rows. When I left, I shook hands and exchanged addresses with George, but the enthusiasm wasn't there like it should have been. I can say only that I am glad that I actually did look George up after he rotated home himself, and in time we forgot about the bad times and started laughing again about the good times. Loyal friend, George Breeding.

Tony Adamo also caught some of my flak. That he did is especially illustrative of my black mood swings, because Tony, then serving as the troop executive officer with brand-new captain bars, was one of the finest men I would ever have the privilege of knowing before, during, or after the war. Tony was a cool head. He'd find me—"Birdwell, let's go do something"—and we'd rustle up a jeep and ramble around Cu Chi for two or three hours, drinking, talking, plotting, planning, drinking some more, checking out the post exchange, and otherwise joking and screwing around. He'd rib me, and I'd rib him.

Unfortunately, and this occasioned a comment from me that Tony had done nothing to deserve, my partner in crime ran afoul of the squadron commander and was booted out of the unit in October 1968. The problem started when the colonel came down to Tony's motor pool—Charlie Troop was getting ready to crank up and move out for the night at the time—to inform the XO that "from now on, when vehicles are outposted on the road, they will button up."

The squadron commander's directive was in response to a mortar attack launched a night or two before on an outpost. One shell had gone through the open cargo hatch of a personnel carrier. It had been a million-to-one mishap, but somebody had gotten killed, and the colonel was hitting the panic button. The real danger was not mortars, but RPGs, and if a rocket penetrated a buttoned-up track, the explosion would be that much more concentrated, the flash burns and fragmentation wounds that much more devastating to the crew.

Tony tried to explain this to the colonel, but the colonel, who had previously upbraided Adamo for running a "sloppy" motor pool, was having none of it. "You go get your troop commander," he finally snapped. "If he doesn't like it, then we'll see."

Captain Harris was in the orderly room. "He's nuts; we're not going to do that!" Harris exclaimed when Tony explained the colonel's new directive to him. Harris headed down to the motor pool, but before he could even open his mouth, the squadron commander, having worked himself into a fine rage, jumped right into his stuff: "If you don't like it, you can find another job!"

End of discussion. The colonel turned and marched off, and a chagrined Harris told his XO to put out the word. "No, I'm not doing it," Tony replied. "I'm not going to do it. If I did, and somebody got hurt because they were buttoned up, I couldn't handle it."

Harris did not argue. He simply issued the order himself and rendered a negative efficiency report on Adamo—the two had never seen eye to eye—who received orders shortly thereafter exiling him to Military Advisory Team 3-72 in the Mekong Delta. It was the worst thing that could have happened to him. Serving with the unmotivated, poorly led ARVN was paramount to a death sentence. They didn't have the gunship, artillery, and close air support available to a U.S. unit at the flick of a radio switch, and if you had the misfortune of getting hit while with an ARVN unit you could pray only that you wouldn't be abandoned in some stinking rice paddy, and even if someone dragged you out of there you didn't know when a medevac might show up. The ARVN weren't exactly top priority.

Misery loving company as it does, I laughed wickedly at my friend's misfortune: "Ha, ha, Tony, what are you going to do now?!"

Tony had a wife and an infant son he had never seen back home. He looked at me, tears in his eyes. "Birdwell, if you don't shut up," he said in a level, no-nonsense voice, "I am going to kick your ass."

I shut up. I had been way out of line, and I knew it.

When Tony shipped out the next day, we hugged. I got choked up. He did too. He still had five months left on his tour.

I could only hope he'd make it.

Chapter Twenty-Two

I was at division headquarters on an administrative matter regarding my pay when a captain came through the office I was in, raising hell with the clerks about some screw-up or another. He stopped when he saw my name tag. "Are you that guy Birdwell with the Three-Quarter Cav?" he asked brightly. I told him that I was. "I understand you're getting a second Silver Star," the captain said. "Well, I'll tell you what. I'm going to get one of our photographers down to the ceremony, and we're going to play it up big in the division paper. That was a hell of a thing you did. We all heard about it."

There was indeed a spec four photographer from *The Tropic Lightning* newspaper at the ceremony—the award was approved in November and pinned on in our motor pool—but he was somewhat less enthused than the captain at headquarters. "What's this guy getting?" he asked as the troop assembled for the show.

"Silver Star," someone answered.

"*Silver Star,* shit!" the photographer said in disgust. "You mean they sent me over here for somebody to get a damn Silver Star?"

Captain Harris was also unimpressed. I had not yet overheard the conversation between him and his lieutenants about getting career-enhancing Silver Stars of their own, or I would have better understood the jealousy beneath the contempt on his face. "Look at that, can you believe they're going to give *him* a Silver Star?" Harris commented loudly to the knot of officers and NCOs standing with him as we milled around waiting for the colonel. "I can't believe we're wasting a *Silver Star* on a piece of shit like this. That's bad enough, but we have to have a goddamn *ceremony* too!"

The squadron commander appeared. This was a new man, a real combat leader in the Otis mold. I came to attention—cleaned up and wearing a fresh set of fatigues, I looked like the soldier I had once been—as did the troops behind me, who were formed up by platoon. "I'm new; I didn't serve with you," the colonel said, "but I know about you, and you're an outstanding soldier." The colonel wound up with "Specialist Birdwell, I salute you," which he did, and after I snapped off my own crisp parade-ground salute, he pinned on the medal, and for all my cynicism and for all the old combat soldier talk about preferring something useful, like a case of beer, to a piece of tin, it felt good. Napoleon had been right when he said that with enough ribbon for his soldiers he could conquer the world. Incidentally, I might mention that my fifteen seconds of fame went unmentioned in the division newspaper.

My last operation was the strangest. In response to an increase in enemy activity to the north in December, the troop was ordered to move up the road and operate temporarily out of Tay Ninh. I had two weeks left to go at that time. "You're going to have to go back out," the first sergeant informed me, the word having come straight from Captain Harris. I snapped that that was fine with me, but it wasn't really. I had short-timer's fever. I didn't want to get killed this late in the game. "That's not the worst part of it," the top continued apologetically. "The worst part is that you're going to drive my jeep to Tay Ninh—and we're going to lead the whole goddamn troop."

Which we did. I'm no better than anyone else to die, but it was nerve wracking to be on point like that when I was so close to going home—I kept waiting for a mine to blow the jeep up, and me with it—and I burned with a renewed hatred for Captain Harris, promising myself that if I actually got through this alive, I would find that vindictive lifer bastard back in the States and kick his butt.

Though the column actually made it to Tay Ninh without incident, I respected the first sergeant for having taken his chances up front with me. In fact, if the truth be told, I liked our peppery old hard-drinking, ass-chewing top sergeant. He might ream you out as "the stupidest, dumbest, sorriest soldier that ever lived," but then he'd turn right around and say, "Let's go get a beer and find a woman."

He wasn't kidding. The first sergeant had more testosterone than even us nineteen and twenty year olds, and telling me to get the jeep, he would make two or three trips a day to our on-base bathhouse and the little shantytown that catered to GI needs just outside the main gate at Cu Chi. The bathhouse had been built late that summer, if I remember correctly. It was supposed to provide the troops with invigorating steam baths and massages—I guess the commanding general thought you'd walk out feeling so clean and limber you'd want to go kill another twenty commies for Christ—but subdivided into private cubicles, it quickly turned into something a little different no matter how many times the division sergeant major ran from room to room, breaking the guys and girls up.

The first sergeant was also always on the hunt for new adventures, and I don't know how many times I hauled him around to find different little whorehouses he had heard about. The chances he took for a fresh piece of ass were amazing—I mean we drove for miles and miles down little cart trails out in the boonies—and I honestly think that I was exposed to more dangerous situations out with the top than I had been in my line platoon. Talking and joking the whole way, he would boldly go where demons feared to tread if it meant getting laid.

If we couldn't get out the main gate because the military police were checking passes or something was going on, the first sergeant would try to bullshit his way out the back gate where the MPs were a little looser because that route led straight into a rubber plantation and only units heading out on missions went that way.

Once, however, we pulled up to the back gate only to have the MP on duty announce, "Top, we can't let you out this time."

The first sergeant thought fast. "You see that cloud of dust over there," he said, pointing to an armored recovery vehicle that was on the move. "I need to catch up with that unit!"

"Top, you're lyin' to me," the MP said sheepishly.

"No, I'm not. *Now, open that gate!*"

The MP did as he was told and off we went. We caught up with the recovery vehicle—and then made a hard left off the main road. When we finally got to where we were going, I was, as usual, so unnerved by the trip that I didn't join the first sergeant inside.

Our first sergeant also liked his beer. That got him into trouble one hot and humid night when he stumbled drunk into the orderly room, passed out, and an ex-tanker clerk who hated our hard-ass first sergeant took his revenge, kicking the hell out of Top as he lay in a heap on the floor. I walked in on the tail end of it and was appalled to see this old soldier who wore as his combat patch on his right shoulder the proud emblem of the 3d Division—Audie Murphy's outfit—being stomped by a young punk when he was down, out, and unable to defend himself. I kept my mouth shut, however, so Top never had any idea who had beaten him. He just woke up the next day bruised and battered and not sure what the hell had happened.

In any event, my buddy the first sergeant almost got me killed during the mission to Tay Ninh. He was in the mood for some action, and even though we had moved north precisely because of a major NVA buildup in the area—they had tried to take Tay Ninh City four months earlier and were preparing to try again—the two of us set out in a jeep for another little tin-shack whorehouse he had gotten wind of. After another harrowing ride through no-man's-land—harrowing, at least, for me—the first sergeant ambled inside the hootch, and as I sat in the jeep waiting for him to get squared away, I kept one hand on my .45 the whole time because we were the only Americans there and the Vietnamese milling around the street included some hard-looking dudes. They had obviously been out in the bushes for a while. They looked weathered, they looked mean, and they were looking right at me. These were some serious mothers, and I didn't take them to be civilians or off-duty ARVN.

Top had once shown me a picture of his beautiful German wife and twin girls. I knew by then that the thirty-year men screwed around as a matter of policy. I had been wised up at my first battalion party in Korea when those good solid Regular Army NCOs I admired, almost all of them married men, showed up with their Korean girlfriends.

I guess I never got used to that mind-set because when I saw the picture of the first sergeant's wife, I said, "Yeah, well, what do you think she'd say if she knew about all those pussy raids of yours?"

"Oh, she knows," he said, grinning. "As a matter of fact, her advice to me was that if you can't be good, at least be careful."

Well, we weren't being careful! Not only had we driven right into what I took to be an enemy recon team, but there was some kind of firefight going on in the distance. I could hear muffled AK fire, and eventually—fantastically—I could see armed NVA in green pith helmets and green fatigues running along a far tree line.

I was in a cold sweat. My God, what are we doing? I thought. What the hell are they going to put on my tombstone—Killed While Waiting on a First Sergeant to Get His Rocks Off?!

The first sergeant finally appeared, hitching up his trousers as he came out of the hootch. *"Man,* that's good stuff," he sang. "That is *goooood* stuff! You want to go in and get some?"

"No, no, no," I shouted, urgently starting the jeep.

We took a little fire on the way out. I thought *that* would get the top sergeant's attention, but I was wrong. He just sat in some silent reverie as we sped off, wearing his boonie hat, which was curled up on both sides, and grinning a dreamy, shit-eating grin.

I didn't think we were going to make it out of there, but we did. I also had my doubts about surviving the return trip to Cu Chi when the Tay Ninh operation folded up, because Harris, whose medal-hunting conversation I overhead when we were up at Tay Ninh, again put the first sergeant and me out in front of the troop column. The joke was on Harris, however. Not one shot was fired. Not one shot. No rockets, either, and no mines. Fuck you, fuck you, fuck you, I thought as we wheeled through the gate of the base camp. I'm alive, Harris! You didn't get me, and you can't stop me! I'm goin' home!

Not yet. Not quite yet. I still had a freak accident to survive. My DEROS—the Date Eligible for Return from Overseas—was December 28, 1968. I drank it up in celebration for three or four days prior to that while going around saying my good-byes and, twisting the Steppenwolf song a bit, singing about the Magic Carpet Ride I was going to take back to the World. Recuperating from all the partying, I was sleeping by myself one afternoon in our ugly little shack by the motor pool, when, groggily coming awake, I had a strange, urgent sensation that I needed to get out of there, something was going to happen—and, bam, just moments after I dragged myself outside, a big old M48 tank noisily crashed through the hootch, crushing my cot. There was no driver in the tank. It turned out that it was being worked on with the engine running when the transmission some-

how got engaged, and off it went. Someone managed to clamber
aboard the runaway tank and drive it back into the motor pool, but
in the meantime, I took one look at the monster bearing down on
me and started running like a madman. I was almost hysterical, because here was proof positive that my luck was all but gone. You
gotta get out of here, I thought, you have got to get the hell out of
here; this is it!

Part of me was celebrating, but part of me was afraid to go home,
because I didn't know what I was going home to. I was determined
to go to college and move up in life, but I was unsure of myself and
wondered if I could ever really escape my roots. College was for the
very best, and I had been told over and over that I was anything but
the very best. People like me weren't destined for success. We got in
trouble. We ended up in the pen. We ended up drunks. One night
near the end there, I was in the barracks, sitting around drinking
with Manuel Lunna, a Puerto Rican buddy of mine, and when we
left, I walked right into a slit trench adjacent to the doorway. It was a
painful fall. I was so jolted that when I looked up from the trench at
a little homemade Christmas tree decorated with lights in the open
barracks door, I thought I was looking at the headlight of a train—
the train that had run over some members of a Cherokee family I
had known as a boy. Wanting to bring a miserable life to a quick conclusion, they'd gotten drunk and lain out on the railroad tracks, and
there they had died. Now I was so frustrated and unhappy that I
thought that train was coming for me, but how could it be, I wondered, I hadn't lain on the tracks, had I?—and then I realized that
Lunna was pulling my arms, and when I finally figured out where I
was and what was really going on, I tried to get out of there myself,
though both of us were so drunk, it was like the blind leading the
blind. It seemed to take forever before I was free of that trench.

Feeling lost, I went to see Sergeant Cooper up at squadron and
asked him if I should stay in the army or at least join the Reserves.
"Dwight, you should get the hell out," he said, as bitter about the
New Army as Dean. "Don't stay in Vietnam. Don't stay in the army,
and don't go near the Reserves. Just get on with your life. I know
you. You'll go a lot further out there than you will in the army."

That was that. I packed my extra uniforms, my medals, and my souvenirs: an NVA canteen, an NVA bayonet, an NVA pith helmet, a silver hockey-puck-shaped NVA weapons-maintenance can with two screw caps (one for gun oil and the other for wood polish), and, finally, of all things, a red-and-yellow South Vietnamese flag that Cowboy Boehm had originally found on a dead enemy soldier at Tan Son Nhut.

I picked up one last souvenir before I left. There was a board in the orderly room on which were nailed wooden silhouettes, painted black, of all the tanks and APCs in the troop. Each cutout was marked with the bumper number of the vehicle it represented and was decorated with little gold stars for every mine the vehicle had hit and a white chalk circle with an X in it for every RPG that had hit the vehicle.

Using a screwdriver to pop off the tank silhouette marked C-36, which had earned three stars and nine circles, someone tossed it to me and said, "It's only fitting that you take this with you."

The morning I flew out of Cu Chi, I was supposed to have been driven to the airfield by a certain Private Schick, a stocky, chubby, clownish guy from Philadelphia who was famous in our outfit for having gone AWOL when he went home on emergency leave in late 1967, and then, having missed all the heavy fighting, suddenly rejoining the troop in late 1968. Everyone wanted to know what had taken him so long to get back, but Schick would never tell. He'd just smile and say that he'd been taking care of business.

Unfortunately, Private Schick had not taken care of his jeep. We ran out of gas halfway to the airfield, and my head throbbing from a hangover, I hefted my duffel bag and angrily trudged the rest of the way. There were several companies of 1st Cavalry Division troops sitting along the airstrip in full combat gear, getting ready to go back out—the cav had been operating out of Cu Chi as of late in response to the enemy buildup in the area—and as I watched them, I thought wistfully that they reminded me of the unit ours had once been. They still looked solid and gung-ho. I envied them. In addition, the Bob Hope Christmas Show was back in town, and while waiting at the airfield for my flight out, I saw Raquel Welch again as she went by on a dusty road in a jeep with a big sign on it. She looked fantastic in her body-revealing outfit, but she avoided eye contact as the guys shouted and whooped it up, and I wasn't interested in her this time around. I just wanted to get home.

During the flight to Bien Hoa Air Base, my boonie hat was sucked out an open cargo hatch of our transport plane as I distractedly watched the scenery go by, and upon my disembarking a major in crisp new green fatigues upbraided me for being out of uniform. He demanded an explanation, but when I told him what had happened to my hat, he simply shook his head and walked away without another word, giving me the impression that he did not believe me.

Ending your tour was like starting it, only in reverse. The group of returnees I was assigned to spent the night at the 90th Replacement Battalion in Long Binh and, having changed into the traveling khakis we had worn when we originally came in-country, were bused back to bustling Bien Hoa the next morning. We DEROS'd out on time, on schedule, and by the numbers, the highest-ranking member of our group, a tall, good-looking army nurse with strawberry-blond hair, being placed in front of our formation on the runway, and leading the loose, happy, single-file march up the steps of the boarding ramp, where a miniskirted stewardess greeted us with smiles.

I sat back as the plane revved up for takeoff.

When I had flown in sixteen months earlier, the view from above was of a green paradise. The landscape we swept over on the way out had been transformed. It was a moonscape, the splotches of dead grayness where all had been shelled, bombed, napalmed, and defoliated spreading cancerlike through virtually every village, every rice paddy, every patch of woods. There were craters everywhere, craters of all sizes, craters that overlapped one another, and I was brokenhearted by the extent of the destruction. We had come and laid waste, but we had not conquered. It was difficult to believe we had accomplished anything at all.

Epilogue

According to my transportation authorization ticket from the Military Airlift Command, which I saved, we departed the Republic of Vietnam at 1155 hours on December 28, 1968, and, gaining a day during the overnight flight across the Pacific because we were traveling with the earth's rotation, landed at Travis Air Base in Fairfield, California, at 1615 on the same date. We were exhausted and exultant.

It took two days of filling out forms and standing in line to clear the U.S. Army Personnel Center at Oakland, California—upon being discharged from the service, we received the traditional meal of steak and french fries—and then I caught a plane to Tulsa, Oklahoma.

For the record, in addition to the usual campaign ribbons, I had been awarded the Silver Star with oak leaf cluster, an end-of-tour Bronze Star, and the Purple Heart. Wearing my beribboned greens, I took the bus from Tulsa down to Sallisaw, the bus station of which was startling because it still had three rest rooms—Men, Women, and Colored—something I had not paid much attention to before Vietnam. From there, I hopped a ride with a couple of high school buddies I had called and headed for Bell. It was a cold, snow-covered day. We were about to turn off onto the gravel road that ran up to my stepfather's place when I noticed his pickup truck parked in front of a little general store on the main road. He had driven down to get his mail—our rural route mailbox was one of twenty or so posted together at the end of his gravel road—and as he often did had then stopped to pass some time at the general store across the main road. It was just another day for him. He knew I was coming home soon, but he didn't know exactly when, and I could not call ahead because the Bell area still didn't have phone service.

We pulled in next to the truck just as Ed Birdwell walked out of the store with his mail in his hand. He was stunned to see me. I was equally shocked. Ed had been seventy-one when I left for Vietnam, but he could have passed for fifty or fifty-five. Up working every morning before dawn, he could put me under he was so strong. His stamina was amazing. He never slowed down. He was never idle.

The Ed Birdwell coming out of the general store was an old man. Sick with worry, he had aged terribly while I was in Vietnam.

When Ed saw me he started to cry, and I started to cry, then he threw my duffel bag in the back of his truck, and we went home.

I didn't stay long. After a tearful reunion with my mother, I changed into civvies and, it being New Year's Eve, I was partying that night with some old friends and their new wives in the rough, tough, cigarette-smoke-filled Elkhorn Bar near Siloam Springs, Arkansas.

Things happened fast after that. I bought a 327 Chevy Camaro two or three days after getting home, started college within two weeks, and by March 1969 I was married, something I had told my buddies I wasn't going to do for some time upon leaving Vietnam. The first night out cruising with my new Camero, however, I was driving past the Dairy Cup in Stilwell when I spotted a girl in a nice tight pair of jeans at the window ordering a Coke. I immediately turned around to ask her if she wanted to go for a ride and realized that the girl was none other than Virginia Bean, baby sister of those wild men I had run with before joining the army. I had always thought she was a cute thing, but she was almost three years younger than me, and anytime I mentioned her name her brothers would let me know loud and clear that I'd better not try to fool around with her. I had bumped into her a few times when I was home on leave before shipping out to Vietnam, but she was sixteen, I was nineteen, and at least in those days nineteen-year-old guys did not go out with sixteen-year-old girls.

That was then. Virginia had written me when I was in Vietnam—one of her brothers had also served there, a helicopter door gunner—and being that she was now eighteen and a senior in high school, she was happy to take a ride in my new Camaro. Unfortunately, I misunderstood her enthusiasm, and, appalled when I jokingly laid out how I thought we should spend the evening, ending it with what we used to call a midnight rodeo, she asked me to take her home.

She did agree to see me again, though. We were of the same clay. I was from Bell, and Virginia from Peavine, another small Cherokee community in Adair County. One of ten children, she, too, had grown up poor—until she was eleven or twelve, they had all lived in a little eighty-year-old log house—and had sometimes gone hungry because when he was otherwise broke her father would hit the taverns with the food money. He was a good man, a proud veteran of the push across Europe during World War II, but he was a drinking man, and it was Virginia's mother who kept everything together. Virginia told me that when her brother came back from Vietnam, he thought he had a nest egg waiting for him because, like me, he had sent most of his pay home to his folks in Treasury checks. Mine put mine in the bank for me. His mother desperately bought groceries and clothes for his bedraggled siblings with his pay, and his father, thinking he was doing a good deed, spent what was left to buy him a new car, which was used so much, however, that by the time his boy came home, it was already burned out and sitting up on blocks in the yard.

Virginia is a loving wife who has stuck by me through good times and bad. There have been bad times. I pity the women who married Vietnam vets because many ended up with troubled husbands and busted lives. Virginia could have had an easier time with someone other than me, and her devotion has been especially appreciated considering how quickly we decided to exchange vows. I had fallen head over heels for her. I was truly in love, so I went to a minister with her—in secret, her family would not have approved because she was still in school—had a motel-room honeymoon that was straight out of *Coal Miner's Daughter,* and then drove her home as if nothing had happened. We kept up the charade until just before she graduated, then moved into a little trailer sitting in the parking lot behind the grocery store where I was bitterly working sixty hours a week to pay for the college classes I was taking, the GI Bill not even beginning to cover the costs like I thought it would. With a wife, I qualified for something like a hundred and fifty bucks a month. I was tempted to drop out and get on unemployment, but I saw too many guys like myself, just back from Nam, who used part of their unemployment as down payment on a hot sports car, then quickly went through the rest on whiskey, cigarettes, and fast living, only to have their car repossessed. Such was the start of their downward spirals, and many ended up with their head in a bottle, living month to month on checks from the Veterans Administration.

It was rough at first. School was good for me in that it kept me focused on what I needed to be doing, but I would often find myself sitting in class thinking that six months earlier I'd been running Highway 1 through a place called An Duc, waiting for my turn to get killed, and that people didn't know, they didn't want to know, and they didn't care. It didn't mean anything. It wasn't real. The dead GIs, the dead Vietnamese, they were just part of some program on TV.

My mother certainly didn't understand. Stern, religious woman that she was, her major concerns when I was living at home before getting married—and this was the source of much bad blood between us—were that I be home by ten o'clock every night, and checking to see if I had beer on my breath when she thought I was asleep.

I can't say that Virginia completely understood what I was talking about when I tried to tell her about Vietnam, but I needed a wife, I needed someone warm to lie with, and that person was Virginia.

We had purchased a mobile home in the Bell area by the time our daughter, Stephanie, was born on December 24, 1969. The nurses presented her to me in a Christmas stocking. I think I was a little overwhelmed by it all—bam, bam, bam, I was in school, married, and a father—but she really brightened the last years of my stepdad's life. He loved to show Stephanie off and took her everywhere with him.

We lost Ed Birdwell in November 1972. The manner of his death was tragic and shocking. Coming home one cold, drizzly day from voting for President Nixon—I did, too, that year, and would also have voted for him in Vietnam had I been old enough—he took his tractor out to work his fields, and had climbed off to adjust the carburetor when the transmission became engaged, and the big right-rear wheel ran him over, breaking his back. The plows hitched up behind the tractor snagged him, and, dragged around by the pilotless tractor, he was terribly mauled and left lying outside for twelve hours before being discovered. He died three days later in a VA hospital.

I had just started law school when Ed passed away. Thanks to Virginia, who was working so I could go to school full-time, I'd graduated the previous May from Northeastern State University in Tahlequah, receiving a bachelor of arts degree in history with double minors in geography and political science. I went from there to the Oklahoma University College of Law, but withdrew when Ed died and moved in with my mom—who stayed on the old homestead until passing away herself twenty years later—to put my stepfather's affairs in order. Virginia and I got a student apartment that summer in a complex owned by OU, which, incidentally, is in Norman, immediately south of Oklahoma City, and I was back in law school for the fall 1973 session. The new and improved GI Bill paid for the whole first year. I went on to graduate in the top 10 percent of the Class of 1976.

Our son Eddie was born that August, and shortly thereafter, as I went to work for an Oklahoma City law firm, we bought our first house in Norman. I eventually started my own practice, Birdwell & Associates, where Virginia keeps the books, having earned a degree in business education at OU. We specialize in energy law, but the oil business being what it is—and as of the early nineties, it wasn't what it used to be—I've been known to chase a few ambulances to try to pay the bills. When I tell my buddies from Vietnam that I'm a lawyer now, they think I must be rich. I definitely am not!

As of this writing, Stephanie has her master's degree in social welfare from the University of California at Berkeley, which is ironic considering how much I hated that place when I was in Vietnam. Unlike her father, however, she's a liberal Democrat. She now works for the Bureau of Indian Affairs in New Mexico.

Not sure what career path he wants to follow, Eddie is a liberal arts major at OU. Like me, he votes Republican, and like me at his age, he's a hardhead with a wild streak, which means we fight almost as much as I did with my parents. At least, however, I never got a tattoo!

In addition to my law practice, I have been involved in tribal politics for the last decade. Specifically, I am one of three justices sitting on the Cherokee Nation's de facto supreme court, the Judicial Appeals Tribunal, in Tahlequah. I was originally appointed as an associate justice in 1987 by then–Principal Chief Wilma P. Mankiller, reappointed in 1991, and elected by the other two justices as Chief Justice of the Cherokee Nation in 1995. The position almost merits combat pay. Ours is a tightly interwoven society, and decisions are not rendered in aloof detachment, but sometimes mean the end of old friendships. Politics being politics, I've also been a little disillusioned with what I consider to be the inefficiency and political favoritism displayed by some of our powers that be, but I've nonetheless valued this opportunity to serve the people of the Cherokee Nation.

There is family and work, and there is Vietnam. It is with me every day, and, unable to let go of this terrible but defining moment in our lives, some of us have kept in touch over the years. We aren't exactly a band of brothers. It wasn't that kind of war. I love some of these guys, dislike others, and have little in common with the rest except Nam, but that is enough. That is everything. No matter how much I'd like to forget the war, we have been forever forged together in the crucible that was Charlie Troop of the Three-Quarter Cav.

We had our first bittersweet platoon reunion at John Rourke's home in McHenry, Illinois, in 1979. Sergeant Dean was there, along with Mike Christie and Bob Wolford. Having found other old buddies in the meantime, most of us linked up again at the Vietnam Veterans Memorial—the Wall—in Washington, D.C., in 1985. Doc Gearhart hosted a troop reunion at his home in Piper City, Illinois, in 1995, and I finally attended a full-scale squadron reunion the following year in Vicksburg, Mississippi.

From these and other contacts, a status report . . .

Lieutenant Colonel Glenn K. Otis. Enlisted in 1946. Commissioned from the United States Military Academy in 1953. Commanding Officer, 3d Squadron, 4th Cavalry, 25th Infantry Division, December 1967–May 1968. Awarded the Distinguished Service

Cross, Silver Star, Legion of Merit, eight Air Medals, and two Purple Hearts.

It was a privilege to have served under Otis. His leadership is one of the few positive memories I have from Vietnam, and it has been gratifying to watch an old-fashioned warrior like Saber 6 rise to the top in the postwar army. He commanded an armor brigade and an armor division in Germany and served as the four-star Commander in Chief, U.S. Army, Europe, 1983–88. He and his wife then retired to Newport News, Virginia, where he is a business executive.

Lieutenant Colonel Otis knew us by our names in Vietnam. He still knows our names. In 1981, when Otis was originally promoted to four-star general and assigned as commander of the Training and Doctrine Command at Fort Monroe, Virginia, I called his office and left a message of congratulations from "Spec Five Birdwell." The next thing I knew, General Otis, in the course of a command-related flight to Texas, made a special stop at Tinker Air Base near Oklahoma City, the sole purpose of which was to thank me for my call. This was no photo opportunity, and this ex-tanker he was visiting was a man of no political or social significance. However, I was important to Otis, as were many like me, because I had been one of his troops in Vietnam.

It was a remarkable gesture, and I will never forget it. Nor will I forget that when General Otis came off the plane, he had a black eye. A real shiner. I've had a bunch that looked just like that, I thought, and wondered if Otis had gotten his in the traditional way. I had a hard time imagining a general in a fistfight. On the other hand, I could see Glenn Otis in a fistfight. In any event, I never got the nerve up during our visit to ask if he'd been at the wrong end of a well-landed punch or had walked into a helluva door, but when we shook hands and he left to reboard his plane, he suddenly turned, pointed to his shiner, and grinned, "Well, if I ever get into another dispute that results in another one of these, I know a good lawyer I can call."

Captain Leo B. Virant II. Enlisted in 1957. Commissioned from the United States Military Academy in 1963. Intelligence Officer, 3/4th Cavalry, August–September 1967. Commanding Officer,

C/3/4th Cavalry, September 1967–January 1968. Supply Officer, 3/4th Cavalry, March 1968–February 1969. Awarded two Silver Stars, two Bronze Star Medals (BSM), two Air Medals, and the Purple Heart.

When we evacuated Virant at Tan Son Nhut, we thought he had either been mortally wounded or would end up disabled with a plate in his head. His wounds had actually looked worse than they were—the fragment that entered the right rear of his head and exited through the left rear had fractured his outer skull and given him a concussion, but miraculously there was no spine or brain damage—and after a month in Japan, he returned to Cu Chi to serve out the balance of his eighteen-month tour as the squadron supply officer.

Virant subsequently served another eighteen-month tour, 1971–72, as a province advisor, for which he received the CIB and a third BSM. Virant went on to retire as a lieutenant colonel in 1988. Life as a hard-drinking, chain-smoking professional soldier who was going through four packs a day as the squadron supply officer resulted in Virant having a massive heart attack five years after he hung up his suit. Having undergone a quadruple bypass, he is now a cardiac rehabilitation patient who works in digital imaging, computer graphics, and commercial photography in Atlanta, Georgia.

First Lieutenant Theo F. Hardies. Commissioned through the ROTC program at Rutgers University in 1966. 1st Platoon Leader, C/3/4th Cavalry, August 1967–February 1968. 725th Maintenance Battalion, 25th Infantry Division, February–August 1968. Awarded a Bronze Star Medal for Valor (BSMv), BSM, and the Purple Heart.

Ted Hardies got married right out of college. Still married and still the lean, athletic, sharp, and to-the-point man he was in Vietnam, he is now a colonel in the New Jersey National Guard, working full-time for the state's Department of Military and Veterans Affairs.

First Lieutenant Richard A. Thomas. Commissioned through the ROTC program at the University of Florida in 1966. Artillery Forward Observer, C/3/4th Cavalry (attached from 6/77th Artillery),

February–July 1968. Awarded the Distinguished Service Cross, BSM, Army Commendation Medal (ARCOM), and the Purple Heart.

His right arm having been amputated, Thomas met his future wife while recuperating at the Medical Center, Fort Gordon, Georgia. She was a WAC corpsman assigned to his ward. They were married in the hospital chapel in December 1968, and still together almost thirty years later, have two grown children. Thomas served a year on active duty in the G3 section at Fort Gordon until being medically retired as a captain in 1970. Obtaining a degree in public administration, Thomas was the Senior Transportation Planner with the City of Orlando, Florida, from 1973 to 1988, and as of 1989 began working as a Transportation Specialist for Seminole County, Florida.

First Lieutenant/Captain Anthony R. Adamo. Enlisted in the Indiana National Guard in 1963. Commissioned through OCS in 1966. 2d Platoon Leader, C/3/4th Cavalry, March–July 1968. Executive Officer, C/3/4th Cavalry, July–October 1968. Military Advisory Team 3-72, Military Assistance Command Vietnam (MACV), October 1968–March 1969. Awarded the CIB, BSM, ARCOM, and the Purple Heart.

Tony's dad, an artilleryman in World War II, was also career army. In fact, the first three months of Tony's Vietnam tour overlapped with the last three of his father's tour, the elder Adamo then a sergeant major serving in an administrative assignment in Nha Trang, 1967–68.

Thoughtful and reflective, strong but soft spoken, Tony is the only one of us who would qualify as a philosopher, and he shrugs off the fact that he was a hero to so many of us in Charlie Troop. "Let me tell you, I never did one brave thing," he says. "I was one of the world's biggest cowards. I was scared every minute I was there."

"I was a soft touch," he wryly continues. "Had I been more mature, had I been more career oriented—had I been more Army—people would be remembering me very differently. . . ."

Tony had a couple years of college under his belt when he put up his bars, but didn't actually graduate for another twenty years or so.

In the meantime, he left the army in 1970 and put another nine years in the Indiana National Guard before going back on active duty in 1979.

Tony was medically retired in 1991 as a lieutenant colonel when he had surgery to remove a brain tumor. He was good people in Nam, and he remains so to this day. "When I got back, I put Vietnam away, and I've had a wonderful life," he says. Tony is still with the woman he married upon being commissioned, has three grown children, and now living in Indianapolis, is employed as the State Equal Opportunity Officer with the Indiana National Guard.

Sergeant First Class James Dean. Enlisted in 1948. C/70th Tank Battalion, 1st Cavalry Division, August 1950–November 1951. Awarded the Silver Star, two BSMv, and the Purple Heart. 3d Platoon and Troop HQ, C/3/4th Cavalry, October 1967–October 1968. Awarded a BSM and the Purple Heart.

Dean bought a house in Salem, Virginia, the week before he shipped out to Vietnam. Retiring from the army on the day he got back, he has lived there with his wife ever since. He is now a grandfather several times over. Dean might be nearing seventy years of age, but having found employment in construction as soon as he settled in Salem, he is still hard at work. "My friends tell me I'll probably die driving a nail," he laughs.

Staff Sergeant Gary D. Brewer. Enlisted in 1959. Receiving Station, Saigon Depot, Vietnam Regional Exchange, USARV, September 1966–July 1967 (tour cut short when he went home on leave to attend father's funeral). 3d Platoon, C/3/4th Cavalry, September 1967–February 1968. Awarded the Distinguished Service Cross and the Purple Heart.

Promoted to E7, Brewer volunteered for another combat tour and served as a platoon sergeant with E/17th Cavalry, 173d Airborne Brigade, 1969–70. He was wounded again during a morning road sweep in June of '70 when his tank—the old reliable M48 had been replaced by then with lighter M551 Sheridans—took an RPG through its thin-skinned side upon starting across a dry streambed. Brewer was temporarily deafened and peppered with fragments, but his Sheridan sped on down the road, clearing the ambush, even as his platoon leader's track behind them was rocketed and burst into flames. Brewer directed his driver to turn around, and they roared back in, dispersing the enemy with .50-cal MG and 152mm main-gun fire, for which he won the BSMv in addition to an end-of-tour BSM.

Disgusted with the protesters and the way the war was going, Brewer quit the army upon returning from Vietnam. Having separated from his first wife between his second and third tours, he remarried then and in 1971 impulsively reenlisted as an E6.

Deciding he had made a mistake, Brewer got out again in 1972, and instead got into the heating and air-conditioning business with his father-in-law. His second marriage also ended in divorce.

Incidentally, Brewer's sons from his first marriage have done well: one is a supervisor for building crews involved in home construction, one served four years in the air force and is now in college, and the third graduated from the United States Air Force Academy in 1989 and is presently a captain flying transport planes.

Why did Brewer's boys go air force when their father had been a hard-charging cavalryman in the U.S. Army? Well, it turns out that our ex-platoon sergeant joined the Indiana Air National Guard in 1979 and, after training as a weapons-system technician for the F4C Phantom jet, switched to the regular Air Guard in 1981. He retired from the smartest of all the services as an E7 master sergeant in 1993, and now, married for the third time, with a fourth, grade-school-age son, is a self-employed heating and air-conditioning repairman, living in Worthington, Indiana.

Staff Sergeant John R. Danylchuk. Enlisted in 1962. Long Range Reconnaissance Patrol attached to D/3/4th Cavalry, February–December 1967. 3d Platoon, C/3/4th Cavalry, December 1967–January 1968. Awarded the CIB, BSMv, two ARCOMv, and the Purple Heart.

Scotty never fully recovered from his wounds, and after multiple operations and a switch to a less rigorous supply MOS—in which he was promoted to sergeant first class—he was medically retired at 70 percent in 1981. Tragically, his disability has since been raised to 100 percent because of Post-Traumatic Stress Disorder (PTSD). Scotty talks at an excited, nervous, rapid-fire rate and, like many others who cannot make peace with the war—my old track commander suffers from intense survivor's guilt—has gone through multiple divorces, though from what I have seen he maintains a good relationship with his children. He has, after all, a good heart. His fourth wife, a Korean woman, also seems to be a stabilizing force in his life, and he is active in PTSD support groups. I might add that though a Scotsman by birth, the Army turned Scotty into a country boy, and in retirement he sports a cowboy hat and cowboy boots, and is a horse cavalryman in a Civil War reenactment unit. He fights for the Confederate side, and lives in Killeen, Texas.

Private First Class/Specialist Fourth Class/Sergeant Russell H. Boehm. Drafted in 1967. 2d Platoon, C/3/4th Cavalry, August 1967–August 1968. Awarded the CIB, two BSMv, and a BSM.

Cowboy returned to ranching after his 1969 discharge. Like many men of honor and dignity who love their country, he drives a Ford pickup! Cowboy presently oversees a 12,000-acre spread in Philipsburg, Montana, on which he and his wife, devout Christians both, live in a log cabin with a wood-burning stove. He tends to 750 head of cattle from dawn to dusk, and then some, and when he isn't working the cattle, he is walking the fence lines or bailing hay.

Time is catching up with all of us, however, and in 1995 Cowboy had a near-fatal heart attack that resulted in open-heart surgery and ruinous medical bills. Despite that, despite Vietnam, he remains unbitter, the best of men. I recently received a letter from my old friend that without even trying spoke eloquently of the spirit inside him: ". . . about 10 or 12 elk came over hill toward me. I set very still [and] they came right to me. When [my] horse moved they ran around me[,] but 3 pairs of cows ran with them. I needed to turn [the] cows. My horse was excited. 'Wow!' he said 'a race!' so away we all went. They managed to sort out. The elk jumped gracefully over the fence. Me and my horse ran a big circle with excited elation. How many people enjoy such experiences? What a lucky man I am!"

Specialist Fourth Class Lucio Herrera. Drafted in 1966. 2d Platoon, C/3/4th Cavalry, September 1967–September 1968. Awarded a BSM.

Lucio got out of the army when he DEROS'd and immediately went back to work as a welder, which he had been before the war, and heavy equipment operator. He got married in 1969, was hired by the local power company in 1970—he is still with them and is presently a supervisor—and a grown son and two grown daughters later, he and his wife are still together. That's the Lucio I remember, solid, stolid, and stable. He and his wife live in Hebbronville, Texas.

Specialist Fourth Class Dean A. Foss. Enlisted in 1966. 3d Platoon, C/3/4th Cavalry, October 1967–October 1968.

Dean was discharged as a spec five in 1970. I thought Dean was one of the best—tough, friendly, innocent, a spark plug of energy—and because I like him to this day, I am sad to say that he has also had a rough time living with the war. He seems a little tired, a little frazzled around the edges. Married with three children, he is employed raising mice for cancer-research labs and lives in Bar Harbor, Maine.

Specialist Fourth Class/Specialist Fifth Class J. Steven Uram. Enlisted in 1966. 1st Platoon, C/3/4th Cavalry, October 1967–October 1968. Awarded the Silver Star, BSM, and the Purple Heart.

Planning on a military career, Steve reupped in 1969, the same year he got married. The army could have used him. At a time when standards were slipping, he had remained an absolute professional in our unit. Sent back to Vietnam for a 1970–71 tour, Steve—who got his orders the day the first of his two daughters was born—served with a mech infantry battalion in the 25th Division until the unit was withdrawn as part of Vietnamization, then transferred to the 101st Airborne Division. He came home with the CIB and another BSM, but, his enthusiasm dampened by his new responsibilities as a husband and father, he left the service in 1973 as an E6. Still married, he is now a police sergeant in Everett, Washington.

Private First Class/Specialist Fourth Class Robert D. Wolford. Drafted in 1967. 3d Platoon and Troop HQ, C/3/4th Cavalry, October 1967–October 1968. Awarded the CIB, two BSMv, and a BSM.

Bob was discharged as a sergeant in 1969. We have kept in close touch over the years. He was a stoic, dependable, low-key guy in Vietnam. He is a stoic, dependable, low-key, and somewhat melancholy guy today who has never married despite several long-term relationships with several fine women. An outdoorsman, bow hunter, and black-powder rifle enthusiast, he works as a plumber and steamfitter and lives in Battle Creek, Michigan.

Private First Class/Specialist Fourth Class R. Franklin Cuff. Drafted in 1967. 2d Platoon, C/3/4th Cavalry, October 1967–October 1968. Awarded the CIB, BSMv, and Purple Heart.

Cuff was discharged in 1969. We have also remained close, and I can report that Fighting Frank being Fighting Frank, he actually joined the VFW, and is a conservative, no-complaints, proud-to-have-served vet who got back on with his life as soon as he came home from Vietnam. He is an oil-field worker and lives in Hillsdale, Michigan. The tragedy of his life is not the war, but that after two divorces, his third wife, who proved a good match and whom he was with for almost a decade, passed away in 1996 from cancer.

Specialist Fourth Class John Rourke. Drafted in 1966. 3d Platoon and Troop HQ, C/3/4th Cav, December 1967–September 1968.

John worked in the orderly room after Hoc Mon. One of his duties was preparing award recommendations, which is one reason why he didn't receive any; he wouldn't submit any paperwork in his name. John went home early, receiving a compassionate reassignment when his mother fell down a flight of stairs and fractured her back. He was discharged two months later. Married with two grown daughters, John now lives in McHenry, Illinois, and works as a ground supervisor for Northwest Airlines at O'Hare Airport in Chicago.

Specialist Fourth Class/Sergeant Daniel W. Czepiel. Drafted in 1966. 1st Platoon, C/3/4th Cavalry, January–June 1968. D/3/4th Cavalry, June–October 1968. Awarded the CIB, BSM, and three Purple Hearts.

Dan went home a little early, his two years of service up before his tour was. Married, with three children, he has been with the postal service for the last twenty years and lives in Agawam, Massachusetts.

Staff Sergeant George S. Breeding. Enlisted in 1962. 2d Platoon and Troop HQ, C/3/4th Cavalry, February 1968–January 1969. Awarded the CIB, two BSMv, BSM, and three Purple Hearts.

George retired in 1985 as a first sergeant. Married before the war, he had three children after his return, but he and his wife eventually divorced. Now remarried with two stepchildren, he works as a high school custodian in Castlewood, Virginia. That is a sedate profession, which is appropriate given that my old tattooed, hell-raising buddy is now a soft-spoken born-again Christian.

Specialist Fourth Class H. Jackson Donnelly. Drafted in 1966. 3d Platoon, C/3/4th Cavalry, February–July 1968. Awarded the CIB, ARCOMv, and two Purple Hearts.

Jack should have been discharged in 1968. Having reenlisted in a hospital bed so as to remain in the army medical system, however, he was not mustered out until 1969. Jack had planned to make a career in forestry, but with a crippled leg—not to mention the discomfort of lesser injuries, to include a metal fragment from his first wound that damaged his nasal passages and is still buried back in his head—he instead sold real estate for several years, started with the post office in his hometown of Willis, Virginia, in 1973, and assumed duties as postmaster in 1974. Still in that position, and still the humble and devout man I knew, he presently lives on the farm on which he was raised, taking care of his elderly and widowed father.

Private First Class/Specialist Fourth Class Russell A. Gearhart. Enlisted in 1967. A/3/4th Cavalry, March 1968. 2d Platoon, C/3/4th Cavalry, March 1968–January 1969. Squadron Aid Station, 3/4th Cavalry, January–February 1969. Awarded the Combat Medic's Badge, Silver Star, BSM, ARCOM, and two Purple Hearts.

Gearhart got married in 1969, was discharged as a spec five in 1970, and utilizing his medical training shortly went to work as a respiratory therapist in a civilian hospital. He and his wife had two children. Doc was drinking heavily at the time, however, "and my wife left me because I was an asshole." It was 1974. Overwhelmed by what would later be recognized as PTSD, Gearhart took an overdose of sleeping pills in an unsuccessful suicide attempt—he was found and rushed to the hospital—underwent detox for alcoholism, "and then

I went to those fucking AA meetings where they teach you God this and God that, and I said, 'Bullshit, God didn't get me into this mess, God ain't going to get me out. I've got to do it myself.'"

Doc has been only partially successful. He ended up working on a garbage truck. Married again in 1975, he had two more children before again being divorced. He attempted suicide two more times.

In 1980, Gearhart went to work as a nursing assistant in a retirement home. In 1982, he married a licensed practical nurse thirteen years his senior who was also working in the retirement home, and this union, which has lasted, has provided some peace. Unable to put all his demons to rest, however, he had another breakdown in 1987, and was awarded a 70-percent disability for PTSD in 1989. Today, Doc, whose manner, though leavened with wisecracks, can be pretty peppery and abrasive—for one thing, he still hates "gooks"—looks like a refugee from the '60s. Beanpole thin, he makes his way through this world in his old jungle boots and bush hat, which is festooned with various pins and badges, and has long wiry hair and a full beard. His beard is gray. He wears a full set of dentures, too, his teeth having rotted out of his head thanks to the hepatitis he contracted near the end of his tour, which left him with a severe calcium deficiency.

Doc is also known to toke up a bit just like the old days. I always remembered Russ Gearhart as a super medic and am left very disheartened by his current state of affairs. I am not alone. In a letter supporting Gearhart's request to the VA for an upgrade to a 100-percent disability, his last squadron commander writes, "In Vietnam, I remember a young, vibrant soldier whose only mission was to serve those in need." After several squadron reunions, the colonel sadly adds that "the Russ that I have seen at these bivouacs is but a shadow of my brave medic. He presents the classic profile of debilitating PTSD: unable to move beyond his Vietnam experience; uncontrollable, erratic behavior at times that precludes him from getting and keeping meaningful employment; low self-esteem . . . Now is the time for the Army to take care of Russ."

Few of us are not still bleeding from the war. Art Parsons, the baby-faced kid who originally helped me transfer into his platoon from the troop communications section went through depression and heavy drinking and subjected his wife and children to abusive rages, as he tried to work Vietnam out of his system. "I finally talked my way through it in therapy," he says, willing to be quoted only behind a pseudonym. "It still bothers me, but it doesn't control me."

Art might consider himself lucky. Another one of the guys already serving in the platoon when I got there, who has been mentioned in this text—he was a hero at Tan Son Nhut—is in a VA mental hospital.

My buddy Richard Johns—fellow Indian, fellow survivor of Tet and Hoc Mon and all the rest—was suffering from debilitating combat fatigue by the time he got out of Vietnam. He is suffering still.

Parsons is a warehouse worker. Richard is unemployed. Mike Christie, who was running the track when I first got to the field, who showed me how it was done, and who I grew to think of as a brother, was a construction worker back in New York the last I heard. I've had only sporadic contact with Mike since we got together in D.C. in '85. Outwardly, he was that day the same tough, handsome, don't-give-me-no-shit guy I knew in Vietnam—hanging Sheetrock will definitely keep you in shape—but he told me that he'd had a hard, hard life since the war. He'd lived with hippies. He'd done whatever else he could to forget, but it was still eating at him like acid, and after we took a group photo in front of the Wall, he said, "Bird, I'm outta here, and I don't know if I'll ever see you again." He started crying and wrapped me in a bear hug and kissed me on the cheek.

And then he disappeared into the crowd.

I feel like I have been living two lives since the war. One part of me has done what I set out to do. Like farming, lawyering is a peaks-and-valleys profession, but I've been able to do a little better for my children than my parents were able to do for me. I have a nice wife. I have a nice house. I have a nice truck—a Ford. I also have sixteen months' worth of bad memories. They are always swirling just beneath the surface—I sleep fitfully—and sometimes they clog the filters of my mind, allowing nothing else through. In times past, I have sat on my back porch in the dead of hot, insect-humming nights, pistol in hand, thinking about Nam. I have been plagued with vivid nightmares, to include a recurring one in which I am looking up from inside my tank turret and realize horror stricken that a ring of NVA soldiers wearing those green pith helmets of theirs are peering down at me through the cupola, having overrun the tank.

I was still in law school when Saigon fell in 1975. The thought that it had all been for nothing—that VC flags were going up over An Duc and Cu Chi and Tan Son Nhut—was almost too much to bear.

The old memories ripped their way to the surface again when the Boat People began showing up around 1978. I still recoil at the ugly jokes I heard about the plight of these uprooted Vietnamese—the people we had been marched off to fight for, the people many of my friends had died for—from my white-collar contemporaries. I frequently traveled on business through Arkansas, where one of the refugee camps was established, and remember, too, the fierce local resentment at the mere presence of the Vietnamese. The basic assumption was that they were going to all end up on welfare, or steal everyone's jobs, or some damn thing, and I was profoundly disturbed to realize that at least some of the support for the war in God's country had been more a knee-jerk reaction to the hippies and yippies and draft-card burners than anything else. These down-home folks had no real interest or understanding of the war, nor any compassion for what our defeated allies were enduring under the communists. I don't think My Lai bothered them either.

There were times when I would hit the road on my Harley-Davidson, trying to outrun these and other realities. I had never worn a flak jacket in Vietnam. I never wore a steel pot, either, when I could help it, and likewise when I went tearing off on my Harley, comforted by its unique bellowing roar, I always went bareheaded.

The idea of dying did not and does not bother me anymore. I've gotten big behind my desk, which, combined with career anxiety and the constant lump in my chest called Vietnam, makes me a prime candidate for a heart attack. I've been worked hard and put away wet too many times to care, however. At least when I check out, I'll finally be able to relax. No more stress, no more strain.

I have sometimes wondered if it wouldn't have been better after all if I'd have caught that quick, clean round through the head that I had so feared. It would have spared me much suffering. I have in my pain returned again and again to the fact that I did not stay in the field for a full combat tour. That has always shamed me, but I finally reconciled that and everything else as well as I could about three o'clock one Saturday morning in December of '79. I had spent the previous seven or eight hours by myself, drinking my way to the bottom of a fifth of bourbon. Except for maintaining limited contact with my friends from the war, I came to the conclusion that the balance of my life would best be served by burying, in my mind, as completely as possible, my tour in Vietnam. I can't say that I totally made peace with myself, but I did stop drinking as of that morning, and I forced myself to accept that nothing could or would come of reliving the past, that I was in a new phase of my life, and that I needed to focus on that in order to move ahead. This I was gradually able to do—the nightmares finally ebbed away after some fifteen years—and though there have been times, as in collaborating on this work, when old wounds were laid open as if with a white-hot knife, I have mostly detached myself from those sixteen months. In the best of times, that boy who came back from Vietnam is gone. He's dead. He climbed up a forested hill in Bell and he's up in heaven with his mother and stepfather. In the best of times, I can talk about the war like it happened to someone else. Sometimes still, though, I cannot talk about it at all.

The war is ancient history to my family. My medals and souvenirs have gotten kicked around over the years. So have I, and my deepest regret is that in carrying the war with me, I never tapped all the talents that I think God had blessed me with. I never lived up to my destiny. Nevertheless, I don't regret having signed my name on the dotted line. I am proud to have served when duty called. When I die, if there's anyone around who remembers me, the only thing I want them to say is that I was a soldier.

Appendix

Killed in Action, Troop C, 3d Squadron, 4th Cavalry, September 1967–December 1968 (this list was compiled by retired MSgt. Robert Maxey of the 3/4th Cav Association from squadron morning reports, and is incomplete given the haphazard nature of such records; for example, in most cases, it does not include those who Died of Wounds after being evacuated):

October 25, 1967
Sgt. Ronnie L. Gros

November 28, 1967
Sp4 Bennie A. Smith

December 17, 1967
Pfc. Richard A. House
Pfc. Martin G. McDonnell
Pfc. Guadalupe N. Zuniga

January 31, 1968
SSgt. Patrick J. Strayer
Sgt. Francis I. Arnett (DOW 13 February 1968)
Sgt. Troy A. Littlejohn
Sgt. Gerald D. Sullivan
Sp5 Harold R. Stafford
Sp4 Roger B. Crowell
Sp4 Norman L. Long
Sp4 Richard J. Rhodes

Sp4 Anthony F. Vanhulle
Sp4 Murray L. Veron
Pfc. Robert M. Finnegan

February 6, 1968
1st Lt. Donald J. Russin
SSgt. Louis J. Orison
SSgt. Michael W. Webster
Sgt. Gregory Jones
Sp5 Alger L. White
Sp4 Donald E. Clark
Sp4 Michael J. Longabardi
Sp4 Robert R. Lord
Pfc. Joe W. Grigsby
Pfc. Charles C. Hale

February 10, 1968
Sgt. Kenneth L. Devor

February 19, 1968
Sfc. William Jenkins
Pfc. Larry R. Moore

February 21, 1968
Pfc. Frank R. Manello

February 28, 1968
Sgt. Klaus D. Egolf
Sgt. Warren G. Harding
Cpl. Robert W. Hunt (MIA/Presumed Dead)
Pfc. James Scuitier

March 3, 1968
Sp5 Daniel L. Penson
Sp4 Eddie L. Pleasant
Sp4 Dennis H. Thompson
Pfc. Dan E. Charles
Pfc. James M. Darby

April 14, 1968
Sp4 Benjamin E. Lennard
Pfc. George A. C. Dillon

April 18, 1968
SSgt. Arnold Pairis
Sgt. Bernard L. Fox
Pfc. Johnny R. Webb

May 7, 1968
Sp5 James R. McDonough

May 9, 1968
SSgt. Frank E. Williams (DOW 1 June 1968)
Sp5 Johnnie W. Davis
Sp5 Charles R. Rosenbusch
Sp4 Barry W. Lewis
Pfc. Steven A. Sommers
Pvt. Ralph Sanchez

May 15, 1968
SSgt. James R. Fisher
Pfc. Frank G. Navarro
Pfc. John R. Oglesby

May 17, 1968
Sp4 Reginald A. Bowman

May 22, 1968
Pfc. George Guerra
Pfc. David W. Moseley
Pfc. Larry J. Samples

June 13, 1968
Pfc. Richard T. Huggett

June 18, 1968
Pfc. Robert M. Woods

July 3, 1968
Sgt. Billy R. Holmes
Sp4 Basil L. Hareford
Pfc. Roy H. McClain

July 7, 1968
Pfc. William E. Watts (DOW 12 July 1968)

October 15, 1968
Sgt. Julius C. Faircloth
Sp4 Joseph H. Riffle

December 11, 1968
Sp4 John Pizzuti
Pfc. Ronald A. Osinski
Pfc. Vincent R. Salemi

Glossary

AIT Advanced Individual Training

AK or AK-47 standard communist 7.62mm assault rifle

APC Armored Personnel Carrier

ARP Aerorifle Platoon

Article 15 nonjudicial punishment usually resulting in a demotion for offenses not serious enough to warrant a court-martial

Arty artillery

ARVN Army of the Republic of Vietnam

AWOL Absent Without Leave

Beehive main-gun ammunition packed with 8,000 two-and-a-quarter-inch steel darts (nicknamed for the sound made when fired)

Bustle rack a pipe framework attached to the rear of a tank turret for the carrying of supplies

Button up to shut and lock all hatches

C4 white, clay-like plastic explosives

C123 transport plane

C&C command-and-control helicopter used by commanders and operations officers to supervise combat operations

Canister can-shaped main-gun ammunition packed with 1,280 metal cylinders (a variety of Civil War–type grapeshot)

CAR15 a U.S. 5.56mm submachine gun (basically a compact version of the M16 with a collapsible stock and a shorter hand guard) usually reserved for officers and special operations units

Charlie nickname for VC and NVA soldiers

Chieu Hoi an enemy defector serving as a U.S. Army scout (from the Chieu Hoi, or Open Arms, program which promised clemency and financial aid to guerrillas who laid down their arms to live under South Vietnamese government authority)

Chinook CH47 cargo helicopter

Claymore standard U. S. antipersonnel mine (set in place above-ground by two metal prongs, it fired 700 steel balls in a sixty-degree arc)

CO Commanding Officer

Cobra nickname for the AH1G attack helicopter

Commo communications

C-rations combat rations (canned meals for field use)

CVC the Combat Vehicle Crewman helmet with a built-in radio headset (also called commo helmet or tanker helmet)

DEROS Date Eligible for Return from Overseas

DMZ Demilitarized Zone

DOW Died of Wounds

Dust-Off slang for medical evacuation, or medical evacuation units

E1 pay grade for recruit private

E2 pay grade for private

E3 pay grade for private first class

E4 pay grade for corporal or specialist fourth class

E5 pay grade for sergeant or specialist fifth class

E6 pay grade for staff sergeant or specialist sixth class

E7 pay grade for sergeant first class

E8 pay grade for first sergeant or master sergeant

E9 pay grade for sergeant major or command sergeant major

Electric Strawberry irreverent nickname of the 25th Infantry Division (based on its patch, a yellow lightning bolt on a red taro leaf)

Grease gun U.S. M3 .45-caliber submachine gun (issued almost exclusively to tankers during the Vietnam War)

Grunt nickname for infantrymen (from the sound they made when lifting their rucksacks)

HE High Explosive ammunition

HEAT High Explosive Antitank ammunition

Herringbone tactical formation used by armor units during halts in column moves, in which vehicles alternately faced right or left so as to overlap fields of fire and provide flank security to one another

Hootch nickname for a native hut or living quarters, or a U.S. personnel tent reinforced with sandbags and a wooden floor

Huey nickname for the UH1 series of helicopter

Illum illumination round or rounds

KIA Killed In Action

Klick kilometer

Laager nickname for a circular defense position (from the Boer)

LAW 66mm Light Antitank Weapon (a shoulder-fired rocket in a disposable one-shot fiberglass tube)

Lifer nickname for a career soldier

LP Listening Post (an early warning element, usually two or three men, placed outside a night defensive position)

LRRP Long Range Reconnaissance Patrol

M14 U.S. 7.62mm automatic rifle, issued to army personnel in training and duty stations other than Vietnam

M16 standard U.S. 5.56mm automatic rifle

M60 standard U.S. 7.62mm machine gun

M48A3 medium battle tank (usually mounted with a 90mm main gun and coaxial 7.62mm machine gun, plus an unshielded .50-caliber machine gun in front of the commander's cupola)

M79 standard U.S. 40mm grenade launcher (a one-shot, breach-loading weapon that fired high explosive and buckshot rounds)

M113 armored personnel carrier (usually mounted with a shielded .50-caliber machine gun in front of the commander's cupola and two shielded M60 machine guns on the back deck)

M577 a variation of the M113 armored personnel carrier with a raised roof for use as a traveling command post

Mad Minute concentrated fire of all a unit's weapons at optimum rate for a set period of time, usually a minute, and usually designed to disrupt possible enemy night attacks

MG Machine Gun

MIA Missing In Action

MOS Military Occupational Specialty (to include 11B for Basic Infantryman, and 11D for Armor Crewman)

MP Military Police

MSR Main Supply Route

NCO Noncommissioned Officer (pay grades E4 to E9)

NLF National Liberation Front

Noncom slang for noncommissioned officer

NVA North Vietnamese Army

OCS Officer Candidate School

Pack nickname for a tank engine

PF Popular Forces (village-level South Vietnamese militia)

PSP Pierced Steel Planking

PX Post Exchange

R&R Rest and Recreation (seven-day, out-of-country leave granted once to every U.S. serviceman during a 365-day tour in Vietnam)

ROTC Reserve Officers Training Course

RPG Rocket-Propelled Grenade (a devastating Russian-made shaped charge capable of burning through armor on impact, resulting in a fireball-type explosion on the inside of the targeted vehicle)

Sapper an enemy soldier trained in infiltration and demolition

SKS a Soviet-made semiautomatic carbine

Slick a troop-carrying Huey helicopter

Starlight Scope a handheld AN/TVS-2 scope which intensified light from the stars or moon to allow its operator to see at night

Straight-leg nickname for infantrymen

TC Tank Commander or Track Commander

Top nickname for First Sergeant

Track nickname for an armored personnel carrier

Tropic Lightning nickname of the 25th Infantry Division (from its rapid windup of the Guadalcanal campaign in World War II)

USMA United States Military Academy at West Point, New York

USO United Service Organization

V-100 armored security vehicle (distinguished by four large rubber tires and a small turret with twin .30-caliber machine guns)

VC Viet Cong

Ville village

WIA Wounded In Action

Wolfhounds nickname for the 27th Infantry Regiment (based on its service in Siberia at the end of World War I)

WP White Phosphorus ammunition

Xenon a 75-million-candlepower searchlight mounted on tanks

XO Executive Officer (a unit's second in command, this staff officer is usually tasked with overseeing administrative matters)